Hegel and Feminist Social Criticism

SUNY Series in Social and Political Thought

Kenneth Baynes, editor

HEGEL
and FEMINIST
SOCIAL CRITICISM

Justice, Recognition, and the Feminine

Jeffrey A. Gauthier

State University
of New York Press

Quotes from *Hegel: Elements of the Philosophy of Right* by G. W. F. Hegel, edited by Allen W. Wood and translated by H. B. Nisbet reprinted with permission of Cambridge University Press. Copyright ©1991 by Cambridge University Press. Quotes from *Hegel's Phenomenology of Spirit* by G. W. F. Hegel and translated by A.V. Miller reprinted with permission of Oxford University Press. Copyright ©1977 by Oxford University Press. Quotes from "Responsibility and Reproach" by Cheshire Calhoun and published in *Ethics* reprinted with permission of the University of Chicago Press. Copyright ©1989 by the University of Chicago Press. Quotes from *The Second Sex* by Simone de Beauvoir, copyright ©1952 and renewed 1980 by Alfred A. Knopf, Inc. reprinted by permission of the publisher.

Published by
State University of New York Press, Albany

© 1997 State University of New York

For information, address the State University of New York Press,
State University Plaza, Albany NY 12246

Marketing by Nancy Farrell
Production by Bernadine Dawes

Library of Congress Cataloging-in-Publication Data
Gauthier, Jeffrey A., 1957-
Hegel and feminist social criticism: justice, recognition, and the feminine / Jeffrey A. Gauthier.
    p. cm. — (SUNY series in social and political thought)
    Includes bibliographiical references and index.
    ISBN 0-7914-3363-3 (alk. paper). — ISBN 0-7914-3364-1 (pbk.: alk. paper)
    1. Feminist theory—Evaluation. S. Hegel, Georg Wilhelm Friedrich, 1770-1831—
    contributions in feminist criticism. 3. Feminist criticism. I. Title. II. Series.
    HQ1190.G385 1997
    305.42'01—dc21
                                                            97-1961
                                                            CIP

1 2 3 4 5 6 7 8 9 10

CONTENTS

Part Three
AGENCY, VICTIMIZATION, AND DIFFERENCE

ACKNOWLEDGMENTS

This book lends expression to the concerns, criticisms, interests, influences, passions, and prejudices of many people, only a few of whom I can single out here. First, I thank Frithjof Bergmann for first suggesting the project and for first impressing the importance of Hegel upon me. I thank Elizabeth Anderson for her support and her very detailed and useful criticisms. Stephen Darwall has provided persistent and supportive critique. I thank Abigail Stewart for broadening my awareness of feminist theory and for her abiding support. I thank David Hills for many useful suggestions and criticisms. To Cecelia Ober, whose friendship, experience, concern, and intense criticism led me to take feminism seriously, I cannot begin to acknowledge my debt. Lisa Schwartzman's innumerable committed, critical, insightful, and supportive conversations have shaped many ideas throughout the text. I wish to thank all of those who have read and provided me with comments on various parts of this manuscript including David Anderson, Mike Buehler, Harry Brod, Janice Dowell, Heidi Feldman, Ted Hinchman, Regan Knapp, Brian Leiter, Louis Loeb, Phyllis Morris, Sherry Ortner, and Peter Railton. I thank the anonymous referees and the dedicated editors at SUNY Press for their many helpful recommendations. In addition, I have benefitted from critical conversations from Laura Bugge, John Doris, Dawn Dougherty, Dan Farrell, Michael Forster, Carol Gilligan, Damon Gitelman, Dan Goldberg, Noelle Guest, Eileen John, Don Loeb, Franz Mayr, Martin Monto, Sarah Patterson, Joel Richeimer, Connie Rosati, Donna Silber, and Jeff Spinner. I wish to thank my colleagues at the University of Portland for their support in my efforts. As always, I owe a great debt to my students who have forced me to think and rethink my ideas through the years, especially the participants in my Philosophy and Feminism classes. To my parents, who have always been supportive of all my academic adventures, I owe a special debt that I can acknowledge but never begin to repay.

vii

Finally, I wish to express my thanks to the many people with whom I have been associated in feminist activism. I owe a special debt to certain men who have struggled with me to bring feminist politics and philosophy together including Dan Douthat, David Reed-Maxfield, and Chris Ahn. In addition, my work has been enriched by my association with members of the University of Portland Feminist Discussion Group, the Feminist Women's Union, Portland Stopping Violence Against Women, the Sexual Exploitation Education Project, Solidarity, the University of Michigan Sexual Assault Prevention and Awareness Center, and the Women's Issues Commission of the Michigan Student Assembly.

NOTES ON CITATIONS

Primary texts from Hegel and Kant are identified by their year on initial publication and cited as follows:

G. W. F. HEGEL (1770-1831)

1801 = *The Difference Between Fichte's and Schelling's System of Philosophy,* trans. H. S. Harris and W. Cerf. Albany: State University of New York Press, 1977. Cited by page number.

1802a = *The Relationship of Skepticism to Philosophy, Exposition of its Different Modifications and Comparison of the Latest Form with the Ancient One,* trans. H. S. Harris. In George di Giovanni and H. S. Harris, eds. *Between Kant and Hegel: Texts in the Development of Post-Hegelian Idealism.* Albany: State University of New York Press, 1985. Cited by page number.

1802b = *System of the Ethical Life,* trans. H. S. Harris. In H. S. Harris and T. M. Knox, eds. *System of the Ethical Life (1802/3) and the First Philosophy of Spirit (Part III of the System of Speculative Philosophy (1803/4).* Albany: State University of New York Press, 1985. Cited by page number.

1802/3 = *Natural Law,* trans. T. M. Knox. Philadelphia: University of Pennsylvania Press, 1974. Cited by page number.

1807 = *The Phenomenology of Spirit,* trans. A.V. Miller. New York: Oxford University Press, 1977. Cited by paragraph number.

1821 = *Elements of the Philosophy of Right,* trans. H. B. Nisbet. New York: Cambridge University Press, 1991. Cited by paragraph number. Remarks are indicated by an "R,'" student additions by an "A." Preface citations refer to page numbers in the Nisbet translation.

1830 = *Logic (Encyclopedia of the Philosophical Sciences)*, Vol. I, trans. W. Wallace. New York: Oxford University Press, 1975. Cited by paragraph number.

1831 = *Science of Logic*, trans. A.V. Miller. Atlantic Highlands, N.J.: Humanities Press, 1969. Cited by page number.

1837a = *Lectures on the History of Philosophy*, 3 volumes, trans. E. S. Haldane and F. H. Simson, Atlantic Highlands, N.J.: Humanities Press, 1955. Cited by volume and page number.

1837b = *The Philosophy of History*, trans. J. Sibree. New York: Dover, 1956. Cited by page number.

1837c = *Reason in History*, trans. R. S. Hartmann. Indianapolis: Bobbs-Merrill, 1953. Cited by page number.

1907 = *Early Theological Writings*, H. Nohl, ed., trans. T. M. Knox. Chicago: University of Chicago Press, 1971. Cited by page number of the German text (inset in the Nohl edition).

1984 = *Hegel: The Letters*, trans. C. Butler and C. Seiler. Bloomington: Indiana University Press, 1984. Cited by page number.

IMMANUEL KANT (1724-1804)

1784a = "An Answer to the Question: 'What Is Enlightenment?" In Hans Reiss, ed., *Kant's Political Writings*. New York: Cambridge University Press, 1971. Cited by page number.

1784b = "Idea for a Universal History with a Cosmopolitan Intent." Trans. C. J. Friedrich. In Carl J. Friedrich, ed., *The Philosophy of Kant: Immanuel Kant's Moral and Political Writings*. New York: Random House 1949. Cited by page number.

1785 = *Kant's Groundwork of the Metaphysics of Morals*, trans. H. J. Paton. New York: Harper, 1956. Cited by page number from *Kants Gesammelte Schriften*, Paul Natorp, ed. Berlin: Königliche Preussische Akademie der Wissenschaften, 1913 (henceforth "Akademie").

1786 = *What Is Orientation in Thinking?*, trans. L. W. Beck, in Kant (1949). Cited by page number.

1787 = *The Critique of Pure Reason*, trans. N. K. Smith. New York: St. Martin's, 1965. Cited by first edition (A) and second edition (B) Akademie page number.

1788 = *The Critique of Practical Reason*, trans. L. W. Beck. Indianapolis: Bobbs-Merrill, 1956. Cited by Akademie page number.

1790 = *The Critique of Judgment*, trans. W. S. Pluhar. Indianapolis: Hackett, 1987. Cited by Akademie page number.

1794 = *Religion Within the Limits of Reason Alone*, trans. T. M. Greene and H. H. Hudson. New York: Harper, 1960. Cited by Akademie page number, followed by Greene and Hudson translation page number.

1797a = *The Metaphysics of Morals*, Part I, trans. J. Ladd. In Kant (1965). Cited by page number.

1797b = *The Metaphysics of Morals*, Part II trans. J. Ellington in Kant (1983). Cited by page number.

1949 = *Kant's Critique of Practical Reason and Other Writings on Moral Philosophy*, trans. L. W. Beck. Chicago: University of Chicago Press. Cited by Akademie page number.

1965 = *The Metaphysical Elements of Justice*, trans. J. Ladd. Indianapolis: Bobbs-Merrill.

1983 = *Ethical Philosophy*, trans. J. Ellington. Indianapolis: Hackett.

INTRODUCTION

It may seem that any book that promises to set Hegel and feminism in something other than a hostile juxtaposition has some initial explaining to do. For few figures in the canon of Western philosophy have done more to explicitly distance themselves from anything resembling feminist goals than Hegel. As with other notable anti-feminist philosophers (such as Nietzsche), however, relatively few feminists have taken this as a reason to dismiss Hegel entirely,[1] and many have actually incorporated at least certain parts of Hegel's writings into their own work on women. Theorists as diverse in time and theoretical outlook as Simone de Beauvoir and Sandra Harding have found Hegel's parable of master and slave an informative guide for understanding the relations between men and women.[2] Likewise, in the wake of Carol Gilligan's positioning of Kantian ethics as antithetical to certain feminist concerns, it may seem natural to rethink Hegel's ethical and political writings in that light, inasmuch as they too begin from certain fundamental disagreements with the Kantian project.[3]

The link that I develop between Hegel's thought and feminism finds its origin in two broad areas of shared concern in these otherwise diverse endeavors. In the first place, Hegel combined a traditional moral and political concern for the justification of actions and institutions respectively with a historical account of the emergence of self-consciousness through social and political practices. Such a project has obvious relevance for those who are concerned with the normative implications of the emergence of women from a history of ethical and political "invisibility." Secondly, Hegel developed the highly original view that while the standards of social and political critique are socially and historically constructed, they can nevertheless yield objective insights into the nature of social reality. This kind of "historicized realism" not only cuts across a still-critical divide in ethics and political philosophy, but it offers an explanation of how feminist social critics can proffer criticisms of concepts such as universality and objectivity, while at the same time implicitly relying upon such concepts to make their criticisms stick.

In part one, I develop some of the Hegelian themes that guide my later discussions of feminist political theory by considering Hegel's project in the context of its complex relation to Kantian moral philosophy. With his various arguments that Kant's formal criterion for testing the will was "empty" in the absence of specific content, Hegel cleared the path for a political and historical account of ethics, where particular historical practices and impassioned acts of individuals play a positive role in determining the content of the universal law. Although Hegel did not abandon universality and rationality as aims of the ethical life, he called attention to the manner in which these must be socially embodied to be meaningful. Moreover, because universality itself must find embodiment in the institutions and practices of certain kinds of social order, rational agency can exist only as the lived expression of such an order. For Hegel, the kind of agency that expresses rational self-determination, to the extent that it can exist at all, can do so only in and through the culturally specific interests and desires that characterize a certain kind of social order, and not merely in the capacity to assume some idealized perspective outside that order.[4]

Because this approach to Kantianism can be taken to cut in two distinct ways, it has been used to ground two divergent approaches in Hegelian political theory. On the one hand, because universalist principles must be embodied in a particular social order to be meaningful, Hegel may be thought to provide a shield for an existing political order against "liberal" criticisms that base themselves on abstract or ideal principles. As I discuss in chapter 3, Hegel himself laid the foundation for this kind of interpretation in the *Philosophy of Right* (1821). Because his approach also asserts the right of the agent to find his[5] interests and desires embodied by the society (for the agent to be "self actualized"),[6] however, it may lend itself to the forces of radical change as well. Hegel's insistence that the moral agent must find respect not only according to the standards of traditional institutions and practices, but as an individual whose freedom must find recognition in those institutions and practices, has consequences that may be profoundly disruptive to a society. Respecting the individual is more than a matter of ensuring respect for formal rights—it is a historical project the full implications of which may be revolutionary.

In part two, I use this approach as an interpretive framework for understanding the political significance of a number of controversial feminist challenges to objectivity and universalism. In short, I aim to show that Hegel's case against Kant's abstract universalism can serve to ground a number of feminist claims as well. My considerations in this section revolve around three issues: (1) the precise roles of feminist appeals to emotions and other "particular" phenomena (e.g., specifically women's point(s) of view) and those to universality or impartiality in developing feminist criticisms of masculine hegemony; (2) the extent to which the agency of unwitting oppressors is impugned by virtue of these transforming political critiques. As regards the first question, I am concerned to explore the issues that underlie many feminist theorists' simultaneous suspicion of traditional appeals to universalism in traditional ethics and political theory and reliance upon some notion of universality in their calls for fairness and equality. These issues have implications both for the tenor of feminist political critiques, with their unabashed endorsement of a particular standpoint (or set of standpoints), and for the project of developing a feminist approach to ethics. I take up those implications in chapters 4 and 6 respectively.

The second issue, while distinct from the first, is related to it in that the justification for agent-criticism hinges critically on the universal accessibility of an act's wrongness. This is important when considering the appropriateness or inappropriateness of labels such as "sexist." Although such an appellation extends a negative judgment beyond the act to the agent, many acts and agents that have been deemed sexist would have been judged quite "normal" prior to specifically feminist criticisms. Indeed, even feminist critics have been quite clear that the sexism of various actions and practices is accessible only by taking up a previously suppressed woman's "voice" or "point of view."

I shall argue that it is possible to resolve the apparent tension between universality and particularity that arises with both of these sets of issues once they are understood in light of Hegel's distinction between universality as an abstract "formal" principle and the particular social and historical conditions that are necessary for gaining access to it. I shall argue that on a Hegelian account of universality, appeals to universal principles by members of oppressed groups may serve to transform a particular historical grasp of those principles. Because the grasp of universal concepts is necessarily an expression of the institutions and practices that govern their application, the historical emergence of an agency that challenges those institutions and practices may also force the agents of a social order to "re-conceptualize" their principles. Moreover, to the extent that persons in a particular social order achieve their ethical agency or "autonomy" by virtue of their relation to the rules or principles governing that order, such a reconceptualization may compel individuals to reassess the condition of their agency as well. Because Hegel links universality to history, the autonomy of the individual itself cannot be formally insulated against the tide of historical change.

Part 3 turns from the problems of universality and objectivity to a distinct area of recent debate within feminism concerning the politics of difference.

Although Hegel's parable of "Lordship and Bondage" in chapter 4 of the *Phenomenology of Spirit* (1807) has long been recognized as a source of insight into conditions of domination, I argue that it has not been employed as creatively as it might have been toward understanding the recovery of feminine difference. I begin by returning to Simone de Beauvoir's pioneering use of Hegelian categories in *The Second Sex* (1980), and argue that de Beauvoir did not fully exploit the critical possibilities of the latter, particularly as concerns the place of fear and risk in relations between women and men. This has particular relevance for more recent debates in both scholarly and popular feminist literature concerning the place of narratives of victimization in feminist theory. I argue that Hegel's well-known narrative of domination may be an important source of insight for this question insofar as it calls attention to how, under certain conditions, a collective history of violent "construction" by a dominant class may be a necessary condition for coming to a new and positive apprehension of the activities and the agency of the oppressed group. For Hegel, the recognition of violent subordination is in no way inconsistent with self-recognition in the characteristic activities and orientations of members of the subordinated group. I use this to suggest that the goals of social constructionist theorists such as Catharine MacKinnon need not conflict with poststructuralists such as Luce Irigaray who advocate a positive embrace of difference.

In defending the claims that Hegel's politicizing of the categories of Kantian morality can serve as a model for understanding feminist critiques of traditional normative approaches and can also serve as a framework for resolving apparent conflicts within feminist theory, I am not claiming that Hegel would have endorsed either of these projects. Although I make reference to his gloss on *Antigone* as well as to his various accounts of women's "ethical" role, it is not my aim to show that these can be taken to reveal a feminist side to Hegel's political philosophy. My claim is, rather, that what was at issue for Hegel in developing a historicized and politicized interpretation of universality and rationality is also centrally at issue in many of the most important ethical and political criticisms of contemporary feminism. Moreover, by developing an alternative approach that endorses neither a "Romantic" version of communitarianism nor a "formalist" universalism, Hegel's political theory offers a framework of particular interest to feminist theorists who would seek to avoid a similar dilemma.

Of course, by taking Hegel's critique of the moral point of view in this direction, I am assuming that his political theory has applications that go well beyond, and indeed sometimes undermine, Hegel's own rather limited use of it. This argument has been made before by those authors who have, often quite convincingly, sought to show that Hegel's political philosophy may be taken to ground radical political movements based on class (an enterprise that would not have much interested or pleased the mature Hegel).[7] Moreover, it is my contention that by investigating the symmetry between Hegel's account and later feminist critiques, certain important elements of Hegel's theory can be grasped in new and possibly more intelligible ways than before. It is not only Hegel who may be of use to feminists, but the concrete struggles of feminism may provide a lens through which certain more obscure aspects of Hegel's thought can come into focus. Such a historical reappropriation should be quite welcome from a Hegelian (if not from Hegel's own) point of view.

EMERGENT AGENCY AND NORMATIVITY IN HEGEL

HISTORICALLY EMERGENT AGENCY
Antigone and Creon

> *You cannot learn of any man the soul, the mind, and the intent until he shows his practice of government and law. For I believe that who controls the state and does not hold to the best plans of all, but locks his tongue up through some kind of fear, that he is the worst of all who are or were.*
>
> —Speech of Creon in
> Sophocles' *Antigone*

Normative theories inevitably rely upon certain assumptions about action and agency. So long as this reliance does not extend beyond the broad sphere of prevailing assumptions, it is not particularly problematic. It may occasion considerable confusion, however, when a conception of ethical acts or ethical agents is less than wholly explicit in its embrace of action-theoretic assumptions that are at odds with the prevailing set of views. This point has special relevance as regards recent investigations of Hegel's ethical and political philosophy. Often these have tended to de-emphasize the "metaphysical" or even "theological" aspects of his thought, and to focus instead upon the implications of his account of *Geist* as it concerns the social development of selfhood and agency.[1] If these implications are taken seriously, there is good reason to conclude that the assumptions of action and agency underpinning Hegel's ethical and social theory are at considerable variance with some of those dominating the philosophy of action as it has developed in Anglo-American philosophy.[2]

In this chapter, I consider certain aspects of Hegel's conception of action and agency that are of particular importance to the explicit discussions of feminist political theory in chapters to follow. It is important to outline Hegel's approach to historical "transformations" of ethical agency in some detail, because it contains some elements of both Kantian autonomous internalism and externalist approaches to justification, while being reducible to neither. I shall contend that this approach to normative justification helps to make sense of similar moves among feminist theorists. If feminists have seemed to waver between a call for "education" on the one hand and a call for "revolution" on the other, this may be a result of exactly the sort of complexities involved in the transformation of human agency on a global scale with which Hegel was centrally concerned.

In the first section, I shall outline some of the basic elements of Hegel's conception of consciousness as activity. In the second and third sections, I shall take up some of the more important ethical implications of this conception. In going about this, I shall make special reference to Hegel's account of the breakdown of ethical life in his discussion of the *Antigone* in the *Phenomenology of Spirit*, an account wherein the transformation of agency is discussed in remarkable detail. I shall identify four basic Hegelian tenets concerning agency which follow from this account: (1) self-ignorance (or "other-dependency"); (2) collective agency; (3) self-knowledge through alienation; (4) the "right of the objectivity of action." All four of these doctrines will be important in clarifying Hegel's conception of the transformation of agency and in showing how Hegel's account of ethical justification differs from more conventional approaches.

From Activity to Agency

Among the most difficult and conceptually fecund aspects of Hegel's account of the self is its assumption that self-knowledge is a collective accomplishment. In his discussion of the development of Spirit, the self or "self-consciousness" comes into being only through the existence and activity of others. Moreover, the possibilities for interaction between self-consciousness and other people are determined by the practices and institutions of culture. Thus, some kind of society is a necessary condition for self-consciousness to come into being at all. This much may not seem terribly interesting, given the prevalence of "social constructionist" accounts in contemporary sociological and anthropological theory. What may be less obvious, however, is that self-consciousness is utterly dependent upon its socially conditioned relationships with others in order to come to particular knowledge of itself, that is, in order to become aware of just what it is doing at any given time. This would seem to have some importance for discussions in ethics, particularly those in which knowing what one is doing has a bearing on moral worth.

On Hegel's account, consciousness is activity. A conscious being first becomes aware of itself as an actor or agent—as one who is already engaged in activities having more or less definite social meanings in its culture. But consciousness cannot arrive at the meaning of its actions on its own. Rather, it must rely on the re-actions of others to learn the meaning of its acts, and thereby come to a more or less adequate reflection of what is initially shrouded in the "immediacy" of its own unthinking activity. This process begins with our birth into a particular culture, but continues throughout life. It is only in this way that we can eventually attain a genuine sense of self-conscious agency, in which the activities in which we are engaged can become truly *self*-expressive. This self-expression is central to Hegel's conception of freedom, that toward which the ethical life aspires.

Charles Taylor (1983) has called attention to a number of important implications of this developmental conception of self-awareness for the philosophy of action. In particular, he is concerned to mark out certain contrasts between a Hegelian theory of action and that deriving from the classical Cartesian and empiricist views. Taylor points out that Hegel's assumptions here require us to understand the perception of our "inner states" as involving a kind of activity on two different levels. In the first place, as discussed above, coming to self-awareness is itself an activity that is carried out in the context of the institutions and practices of culture. As such, it is "something we can altogether fail to do, or do in a distorting or partial or censored fashion" (85). Secondly, the mental phenomena that are the result of this activity of "self-formulation" are not merely data or "givens," but are themselves "bound up with activity" (86). For Hegel, our desires, intentions, purposes, and so on are not simply so many "feelings," but reflect the purposes and values of the wider society of which we are a part. Just as our activities have social meanings (of which we are initially unaware), so the mental phenomena associated with them mirror wider life processes.

Among the most important implications of this account is that, contrary to the classical Cartesian and empiricist views, particular forms of self-awareness (awareness of my desires, intentions, perceptions, etc.) are neither incorrigible nor given directly to consciousness.[3] It is exactly to the extent that elements of self-knowledge are direct or "immediate" that they are *unknown*, not reflected back to consciousness from others. Moreover, once such awareness begins to take place, far from being incorrigible, it is ever subject to correction and revision on the basis of our interactions with others. This revision may come about because of our initial awkwardness in coming to a grasp of how our actions are actually reflected in our culture (from our initially poor grasp of language, for example), or because the institutions and practices of society themselves offer vague or ambiguous readings of our activities. Hegel was himself particularly concerned with those periods of historical upheaval where social meanings are in flux, the times when new shapes of conscious awareness become possible.

Taylor also contends that among the consequences of this approach to the philosophy of mind is a repudiation of causal accounts of action. The

Cartesian and empiricist accounts distinguish actions from other kinds of events by reference to their peculiar mental causes (desires, intentions, purposes, sensations, emotions, etc.). On some classical accounts these mental causes may be further reducible to physical phenomena, but they are, in any case, ontologically distinct from the actions to which they are causally related (1983: 78). Because action is a "primitive" on Hegel's account, Taylor argues that the mental component is inseparable from the action and thus incapable of standing in a causal role with respect to it. Although actions are "qualitatively distinct" from other events, this is in virtue of their being "inhabited by the purposes that direct them" and not their being caused by such purposes (78).

According to Taylor, this links Hegel's conception of action to that of Wittgensteinian action theorists who call attention to an irreducible distinction between our knowledge of actions and that of other events. According to these theorists, to the extent that I am performing an action, and am not merely being acted upon, I must, in some primitive sense, "know what I'm doing." For example, I experience a distinction between *raising* my arm to reach a shelf that is over my head, and merely noticing the arm *being raised* to the shelf (say, by means of a cable). I know that the former is my doing in a sense that the latter is not.[4] Taylor, however, distinguishes this knowledge from that of experiencing mental phenomena as causes of action in that the latter involves perceiving the intention in a contingent relation to the subsequent act.[5] Although actions are distinguished from other events by their fundamentally "purposive" character, this character cannot be captured by reference to their antecedent causal history.

Taylor's discussion goes far toward clarifying Hegel's discussion of agency in the context of contemporary analytic philosophy, and I shall be indebted to it in much of the discussion to follow. Nevertheless, his attempt to link Hegel's account to the debate over causal and non-causal accounts of action raises certain important difficulties. In particular, Taylor's contention that Hegelian agent-knowledge may come to something like "non-observational knowing," and thus rules out "causal" accounts of action, seems to cut against some of the more striking features of Hegel's descriptions of transformations of agent-knowledge. Most importantly, insofar as non-causal accounts must invoke some sense of the agent's "knowing what she's doing" in their descriptions of action, this would appear to introduce an element of "self-awareness" to the Hegelian account which could compromise its doctrine of "other-dependency." As will become clear below, this social dependency has important implications for the relationship between politics and moral responsibility.

In the next section, I shall argue that some of Hegel's most interesting discussions on agency and self-awareness in the *Phenomenology* and the *Philosophy of Right* rule out even the limited form of self-access to which Taylor alludes. By making awareness of our mental states a socially mediated activity, Hegel allows for the possibility that our intentions may be entirely opaque to us in the absence of such activity. Moreover, Hegel's discussion of the self-transformation occurring with the move from complete opacity of intention to what may be a shocking and even tragic grasp of our purpose, is one of his most original and important contributions to our understanding of ethical agency.

Self-Awareness and Self-Ignorance in the Antigone[6]

In his account of the breakdown of the original Greek *Sittlichkeit* near the beginning of chapter 6 of the *Phenomenology* ("Ethical Action. Human and Divine Knowledge. Guilt and Destiny."), Hegel provides a rich and profoundly unorthodox account of agency and self-awareness. This breakdown of the ethical life is the necessary condition for emergence of the individual, who does not yet exist in the unity of the early Greek city-state:

> [S]elf-consciousness has not yet received its due as a particular individuality. There it has the value, on the one hand, merely of the universal will, and on the other, of consanguinity, *This* particular individual counts only as a shadowy unreality. As yet, no deed has been committed; but the deed is the *actual self*. It disturbs the peaceful organization and movement of the ethical world. (1807: 464)

It is only with "the deed" *(die Tat)* that self is brought to actuality, and this deed, by its very nature, must upset the harmony of the extant community. Hegel takes up the dramatic events of the *Antigone* to illustrate the destructive process by which the individual comes into being at the end of Greek antiquity. Here, human law, embodied in Creon's command that the bodies of the attackers of Thebes remain unburied, comes up against the divine law, which Antigone obeys by burying her dead brother Polyneices. In upholding the bonds of the family and the gods over against the laws of the state, Antigone disrupts the ethical unity in which the community has subsisted. Moreover, in taking such a stand against human law, she exercises what is for Hegel a uniquely "feminine" agency. Women's unity with the divine law—"unconscious Spirit"—makes them a divisive force for Hegel, "the everlasting irony [in the life] of the community" (475).[7]

What is more important as concerns the relationship between politics and agency, however, is his detailed description of the manner in which the previously undisturbed unity of the state breaks out of its immediacy through feminine agency. The "universal self-conscious Spirit" which is manifest in Creon's decree knows itself only as the expression of the law of the state. In acting as he does, Creon merely expresses the right of the community, through its law, to protect itself. Conflicts arising out of the exercise of the community's prerogative (e.g., Antigone and her sister Ismene's horror at the order that Polyneices go unburied) are unfortunate but involve no ethical dispute. The state, in its original unity, must see its actions as expressive of the right, and, in Antigone's action, "only the self-will and disobedience of the individual who insists on being his [sic] own authority" (466).[8]

In violating the divine laws regarding burial, however, the state has, albeit in an entirely *unconscious* manner, occasioned a divided attitude toward the law.[9] Though it would "one-sidedly" claim the right to recognize in its action only a legitimate decree, only that which was consciously intended, by acting, the state renounced such claims to innocence:[10]

> By this act it gives up the specific quality of the ethical life, of being the simple certainty of immediate truth, and initiates the division of itself as the active principle, and into the reality over against it, a reality which, for it, is negative. (468)[11]

Creon's decree violates the divine law, and this is embodied in the outrage of the women, that law's "natural" guardians. The state's action, by turning "its back on the other (Antigone)," and violating her, is responsible for establishing its own "negation" and thereby passing over into "crime" (468). The state can in no way escape this responsibility, although in initially fashioning its decree it did no more than act according to its nature.

Clearly, Hegel's example is fanciful. Nevertheless, it expresses certain principles that are basic to his conception of agency and the development of self-awareness. In the first place, it is a classic example of a shape of consciousness developing through a process of "negation." This process has several identifiable steps: (1) an existing form of consciousness *(C)* exercises its agency (i.e., brings itself into actuality) in such a manner as (unconsciously) to set itself in opposition to an other *(O)*; (2) *O* rebels against this opposition (literally, it re-acts), so as to reflect the nature of the negation back to *C*; (3) *C*, because it cannot escape the judgment of *O* (in the present case, whose "nature" has been violated), is compelled, contrary to all previous expectation, to grasp its action in a negative light; (4) *C*'s agency, that by which its nature was brought into "actuality," is now transformed into "guilt," and/or "crime."[12] This process, of course, depends critically upon the assumption at (3) that *O*'s expression of outrage will be taken in such a manner as to transform *C*'s agency to guilt. Otherwise, *C* may simply dismiss the claims of *O* and go on interpreting her rebellion as "self-will and disobedience" (Hegel 1807: 466). I shall return to this point below. Before turning to that issue, however, it will be useful to consider some of the implications of this account for Hegel's conception of agency.

The Transition from Self-Ignorance to Agency

In the first place, Hegel suggests a scenario where consciousness not only lacks full awareness of what it is doing before it acts, but where its agency is utterly transformed by the "intersubjective" implications of its action. It would not be strange to say that one cannot always know fully the consequences of a particular action in advance, or even that an action may have unforeseen or surprising consequences. Presumably, no plausible account of action would deny that. The transformation that Hegel depicts here—from ethical consciousness to crime—is far more shocking, and entails a kind of "self-ignorance" that goes far beyond the usual sense of our inability accurately to predict the consequences of our acts. It suggests that, at least in certain pivotal historical circumstances, one's appreciation of agency may be entirely reversed by virtue of an act or a set of acts and the consequences which they occasion.

In order to understand how such a transformation of agency is possible, it is necessary to consider a second implication of Hegel's account, that of collective agency. In Hegel's gloss on the *Antigone*, the masculine agency of the human law embodied by Creon's decree violates the divine law. As such, it stands under the judgment of the latter, embodied in the action of Antigone. In this conflict, it is not primarily the guilt of a certain individual (Creon) and his act which is at stake, but that of an entire class (men) before the judgment of another class (women). Although an individual man experiences guilt:

> [I]t is not *this* particular individual who acts and is guilty; for as *this* self he is only the unreal *(unwirklich)* shadow, or he exists merely as a universal self, and individuality is purely the *formal* moment of action as such, the content being the laws and customs which, for the individual, are those of his class and station. (1807: 468)[13]

For Hegel, the activities by which an individual achieves a concrete determination within a culture are not initially, if ever, her own doing. Her individual agency (the sense in which her act is genuinely self-expressive) is merely *formal* in that the *content* of her action takes on its meaning within the cultural institutions and practices in which she merely plays her part. The particular individual at this stage of social history is a mere placeholder in a collective system, and it is the system that is the actual locus of agency.

Hegel's conception of collective agency underpins the discussion of responsibility in the account. Were it the case that an individual's action represented only *her*, that is, *her* particular interests and desires, she could escape the judgment of the community and the meanings it assigns to her acts. She could not be so utterly mistaken with respect to an agency that was wholly her own. For Hegel, however, this kind of self-knowledge would reverse the actual developmental order of the social world, placing the individual and its interests prior to those of culture. The judgment of others is inescapable because the content of an individual's actions is not initially her own, but embodies publicly identifiable social practices and thereby asserts those within the society.[14] To the extent that she does come to a sense of these interests as her own, it will be only through the reciprocal actions (judgments, punishments, rewards, etc.) of members of other classes in the society.

The importance of this point in coming to a grasp of Hegel's conception of self and agency can scarcely be overemphasized. To perform an action within the context of a society is fundamentally different from simply "acting out" a set of physical motions. Contrary to Taylor's assertion, however, this is not because of any special sense in which "I know what I'm doing." As the gloss on Sophocles' play makes clear, the agent may be utterly in the dark as to what she is doing as she performs the act.[15] Moreover, this inseparability of private intention and the public reception of an action is not limited to the historical characters of the ancient world. As Hegel details in the *Philosophy of Right*, what is unique about actions within the context of society is their "universal" *(allgemein)* character, that is, their function within a meaningful system of social practices:

> [T]he determinate character of the action for itself is not an isolated content confined to one external unit, but a *universal* content, containing within itself all its various connections. (1821: 119)[16]

As the embodiment of a wider system, my action is never isolated, but is part of and serves the interests of a group within that system in ways that may be unknown to me (and to everyone else as well) at the time of my acting.[17] Nevertheless, because my action has effects upon members of other groups within the system, and because I cannot escape the judgments of those groups, my self-ignorance is not invincible. By virtue of the effect my action will have on others (in the case of Creon's action, evoking "a volatile and now hostile enemy demanding revenge" [469]), I have, according to Hegel, implicitly willed the necessary condition for coming to know the content of my act. As I shall discuss in the chapters of Parts II and III, men's violations of the agency of women establish a similar set of conditions in which men may come to know the content of their character.

This suggests a third and critical implication of the account, the claim that self-knowledge arises through a process of "alienation." If I am to come to know the nature of my action, that knowledge is possible only through the action's estrangement from me—its reflection back to my consciousness through the action of certain others who are victimized or otherwise affected by it.[18] Hegel states that in the action of Creon:

> [O]nly one aspect of the resolve as such is clearly manifest. The resolve, however, is *in itself* the negative aspect which confronts the resolve with an "other," with something alien to the resolve which knows what it does. (1807: 469)

Thus, alienation, the splitting of the initial unity of the agent's "resolve," is a necessary condition for the agent's coming to conscious awareness of her action. Without it, the content of an action remains unrecognized, immersed in "the simple certainty of immediate truth" (468). In the absence of the reciprocal action of Antigone, the criminality of Creon's action remained unknown to him.

For Hegel, however, this kind of antecedent "self-ignorance" does not excuse the *agency* of the ignorant actor. Because the reciprocal action by which the original act is alienated is "in itself," or implicitly, included in the original willing, it is, for Hegel, within the agent's "intention." This suggests a fourth and most interesting implication of Hegel's account, his "right of the objectivity of action." This aspect of Hegel's concept of agency will prove most important in coming to a grasp of his approach to Kantian ethics, with its concern for the quality of the agent's intention in its assessment of moral worth.[19]

In the *Philosophy of Right*, Hegel argues that for a consequence or set of consequences of my act to be a part of my purpose or intention, it is not necessary that I consciously will it prior to the act:

> The external essence *(Dasein)* of an action is a varied set of connections which may be regarded as infinitely divided into *individual units (Einzelheiten)* . . . . But the truth of the individual *(des Enzelhen)* is the *universal,* and the determinate character of the action for itself is not an isolated content confined to one external unit, but a *universal* content containing within itself all its various connections. The purpose, as emanating from a *thinking* agent, contains not just the individual unit, but essentially that *universal aspect* already referred to—the *intention.* (1821: 119)[20]

For Hegel, the purpose of the thinking or rational agent (the nature of which I shall address shortly) is inseparable from her action's "universal side," i.e., its reception by the community. The public meaning of the action thus plays a decisive role in determining its nature for the agent. This is consistent with the conception of meaning developed in chapter 1 of the *Phenomenology,* where Hegel argues that in order to mean anything at all, even to itself, consciousness must appeal to the universality of language (that which is *mein* is a function of that which is *allgemein*). Because self-conscious awareness can exist only as the reflection of a community of meaning outside itself, self-consciousness is in no position to repudiate the perceptions of that community.[21] Such a repudiation would be, in a quite literal sense, "self-defeating." The development of a "self" is nothing other than recognizing that self, in perhaps a very unexpected or unpleasant manner, as it is alienated in action. "The accomplished deed completely alters its point of view" (1807: 470).

If the community has a right to name (universalize) the action of self-consciousness, however, self-consciousness has a reciprocal right that the universal meaning of its act be recognized as part of its intention.[22] As a rational agent, that is, one with the capacity to come to a grasp of my action in its universal character, I can claim this character as my intention:

> The *right of intention* is that the *universal* quality of the action shall have being not only *in itself,* but shall be known by the agent and thus have been present all along in his subjective will; and vice versa what we may call the *objectivity* of the action is the right of the action to assert itself as known and willed by the subject as a *thinking agent.* (1821: 120)[23]

Hegel puts an interesting spin on the concept of autonomy here. The latter is usually understood as a capacity or set of capacities to evaluate and to guide one's actions according to motives and principles that a rational agent, under some description, could unqualifiedly endorse. To be "self-legislating" or "self-regulating" in this sense, one must be able to act independently of certain kinds of alien influences.[24] For Hegel, however, the autonomy of the agent is expressed in her capacity to accept the consequences of an action as falling within the compass of her intention after the fact (or after the "act").[25] This follows, once again, from the priority of action in constituting both its objective consequences and the subjective agency by which it assumes "moral" significance.[26] Before acting, the agent does not know the content of her desires and intentions and is thus in no position to render a judgment as to their rationality. The guilt occasioned by Creon's act, for example, does not derive from his failure to act according to a set of endorsable principles, but from an unforeseeable and tragic breakdown resulting from action in accord with those principles. Still, as a "thinker," the rational agent has the capacity to grasp the consequences of the act as her own once they have been publicly constituted.[27]

As self-conscious agents, persons whose agency has developed through the meanings of a particular culture, all of us have the capacity to embrace our action, however blind or misdirected it may have been in its particular origins, from the "universal" point of view, i.e., that of the community.[28] To do this (at least within the context of our own culture), however, entails more than just recognizing another point of view on our acts. This is because, if I am to claim any meaning for my action, I must rely upon (must "posit" in Hegel's sense) others who will comprehend my meaning. To act so as to evoke condemnation from those others with whom I am in this relationship is nothing other than for me to posit the action's condemnation. It is thus that I experience the wrongness of the act as not merely an unfortunate consequence, but as the content of my own intention. Because my motive and intention come into "actuality" simultaneously with the social reception of my action within the community, my individual motivation is never clearly distinguishable from the social meaning of my acts: "Ethical self-consciousness . . . learns from its deed the developed nature of what it actually did."[29] The self-conscious agent, should its action occasion a breakdown in certain essential relationships in its society (e.g., if it is condemned for the act), experiences this break in such a way that it "cannot deny the crime or [its] guilt" (1807: 469).[30] Denial could issue only from a point of view outside the nexus of relationships within our community, and thus, in a real sense for Hegel, outside ourselves. On the other hand, to recognize our intention in the social reception of the act has a transformative effect upon our agency.

It is just such an "internal" transformation brought about by a certain "external" assessment of one's agency that was described at step (3) in the outline of the *Antigone* account above. If consciousness *(C)* cannot escape the judgment of an other *(O),* this can only be because *O*'s reading of *C*'s action expresses a socially accepted meaning of that action. In the sequence of events in Sophocles' play, the social definition of Creon's act takes shape through the series of confrontations in the play. We find the chorus first expressing sympathy toward Creon's apparently accurate grasp of his decree, then growing concern as Haemon, Antigone, and finally Teiresias expose the tragic nature of that understanding. As with other critical transitions in the *Phenomenology*, we find a major historical shift in Spirit's self-understanding contained within the space of a single dramatic event. While actual historical shifts in social meaning may be far slower and more uncertain in their movements, on Hegel's account they too are marked by epic, and often tragic, transformations of agency.

I shall take up the normative implications of Hegel's conception of rational agency in greater detail in chapters to follow. Before concluding this discussion, however, it is important to address what may seem a glaring omission in the account as outlined so far. It may be objected that whatever the merits of Hegel's descriptions for moral psychology, the only *grounds* offered for ethical transformation are those of a defunct theology. Moreover, even if the theology is taken to be grounded in a broader set of institutions and practices guiding society, it is unclear how a Hegelian account could ever justify a critical stance toward those institutions and practices. By focusing upon the agent's emergence in and through cultural practices, Hegel's ethics seems uncritically bound to them.

Although it is impossible fully to address this issue here, it is important to outline two related, though distinct, Hegelian arguments against any conservative "communitarianism" such as that suggested by this objection. In the first place, it must be emphasized that the capacity to apprehend the public meaning of one's action as one's own entails constraints on what that meaning can be. It does not follow from the fact that an agent cannot develop rational agency apart from the institutions and practices of a particular social order, that *any* set of institutions and practices will suffice to develop that capacity. The institution of slavery, for example, constitutes an extreme example of failing to effect such development for the slaves On this account, when ancient Greek society "universalized" an agent's actions as those of a slave, it failed utterly in respecting that agent's capacity as a self-determining individual. To be a slave is to find one's action, one's labor, defined as belonging to another—the master.[31] To experience one's act publicly reflected back to oneself as that of a slave is to be *unable* to embrace it as one's own, as that would contradict its public meaning. My act belongs to another. In this extreme case, the agent's attempt to embrace the public meaning of her action as her own can generate only frustration, leaving her with the options either of trying to repress her capacity for autonomy altogether, or of rebelling against the society that would define her action in such a way that she cannot take it up as her own.[32] As I shall detail in chapters 4 and 7, Hegel's description of the failure that slavery embodies has special relevance for feminist normative claims. Of course, not all ineffective social systems are so confining as that of slavery, and, consequently, they may not occasion conflict quite so readily.[33] This has been the case with a variety of accepted social practices by which women have effectively been deprived not so much of their labor as of their bodies, thereby rendering them peculiarly deprived of agency.

Secondly, Hegel holds that the procedural constraints of the moral point of view can serve as an important, though underdetermined, "starting point" toward social recognition of the demands of self-actualization. Although, contrary to moral philosophers such as Kant, Hegel does not think that the simple *application* of a formal criterion of right action can ensure the universality of an agent's willing, universality remains the goal of modern social and political orders, a goal that is manifest in the demand that the individual be respected in her freedom. Although no moral procedure can assure in advance that this goal is met, unlike the case of the ancients, we "post-Kantians" have the reflective capacity to recognize the formal demands of self-conscious agency.[34] I take up Hegel's assessment of the moral point of view as a starting point, and how that discussion intersects with the conception of agency developed here, chapters 2 and 3.

Conclusions

Some of the most unique aspects of Hegel's conception of action and agency develop around the basic themes of self-ignorance, collective agency, self-knowledge through alienation, and the right of the objectivity of action. The first three of these concern primarily the means by which self-consciousness emerges from a state of mere potentiality to actuality within a society. The right of the objectivity of action, however, concerns the capacity of self-consciousness to grasp the socially determined purpose of an action as its own, even where such a grasp was entirely absent prior to the act. Moreover, this capacity exists as a consequence of our membership in a community that assigns "universal" meaning to our acts, and of our ability, as rational agents, to take up that meaning as our own. Thus, contrary to Taylor's contention, agency for Hegel does not demand that "we . . . already have some sense, however dim, . . . of what we are doing" (1983: 80).[35] Even such a limited dependency on introspective awareness would place the individual before the social in the development of agency, and would represent a return to the "Cartesian/empiricist" picture. The most original and important aspect of Hegel's conception of action lies with its attempt to account for direction and purpose without any recourse to socially "unmediated" phenomena.

In the following two chapters, I shall turn to a more specific discussion of Hegel's conception of moral and political justification. This will complete the groundwork for parts 2 and 3, where I argue that a Hegelian framework is useful for coming to an understanding of certain key aspects of a feminist critique of sexist society. To the extent that Hegel's framework can be applied to a wider body of social and political criticism, it may serve both to provide a coherent conceptual underpinning to that criticism and to expand our understanding of the framework itself. It is to these tasks that I now turn.

HEGEL'S CRITIQUE OF "EMPTINESS"
Politicizing the Moral Point of View

> Many . . . in the Kantian tradition say that if a dis-
> course is not generalized, universal, and agreed upon,
> it is exclusionary. The problem, however, is that the
> generalized, universal, or agreed-upon never did
> solve the disagreements, resolve the differences, cohere
> the specifics, and generalize the peculiarities.
> —Catharine MacKinnon,
> *Toward a Feminist Theory of the State*

In what must appear to ethical universalists as a paradoxical move, feminists have developed a sustained ethical critique of a wide range of dominant institutions and practices and, at the same time, assailed some of the key moral categories upon which that critique relies. In fact, this simultaneous employment and critique of normative categories suggests a fertile point of intersection between Hegel and feminism. Hegel's assessment of Kantian universalism includes both an attack on its alleged "emptiness" and a qualified endorsement of it as the beginning or starting point for the complete ethical life *(Sittlichkeit)* (1821: 135R). These two appraisals are, in fact, related, as Hegel believes that it is precisely when we would try to read a moral imperative as something *more* than an abstract and underdetermined start toward a genuine grasp of the nature of the right, that the emptiness of morality becomes manifest. The critique of the hypocritical "moralism" that Hegel develops at the end of chapter 6 of the *Phenomenology* details the psychological consequences of such a misplaced adherence.

This critique alone, however, offers little toward the development of a positive account of how the "universal" point of view is supposed to function within Hegel's broader conception of the ethical life. In this chapter and the next, I take up some of the important points necessary for coming to an understanding of how *Sittlichkeit* is not only a contrast to, but a completion of Kantian morality. This will involve taking up both the early and well-known critique of the Formula of the Universal Law, in the essay *Natural Law* (1802-1803), and the account of the transition from "morality" *(Moralität)* to *Sittlichkeit,* in the *Philosophy of Right* (1821).[1] In this chapter, I shall focus upon the former critique. In particular, I argue that Hegel's much maligned charge of "emptiness" against Kantianism may be plausibly re-interpreted as an argument that Kant's Formula of Universal Law cannot function as a guide to action in the absence of socially particular background assumptions. By calling attention to these assumptions, Hegel attempts to show that Kant's universality test cannot attain the standards of universality that it sets out for itself. This discussion will form the foundation for my eventual claim (developed in parts 2 and 3 of the book) that the feminist critique of masculine conceptions of morality and justification is best understood as a similar questioning of the background assumptions governing the application of moral and political concepts in a patriarchal order.

My approach to the subjects of this chapter and the next is importantly limited. In the first place, by focusing upon Hegel's conception of the transition from morality to the ethical life, I cannot and do not purport to encompass any number of other possible approaches to Hegel's very rich and complex assessment of Kantian moral philosophy. For example, by pursuing the line of interpretation outlined above, I shall be largely setting aside the complex and interesting psychological analysis of Kant's moral philosophy in chapter 6 of the *Phenomenology of Spirit*.[2] Secondly, I am less interested in showing that any of Hegel's criticisms constitute decisive "blows" to Kant's system than I am in clarifying and developing Hegel's conception of his approach as the "completion" of Kantian morality. If my interpretations here are correct, at least some of Hegel's objections to Kantianism are most interesting when they are taken as calling attention to critically important *limitations* of universalistic moral theories, and not when they are taken as attempts to defeat them conceptually.[3] This, of course, is entirely in keeping with the "dialectical" character of his own account.[4] It may also place Hegel's ethical philosophy among Kantian "constructivist" approaches, although in rather unorthodox fashion.[5] I shall briefly address this interpretation of Hegel in chapter 3.

In the first section, I discuss the "emptiness" critique developed in the early essay *Natural Law* (1802-1803) in detail, and suggest that it can be plausibly extended to include the charge that the universalizability test cannot be employed in the absence of socially specific background assumptions. After this, I consider some of the broader implications of this charge when it is taken in the context of Hegel's social and political philosophy. I conclude my discussion by sketching Hegel's own approach to universality in ethics, and contrasting it with that of Kant. This will serve both to clarify Hegel's own account of rationality and to link his critique of Kantian universalism to certain themes developed in chapter 1.

Universality and Emptiness

In his essay *Natural Law* (1802–1803), Hegel argues that it is impossible from the "absence of contradiction" alone to derive determinate action-guiding principles.[6] This leads to the well-known, if less well received, Hegelian charge that Kant's ethics of duty is "empty." Hegel later develops this theme in terms of moral psychology, arguing that the attempt consistently to will "duty for duty's sake" leaves the moral agent entirely unguided and driven into hypocrisy.[7] For Hegel, these two critiques are related in that consciousness's discovery that it cannot attain purity of will except by purging its willing of all content (i.e., its realization that it is obliged to be "empty") drives it on a hopeless and inevitably hypocritical quest to achieve pure "conscientiousness."[8] Though Hegel has reason to link the emptiness charge with that of hypocrisy (as I note in the next section), my focus here is on the plausibility of a charge of emptiness against the test of the categorical imperative.

In his widely discussed criticism of the Kant's Formula of the Universal Law, Hegel takes up Kant's question as to whether or not it would be morally permissible to keep a deposit that has been left with him (Kant 1788: 27–28). Kant had argued that an agent could not universalize a maxim to increase her property by stealing deposits left with her when she could safely do so. He argued that "taking such a principle as a law would annihilate itself, because its result would be that no one would make a deposit" (27). Hegel questioned the normative significance of this conclusion, asking why the elimination of the practice of leaving deposits need be taken as immoral. Inasmuch as this practice is an essential part of a wider system of private property, it might be thought that it is the private property system that Kant is enjoining us to preserve. To show that undermining the practice of leaving deposits is inconsistent with the existence of private property, however, sheds no light on the morality of that system of social relations. It would be equally true, Hegel points out, that a universalized maxim of respect for property would be "inconsistent with the non-existence of property," but, in the absence of an independent judgment as to the rightness or wrongness of private property, we are no closer to knowing the morality of keeping or of not keeping deposits (1802–1803: 436–437, cf. 1807: 430, 1821: 135R).[9]

The argument that the formula of the universal law cannot, by itself, offer any guidance for the moral agent lays the foundation for a second charge.[10] Not only is Kant's procedure devoid of content when properly applied, Hegel argues, but it permits content to be surreptitiously "smuggled in" *(untergeschoben)*. Hegel caustically remarks that "in this perversion and trickery lies the nerve of pure reason's practical legislation" (1802–1803: 438). The immorality of the abolition of deposits or of the system of private property derives not from any deliverance of the categorical imperative, but from the fact that it is implicitly assumed in advance that deposits and the bourgeois property system ought not to be destroyed. Hegel further charges that by so *presupposing* the rightness or wrongness of particular actions or practices, "anything specific can be made into a duty" (438).

Hegel also takes up the opposite route in challenging Kantian universalization, arguing that apparently virtuous activities might actually fail such a test. A practice such as charity toward the poor, though apparently moral when engaged in by particular individuals or groups of individuals, will in fact prove to be immoral when thought of as universal. Hegel argues:

> The maxim, "Help the poor," expresses the supersession of the specific thing, poverty. The maxim, "Help the poor," tested by being elevated into a principle of universal legislation, will prove to be false because it annihilates itself. . . . [E]ither there are no poor left or there are nothing but poor; in the latter event no one is left to help them. In both cases the help disappears. Thus the maxim, universalized, cancels itself. (1802–1803: 80)

Not only does Kant's procedure of universalization fail to specify a particular course of action in the case of stealing loans, but it would seem also to forbid apparently moral acts such as helping the poor.

This much of Hegel's critique is well known and, many defenders of Kantian ethics have argued, is far from a decisive case against Kant.[11] Most importantly, Hegel's criticisms appear to trade on the assumption that the Formula of the Universal Law calls on the agent to inspect the universalized form of her maxim and then to judge whether or not the maxim contradicts itself in that form.[12] Kantian critics have pointed out, however, that when Kant enjoins the moral agent to "act only on that maxim through which you can at the same time will that it should become a universal law," what is critically at issue is whether or not an agent can simultaneously *will* her maxim and its universalization (Kant 1785: 422). It is when the agent who would steal a deposit attempts such a willing that a contradiction seems to arise. As Christine Korsgaard (1985) argues:

> [T]he contradiction lies not in envisioning a society in which there are no deposits, but in envisioning a society in which the agent and the others with his purpose are making use of the deposit system even though there is no such thing. (31)[13]

The conflict in the agent's will derives not from any independent normative judgments about either deposits or the property system, but from the agent's implicitly willing the existence of those practices in seeking to benefit from them.

Such a reply also addresses Hegel's concern regarding apparently moral practices such as succoring the poor (39). To the extent that the agent's purpose in giving to the poor is the alleviation of poverty, there is no contradiction in her willing that all so act and bring it about that there are no poor.[14] Such purposes in no way compel the agent to will the existence of the particular *practice* in which she is engaged. This differs from the case of stealing deposits so long as one can, because there, if the agent *wills* a world in which every person use the practice of leaving deposits to enrich themselves, no one will leave deposits, thus contradicting the agent's initial purpose in keeping the loan.

This line of response takes for granted, however, that an agent's purpose in keeping a deposit is restricted to a greedy or self-seeking aim. Clearly, this need not be the case. Were the act of keeping the loan motivated by a political end such as bringing about communism or anarchism, for example, willing that all agents act on that end, dishonestly procuring deposits and thus "destroying the practice," would be entirely consistent with the antecedent intention to eliminate private property. Precisely because the deliverances of the contradiction in will test are contingent upon the agent's particular intention, it cannot rule out *a priori* the possibility that an agent's purposes may be consistent with the elimination of the practice in which she is engaged (as was illustrated in the case of the agent who would aim to eliminate poverty by means of a charitable practice).

To see this more clearly, it is useful to consider the structure of Korsgaard's (1985) argument defending Kant against Hegel's charges. She argues that from,

> (1) *A* cannot rationally will an action that would become ineffectual for the achievement of *A*'s purpose if everyone employed, or tried to employ it for that same purpose (p. 25),

it follows that,

> (2) *A* cannot rationally will to use a practice *(P)* as a means to achieve her purpose, if willing *A*'s maxim universally would destroy *P*. (38-39)[15]

Claim (1) states a version of Kant's contradiction in will test (Korsgaard's "Practical Contradiction Interpretation"). Claim (2), however, is stronger than (1), and follows from it only on the further assumption that it would be irrational for *A* to will the destruction of *P*. So long as *A*'s purpose is not inconsistent with destroying or undermining *P,* and so long as no independent assumptions regarding the rationality of that purpose are called into play, there is no contradiction in will.[16]

This suggests that the Hegelian charge of underdetermination against the categorical imperative is defensible, though in rather a different form from that for which Hegel explicitly argued. Although Hegel is right that some "content" is presupposed in his example of the test, this is not because the Kantian must antecedently assume that the particular actions or practices up for review are justified. Rather, it is the range of subjective principles for an agent's proposed action that reflects particular normative assumptions on Kant's part.[17] In order to specify an agent's maxim and to rule out an indefinite range of socially and psychologically possible principles of action, Kant must assume the morality or immorality of certain lines of conduct.

It is important to distinguish this charge from an apparently similar, and more readily defeasible, claim sometimes associated with it.[18] It might be thought that in charging that the application of the categorical imperative enjoins the agent illicitly to "import" particular content into the procedure, Hegel was making the relatively innocuous claim that it is impossible to apply the test of the categorical imperative without some appeal to the particular content of an agent's willing.[19] By itself, it is hard to see what force this is supposed to have against the test of the categorical imperative, since the impossibility of determining the morality of one's action in the *absence* of the agent's particular purpose is implied in the very form of Kant's test. Much as theoretical reason depended upon the manifold of intuitions in coming to a knowledge of the conditions of possible experience, so practical reason's grasp of the "moral possibility" of a given action may be understood to require a particular principle of the will that is subjected to moral scrutiny.[20] So long as it is the particular content of the will that is subjected to the moral law, and not the other way a round, there need be no inconsistency in a test for universality relying on that content.[21]

Because the particular content of the agent's maxim cannot be specified as narrowly as Kant held, however, the range of potentially universalizable action may be far wider than he thought it was. Though this kind of criticism does not render judgments based on a "formal" standard such as the categorical imperative entirely insignificant, it does call attention to important limitations of such judgments. While the categorical imperative may prove a most useful tool in grasping why a particular course of action involves a socially unacceptable violation of my own agency or that of another, it remains tied to the perspective of a given social order in its formulation of principles of the will.

This has two distinct implications of normative significance. First, owing to concrete differences in the *cultural* construction of the will, persons in one kind of social order may find it "morally possible" to will maxims, which might be impossible in other social situations. Across different cultures, and even within a single culture over time, there exist a multiplicity of institutions and practices in light of which individual agents can make sense of their actions.[22] In an honor-based social order, for example, an agent might be able to universalize a maxim of blood revenge for crime, even where doing so entails the possibility of bringing about the agent's own demise.[23] In such a society, the possibility of dying with honor might be an acceptable risk, even if it could not be for agents in a law-based society.[24] Because the institutions and practices by which we make sense of our activities vary cross-culturally, the background assumptions governing the application of the categorical imperative may vary, and, along with them, what actions are or are not procedurally justified.

By itself, the fact that the moral law might be expressed differently in different cultural settings might not seem so troubling.[25] To the extent that our ability procedurally to judge our acts relies upon the norms of a changing social order, however, this may pose serious difficulties for gaining access to the demands of universality even within a particular culture. Because our access to the moral law via the procedure of the categorical imperative is grounded in social practices, *violations* of that law that are embedded in those practices may be procedurally inaccessible to us.[26] Where the application of a formal criterion of the right requires culturally specific background assumptions, the successful application of the criterion alone cannot guarantee the universality toward which it aims. Hence, it cannot ensure that the agent has freed her willing from all alien content and acted autonomously. Inasmuch as it is the concern for autonomous willing that guides other aspects of Kant's moral philosophy, it is worth considering the ramifications of this dimension of Hegel's critique in greater detail.

The Political Implications of Hegel's Critique

As noted above, Kant and Hegel share a commitment to universality as the standard of normativity in the ethical life. To the extent that the test of the categorical imperative relies upon particular content in stipulating possible principles of action, it cannot, or at least it cannot always, serve as an adequate means of *access* to such universality. So long as the exceptions to the application of the test are restricted to the unsavory purposes of certain misanthropic individuals, or even to certain kinds of "revolutionary" maxims, however, the implications of this fact may not be fully apparent.[27] When specific sets of social relations function as hidden background assumptions for the application of a formal criterion, even acts can be "universalized" may nevertheless fall short of the demands of universality.

Should private property, for example, play a functional role in an oppressive system where one group of persons is enslaved, exploited, or otherwise subordinated by another, an agent who decides upon moral reflection to repay her deposits, even if her action is not egoistically motivated, may embody those violent relations in her act.[28] The particular *interests* her actions express may violate those of a certain group.[29] Where oppressive relations come to form part of the accepted background assumptions for applying a formal criterion of right, it will be impossible within the purely formal mechanisms of the criterion to come to an awareness of the objectionable relation. No matter how conscientiously an agent attempts to apply the test, no matter how searching her introspection may be, unless the system of social relations that informs her judgment comes to light, she may remain blind to the oppression her agency embodies. Like Creon in Sophocles' play, she may come to find her action taking on an altogether unexpected and unwanted shape.

On the other hand, to the extent that an agent's maxim embodies a challenge to widely held but objectionable background assumptions operational in the application of a formal test, that maxim's apparent failure to pass the test need not entail that it violate the agent's autonomy. Hegel held that in certain pivotal historical circumstances, violations of social conventions that were previously considered justified (i.e., conventions that would have passed a universalizability test given the background assumptions operative in the society in question) may be precisely what is needed to "mediate," i.e., to embody in a socially meaningful way, the violent nature of those conventions, and thereby to express the autonomy of the violated agents.[30] This will occur when the state of affairs occasioned by an apparent violation of the moral law can serve as the causal condition for making a violation of the moral law accessible to moral reflection.[31]

Suppose, for example, the state of affairs occasioned by a mass refusal to repay debts in a particular society could function as an effective public expression of the violence done to an impoverished class in that society. If an agent who is a member of that class acts upon a reflective judgment that she ought to repay her debts (e.g., a judgment that she could not simultaneously will a maxim to withhold payment and its universalization), this may be morally suspect. Not only could such an action fail to respect the agency of the member of the impoverished class but, ironically, it could limit access to more impartial judgments with regard to poverty in society at large. Perhaps the agent's assertion of outrage, and refusal to abide by the demands of a conception of impartiality that is tied to the assumptions of an intransigent economic system, will serve to publicize the violence of that system.

The Kantian may object to this point, maintaining that even if an agent serves as the unwitting vehicle of a particular, and even a heinous interest, so long as she has done her best to take an impartial perspective with regard to her proposed action and to act out of that point of view, her willing retains its purity. Moral worth, after all, consists not in the actual consequences of an action, but in the condition of its willing.[32] To hold an agent responsible for the effects of actions to which she lacked reflective access, whatever that comes to, is simply alien to the Kantian emphasis upon the good will.

If Hegel is right, however, that any application of the categorical imperative must, however opaquely, appeal to the content of particular social practices, then Kantian agents are obliged morally to take that fact into account in assessing the worthiness of their acts. If I take seriously the possibility that, perhaps entirely unbeknownst to me, my morally reflective judgments express immoral agency, this must affect my certainty with regard to an action based on such judgments. To insist stubbornly that my willing remains pure when I am fully aware that my action might express an immoral will (even if I am not aware just *how* it might) suggests the duplicity of which Hegel was critical in his account of "Morality" in the *Phenomenology of Spirit*.[33] It is precisely when the agent would adhere to Kant's doctrine of moral worth *and*, at the same time, reject his contention that it is possible to test one's maxim without appeal to alien content that she is susceptible to the charge of hypocrisy.

It is important to emphasize two points with regard to this discussion before taking up Hegel's alternatives. First of all, the threat to autonomy that it suggests directs concerns about "particularity" away from the Kantian focus on the individual and toward the social conditions of action.[34] The test of the categorical imperative assumes that the "dear self" and its egoistic nature constitutes the primary threat to an agent's autonomy.[35] Hegel, by contrast, draws attention to specific social conditions operative in the agent's willing. In the case of leaving deposits, it is quite possible, and no doubt usually the case, that the agent who judges upon moral reflection that she ought to pay back a loan, does not do so out of what we would ordinarily call a *selfish* inclination. Her judgment, nevertheless, relies upon the assumptions of a historically particular set of social relations, and one that embodies particular sets of interests.

Secondly, with regard to the last example, even if *A*'s *apparent* violation of the moral law was the causal condition for expanding a social conception of the moral law in *S*, it does not follow from this that *A* violated the moral law as it comes to be understood in its later form. To the extent that the background assumptions governing the application of a formal criterion are successfully altered, the justification of what appeared previously to be a violation of the law will be apparent to impartial reflection, as will the unlawful nature of what may previously have appeared to be right. Hegel considers this aspect of moral transition in *Reason in History* (1837b):

> The later universal, so to speak, the next higher genus of the preceding species, is potentially but not yet actually present in the preceding one. This makes all existing reality unstable and disunited. (38)[36]

Hence, it would not seem strictly correct to say that those persons and movements that challenge a historical conception of morality by violating its ordinances are necessarily acting "immorally" in doing so.

If this is right, then Hegel's criticism of the moral point of view does not count against universalizability as a *purely abstract* criterion of justification, but it does serve to draw attention to that criterion's limitations in affording reliable access to the content of a truly "impartial" point of view at any given stage of history. On the one hand, the deliverances of a principle of universalizability cannot guarantee that an action is in accord with the moral law. On the face of it, this may not appear to be a very serious charge, in that Kant's first formulation of the categorical imperative need not be understood as providing a sufficient condition for moral action unless it is understood to include a principle of respect for persons as ends in themselves as well. In fact, however, the limitation is more serious. Because an agent may run afoul of the true demands of morality even when she adheres to the demands of a principle of universalizability, the categorical imperative may fail to specify necessary conditions for moral action.

Moreover, if *moral reflection,* where that is understood as the attempt procedurally to subject one's proposed actions to impartial judgment, is subject to this kind of error, then its value as a guide for autonomy must itself come under scrutiny. If apparent violations of the formal criterion are not really immoral, or, conversely, if acts that are apparently justified are not really moral, then acting in accord with the demands of morality is not a reliable standard for autonomous agency. The motivation to subject one's desires to an impartial standard may be precisely what is not needed in advancing our access to a truly universal point of view.[37] It may be that it is precisely through the mediation of those desires or interests that a new and more encompassing grasp of the right is made possible.[38]

In arguing that we can move toward a more universal perspective by means of particularity, Hegel anticipated the moves of certain feminist philosophers of science who have argued for the importance of particular points of view for expanding objectivity in the sciences. As Helen Longino (1990) has argued, because "experimental results can be taken as evidence for hypotheses only in the context of some set of background beliefs," merely following scientific procedures is not adequate to ensure objective results (48):

> [T]here are standards of rational acceptability that are independent of particular interests and values but . . . the satisfaction of these standards by a theory or hypothesis does not guarentee that the theory or hypothesis in question is value- or interest-free . . . . [T]he development of knowledge is a necessarily social rather than individual activity, and it is the social character of scientific knowledge that both protects it from and renders it vulnerable to social and political interests and values. (12)

For Longino, it is precisely when the background assumptions governing the acceptance of experimental results as evidence for hypotheses are up for debate, i.e., when political conflicts of interest call assumptions into question, that scientific "objectivity" is advanced.[39] Following a Hegelian line of thought, Longino holds that social conflict can serve as the means toward achieving better theory. By the same token, the fact that a theory fails to occasion social debate need not indicate that it is more "universal," but may, on the contrary, show that a particular set of background assumptions remain transparent and outside the sphere of critical inquiry.[40]

Seen in this light, Hegel's abiding concern for universality need not be inconsistent with the fact that the key figures and movements in his account of world history are characterized by acts that defied or challenged rather than respected the standards of their ethical world. From Antigone's familial devotion to the passionately individualistic desires of the "world historical individuals," it is through the mediation of non-ethical motivations that the dramatic actors of Hegel's writings transform the assumptions underpinning the ethical life at the times of the acts.[41] Altlthough the "universality" of these epic acts may be subject to a formal grasp *after the fact*, because that grasp is itself informed by the transformed ethical categories, no formal procedure can reliably assess them in advance (cf. 1837b: 34-43). Moral philosophy's "owl of Minerva" too arrives with the dusk, when it is too late for counsel.

Thus, the Hegelian charge that the application of the Formula of the Universal Law requires socially particular background assumptions, when that charge is understood in the context of certain aspects of his doctrines of "self-ignorance" and collective agency, points to critical limitations of the Formula. The fact that I can consistently will a maxim at the same time as that which is, to the best of my knowledge, its "universalization" is no assurance that my willing does not embody a particular agency, even an agency that is oppressive. The background assumptions necessary for the application of the formula (e.g., economic conditions) may conceal collective relations of oppression. Likewise, my apparent inability consistently to will my maxim simultaneously with its universalization need not show that my action would not express universality, or at least a higher stage of it.[42] It may, independent of any conscious intention of my own, mark a historical challenge to the existing moral categories.[43]

Hegelian Universalism

As discussed so far, Hegel's criticism of the first formulation of the categorical imperative has focused upon its failure as a procedure for specifying a point of view that is truly impartial. Because the application of its criterion for right action must take place against a backdrop of particular social and political assumptions, the categorical imperative cannot ensure that the judgments it yields do not embody objectionable content.[44] As such, this criticism points to a critical limitation of Kantian moral theory. Even if Hegel is right about the shortcomings of Kant's *procedure*, however, it is not immediately clear how this criticism bears on the considerations that motivated the procedure in the first place. In particular, to show that the moral agent cannot specify the content of the universal point of view by means of a formal procedure (such as the categorical imperative) does not show that the content of this point of view is not ethically relevant.[45] In other words, it does not support, or at least does not obviously support, the stronger claim often associated with Hegelianism that Kant's conception of impartiality is itself mistaken as a standard for the ethical life.

The set of issues surrounding Hegel's conception of "universality" raises deep and important questions regarding not only the scope and nature of a Hegelian critique of Kantianism, but the manner in which a critique of universalism can simultaneously be governed by universal principles. This issue is of critical importance for the feminist social criticisms that I shall take up in the chapters to follow. As suggested above, and as I further discuss in chapter 3, even if Hegel's argument is limited to showing that the application of a formal criterion cannot ensure immediate *access* to an impartial point of view, this has significant consequences for social and political theory. Indeed, none of my critical points to follow will entail going beyond this weaker claim. It is important, nevertheless, at least to sketch some of the reasons why Hegel may appear to have embraced the stronger and more controversial claim that impartiality is mistaken, even as an abstract standard for the ethical life. This will both tie his critique to some of the considerations taken up in chapter 1 and help to clarify his peculiar use of certain terms.

In the first place, it is clear that Hegel never eschewed what he termed the "Universal" as the goal of the ethical life. In the *Philosophy of Right* (1821), he states that the goal of the ethical life is "rationality," and "the universal which has being in and for itself in general is what is called the *rational* (*vernünftig*)" (24R).[46] Moreover, as I shall emphasize in chapter 3, Hegel is adamant in his rejection of a Romantic "intuitionism" that would eliminate rationality from the ethical life.[47]

Just as importantly, his objections to the application of the categorical imperative in *Natural Law* (1802-1803) do not appear to count against a procedure of universalization *per se*. Even if Hegel is right that the Formula fails in Kant's case of the loan, for example, this does not show that my inability consistently to will *M* simultaneously with its *genuinely* universalized counterpart (e.g., *M* universalized over all times and social situations) would not show *M*'s "moral impossibility." Though a moral agent may be ever subject to error, even disastrous error, in applying the Formula (due to her finite knowledge of society and history, for example), that need not count against universality as an abstract criterion for right action.[48] Just as the attempt to apply a standard of objectivity in empirical science may fall prey to a variety of experimental errors without thereby challenging the criterion, so the failures of historically situated moral agents do not, by themselves, constitute an objection to a universalizability standard.[49] Such error might in fact suggest that success could be ensured only at "the end of history," a view that could situate Hegel's own project in the context of a broader Kantian conception of justification. For example, Hegel's "dialectical anthropology" could be interpreted as "deducing" the social and historical conditions for achieving the impartiality at which Kant's moral philosophy aims.[50]

It would be seriously misleading, however, to take Hegel's commitment to rationality or universality as a simple endorsement of Kant's understanding of those concepts. As noted in chapter 1, Hegel conceives the true "universal" *(allgemein)* to be a reflection of the life, institutions, and practices of a certain kind of community *(Gemeinschaft)*. This conception informs his distinction between "abstract" or "external" universality and the absolute universality that characterizes the fully developed ethical life. In his formal dialectical account of the "universal," Hegel distinguishes three "moments" or functional divisions of that concept: universality, particularity, and individuality.[51] At the level of the "Understanding" *(Verstand)*, universality is simply contrasted with particularity, and does not move on to the synthesis of the two in individuality.[52] At this "abstract" level, universality expresses abstraction "from everything determinate," expressing a common *[gemeinsam]* property [1821: 7R]. "Reason" *(Vernunft)*, in its cunning, however, overcomes the opposition between abstract universality and mere particularity by embodying the universal in the particular desire of the individual.

It is, of course, Hegel's contention that Kantian morality remains at this abstract level, where universality is simply opposed to particularity. The test of the categorical imperative, by exploiting the contrast between a merely egoistic determination of the will and a will that would take as its maxim only a principle that could hold for all rational agents, fails to get beyond abstract concepts of particularity and universality. Thus, the test falls short of the moment of "Individuality," where Reason prevails over the apparent inconceivability of an action that would simultaneously embody both the universal and the particular (7R).[53] By not attempting to grasp how the individual will, in all its "particularity," could adequately embody the universal law, Kant's discussion does not get beyond the abstract analyses of the Understanding.[54]

Hegel is centrally concerned here that the demands of the moral law find expression in and through the desires of the individual, and with the arrangement of institutions and practices that would make such a coincidence likely to occur. Here, ethics and socio-political thought merge. By reducing ethics to the application of a formal criterion to the desires of the agent, Kantian morality licenses the trampling of individual desire, and effectively short circuits the complex *social* task of transforming uncultivated sensuous desires into a desire for the right. Hegel's concept of absolute universality, or "Individuality," seeks to express the unity of particular desire and universal right, and the transcendence or completion of the stage where these are understood as opposed—capable of unification only by the domination of one by the other.

I shall attempt to specify more concretely what this transformation might come to in the next chapter. What is important for the discussion at hand is the way in which the distinction between Kantian justification and Hegelian transformation points to a basic divergence in their respective conceptions of reason and universality. Both Kant and Hegel acknowledge the capacity of reason to transcend a "merely particular" perspective on the world by taking up a new and more encompassing grasp of reality. On a Kantian account, rationality is expressive of my ability to take up a new, more or less impartial, point of view on the world, and to act on the basis of that view. *Qua* moral agent, I can leave my limited, personal perspective and take up a more universal vantage point from which to assess my personal interests and so judge my action. I express my rational agency to the extent that I adjust my action in accord with my reasoned judgment.

For Hegel, on the other hand, rationality turns on the self-conscious agent's ability to re-conceptualize, or transform her *particular* grasp on the world. My capacity as a rational agent is realized insofar as I can, without compromising my self-consciousness, apprehend the universal meaning of my act (i.e., the meaning that it has in the context of the institutions and practices of my community). As discussed at the end of chapter 1, this interpretation of universality places constraints on both the agent and the community. If the community's description of an agent's activity is not one that a self-conscious agent could take up (if, for example, it fails to ascribe the activity to the will of the agent at all, as in a slave society where the slave merely embodies the master's will), then that description fails the demands of rationality.[55] It will be met by the rebellion of the agent and a breakdown of community. If, on the other hand, the agent's grasp of her action is inconsistent with that action's description in the community *and* that description is one that respects her agency as a self-conscious agent, then she will find her grasp transformed.[56] She will recognize the violation of the law in her action, and grasp it as such. "The doer cannot deny the crime or his guilt" (Hegel 1807: 469).

I discuss these transformations in greater detail in chapters 3 and 6. It is clear, however, that for Hegel there can be no genuine universality (i.e., "concrete" universality) that is not simultaneously the expression of the self-conscious agent's particularity. If the agent finds her desires and beliefs regarding her action at odds with universality, such that she would have to *impose* the moral law upon herself, then this signals a breakdown in the life of the community.[57] A Hegelian account could not privilege a point of view that is universal in the sense of being simply "impartial," where that is understood to abstract from particular interests, and present its judgment as a "demand" on the agent. The concept of impartiality still assumes a duality between the particular and the universal in which the agency of the individual can remain untransformed.

On the other hand, Hegel conceives of "transformation" as more than a retreat into particularity, since it is in the power of Reason (as opposed to

Understanding) to remake what was hitherto "alien" and "heteronomous" into its own willing: "It [the will] is *universal*, because all limitation and all particular individuality *[Einzelheit]* are superseded within it" (Hegel 1821: 24).[58] Rather than an ability to take up a standpoint removed from particular interests and desires, Hegelian universality or rationality might better be thought as the capacity to realize (or recognize) my freedom in what was formerly alien to me.[59]

It is a further implication of this account of universality (at least in Hegel's view) that the concrete universal will cannot be a distant goal, achievable only at some later date, as was suggested above. Reason is always present in some form in the institutions and practices of any social order.[60] To put universality off to another time would make of ethics an "ought-to-be" that never "is," or at least never is before a final reckoning. It is among the explicit aims of Hegel's ethics to show that the ground for the ethical life is actual: "The rose in the cross of the present" (1821: preface, 22). However inadequate the embodiment they offer, reason can come to actuality only through the particular institutions and practices of society as these develop dialectically through the struggles of self-consciousness. The point in calling attention to the background assumptions necessary for applying the Formula of the Universal Law was not to recommend a distant ideal ethics that would have *no* particular background assumptions, but rather to show that any meaningful account of the ethical life *must* have them. The transition from morality to *Sittlichkeit* is a move *from* the merely formal starting point of an impartial point of view *to* that of a socially specific, functioning community.

This is, of course, consistent with Hegel's own description of the "Ethical Life" in Part Three of the *Philosophy of Right* (1821). Although the latter is clearly intended to express universality, it is far from eschewing particularity. Hegel's description includes not only an internal social order characterized by clearly identifiable classes or estates *(Stände)*, but a nation that itself exists in a context of other rival, and even warring states (324f). Regardless of one's assessment of the plausibility of this as a description of "rational" order, it is clear that Hegel never conceived universality as excluding the particular identification of an agent's interests—either as a member of a class or of as the citizen of a state. This is manifest in his endorsement of a political order in which class identifications would be maintained and play a central role in the self-identification of groups of citizens (and not be eliminated, as in Marxism, for example).[61]

There is, however, a critical ambiguity in Hegel's identification of the rational and the actual, and his consequent rejection of a morality of "ought-to-be." As I argued in chapter 1, and will further elaborate in the next chapter,

Hegel's account of the political development of agency has the resources to make "formal" distinctions between more and less effective political orders. This is clearly evidenced in the divisions of the *Philosophy of Right* where certain social practices (e.g., revenge) are given an early place in the dialectical chronology, and thus deemed less rational than later ones.[62] Likewise, the inadequate structure of certain relationships such as that of "Lord and Bonds-man" may be identified and employed as a basis for social critique. Thus, it is not strictly true to say, even of Hegel's system, that it eschews all formal normative judgments.

At least part of what Hegel had in mind in rejecting an ethics of merely "ought-to-be" *(Sollen)* appears, once again, to concern a morality that would pretend to base itself on formal judgments alone, and thus fail to acknowledge the socially particular background assumptions that must inform it. Although Hegel attempted formally to "deduce" the various stages of self-conscious development, the "actualization" of those stages is entirely dependent upon the contingencies befalling the historical development of society. That a particular action will meet or fail to meet the demands of Reason is, in the end, determined by the institutions and practices of a given society. It is impossible via any formal procedure reliably to anticipate how those institutions and practices will engender future transformations of agency, or concretely to predict the precise shapes that Spirit will take.[63] "[No] individual can overleap his own time or leap over Rhodes" (Hegel 1821: "Preface" 21-22 [see also 1837c: 37]).[64]

This reading, however, is consistent with an indefinite progression of shapes of consciousness through history, each embodying a more or less rational concept of agency. In other words, there might indeed be an everlasting "ought-to-be," in the sense that judgments of that form are understood to refer to the future dialectical resolutions of continuing conflicts (cf. Hegel 1837c: 38-40). This would not be an abstract ideal, since its content would be mediated by the causes, interests, and "passions" of particular persons and groups in history.[65] Barring some special metaphysical access to the "End of History," however, Hegel's account cannot eliminate the "ought" of the ethical life. (See note 52 above.) What it can do, on the contrary, is specify how limited the Understanding is in gaining a fix on just what it is that ought to be.

Conclusion

In this chapter, I have attempted to specify Hegel's critique of Kant's formal procedure of justification, and to suggest some of the political implications of that critique. I have also sketched how Hegel conceives himself to have maintained a commitment to "Universality" despite his critique of "universalization" as a method. Though Hegel does make appeal to Reason and Universality in his ethical philosophy, his use of these terms is highly idiosyncratic, and must be understood in the context of other aspects of his system.

In chapter 3, I shall go beyond Hegel's explicit criticisms of Kantianism, and discuss in greater detail how certain aspects of the normative account developed in chapters 1 and 2 might be applied to problems of social and political philosophy. In particular, I shall be concerned to show that certain aspects of a specifically Hegelian approach to the ethical life may be fruitfully employed in political critique. This will involve showing how, despite the methodological conservatism that Hegel's link between "absolute universality" and actually existing social orders appears to entail, his approach can be employed toward radically re-conceptualizing existing social relations. These considerations will lead directly into my discussion of feminist critique in parts II and III.

HEGEL'S PHENOMENOLOGY AND IMPARTIAL JUSTIFICATION
Toward a Historical Realism in Ethics

> *Here my friend Dorothy has protested: "Morality! I'd call it ethics." She hates the word, it having been used against her often. It's true: her Baptists, and my Presbyterians, not to mention others we could name, have turned the word on us too much. But Dorothy, ethics sounds like classical Greece to me. What if I say, not morality but —I'm trying to talk about struggling against racism and anti-Semitism as issues of how to live, the right-and-wrong of it, about how to respect others and myself. It is very hard for me to know how to speak of this struggle because the culture I was born and raised in has taught me certain ways of being that reduce the process of change to ought-to, that reduce the issue of how to live to ought-to.*
>
> —Minnie Bruce Pratt
> "Identity: Skin Blood Heart"

In his dialectical account of Kantian morality, Hegel not only raises a set of criticisms against Kant's approach to the ethical life but attempts to resolve the contradictions to which he saw Kant's account giving rise. Hence, it was not Hegel's aim to scuttle either Kantian morality or the place of a formal criterion of the right in modern ethics more generally. By contrast, he sought to *situate* "morality" within his own broader approach, one that purported to take into account the contribution of the moral point of view to the historical development of self-consciousness.[1] Under the influence of writers such as Friedrich Schiller, Hegel could not accept the moral psychology of the agent who seeks to conform to the strictures of impartial morality as properly expressing the nature of the ethical life. In contrast to some of his Romantic contemporaries, however, Hegel insisted that this life was altered decisively by the appearance of the moral point of view. It was in this spirit that he declared that perspective to be the necessary starting point, but no more than that, for all modern discussions of ethics.

In chapter 2, my discussion focused upon Hegel's highly negative assessment of Kantian morality with its charge of "emptiness." In this chapter, I shall expand upon that discussion by considering the manner in which Hegel took

Kant's universalist ethics to be importantly superior to alternative methods of justification, and saw it as the "starting point" for his own approach. In clarifying this mixed tribute, I shall focus attention upon the reconceptualization of the moral categories that must occur with the historical emergence of novel "shapes of self-consciousness." Of central importance for determining the "background assumptions" governing a historical concept of universality is the relationship of members of different groups within a given social order. As previously silent or suppressed forms of consciousness emerge, our access to the universal is also transformed. Although my discussion of the collective emergence of historical shapes of consciousness draws from Hegel's own treatment of those issues in the *Philosophy of Right* (1821) and the *Phenomenology of Spirit* (1807), it is not my intention to argue that Hegel would himself have endorsed the particular *applications* to which I shall put this theory. As I point out in the second section below, there is little question that, at least in his mature writings, Hegel was far from advocating the kind of "revolutionary" political changes that I shall employ certain aspects of his political theory to explain.[2] Interestingly, however, his "phenomenological" account of past transformations of social consciousness, and, even more ironically, his political counsel on how to *prevent* the development of the rebellious "rabble," lend themselves to interpretations that go well beyond his specific political ends.[3]

It is worth noting that by integrating a positive account of the regulative capacity of moral concepts with the claim that such a capacity requires historically contingent and changeable content, Hegel embraces the very considerations that have inspired both moral realists and moral skeptics. To the extent that Hegel's acceptance of the universal regulative capacity of moral concepts presupposes the existence of an experience-transcendent moral reality, he must be counted a realist in ethics. Unlike conventional moral realists, however, Hegel rejects the view that such a reality can make itself felt independently of our conceptual scheme and, as a corollary, asserts that ethical knowledge is a socio-historical phenomenon.[4] In the pages to follow, I shall outline Hegel's justification for this position, which I dub "historical realism," with an eye toward how such a view can function to explain certain important aspects of feminist political critique.

In the following section, I describe Hegel's positive approach to the moral point of view, drawing out some of the implications of his argument that it must find "completion" in the ethical life of a community. In the next section, I go on to describe how such a completion can occasion the collective reconceptualization of the moral point of view. In such a process, the background assumptions for the application of moral categories are effectively altered such that the categories themselves undergo a change in scope and/or meaning. In the next section, I return to the question of universality with which I concluded chapter 2. I discuss how the process of reconceptualization involves an appeal to the constraints of impartiality which, while strikingly different from that of Kant, nevertheless retains much of the conceptual apparatus of his critical philosophy.

Toward a Historical Realism in Ethics

In coming to an understanding of Hegel's complex assessment here, it is useful to begin with his dialectical account of the point of view associated with Kantian morality.[5] Specifically, Hegel credits that perspective for its assertion of "the pure unconditional self-determination of the will as the root of duty" (1821: 135R). He identifies this respect for the capacity of the will self-consciously to embody universality in its individual action (autonomy) as an epic advance in the historical development of self-consciousness. Indeed, it is the final stage in the ethical development of Spirit from its initial breakdown at the end of Greek antiquity *(Antigone)* to its new unity in the *Sittlichkeit* of the modern state.[6] Whereas in previous ages, the *universal will* always assumed its shape in a political, cultural, or religious form, it can now find a home in the agency of the individual.[7] In previous epochs, standards for the ethical life were simply functions of the social system of which the individual agent was a part. With the shape of self-consciousness emerging out of the French Revolution and its destructive aftermath, however, Hegel asserts that the barrier between these has decisively been broken: "Absolute freedom has thus removed the antithesis between the universal and the individual will" (1807: 595).

For Hegel, there is no question of going back on this development. The freedom of the individual, and the ever-changing manner in which that freedom is understood, is the proper locus of modern political theory. Moreover, by insisting upon the "absolute" link between the purposes of the individual and the moral worth of her action, Kantian morality embodies the central importance that the freedom of the individual has properly taken on. It is emblematic of the advance from self-less immersion in the "objectivity" of social institutions and practices to reflective self-conscious awareness.[8]

This advance, however, must be understood dialectically, i.e., as representing a triumph over a previous shape of consciousness. Kantianism's expression of the spirit of Enlightenment individualism, while important, like all "narratives of victory," presents a one-sided account of the struggle. To pay homage to the freedom and autonomy of the individual without attending at least

equally to society, the actual medium that must concretely embody that freedom, leaves us with only an abstract and formal conception of autonomy:

> [T]o cling on to a merely moral point of view without making the transition
> to the concept of ethics reduces this gain to an *empty formalism,* and moral
> science to an empty rhetoric of *duty for duty's sake.* (1821: 135R)[9]

As discussed in chapter 2, Hegel argues that the form of the universal law
remains underdetermined unless it is informed by the content of the particular
social institutions and practices that characterize the ethical life of a society.

Respect for the individual will embodied in the moral point of view can
take on a concrete meaning, "actuality," only when it assumes a shape within
the ethical and political life of a certain kind of community. Although the moral
agent has a right to have her rational capacity (her ability to be a "thinker")
respected and expressed in that community, such a right assumes that social
practices will determine a set of conditions for its exercise. This is the balance
that Hegel thinks must be maintained between the "right of intention" and the
"right of the objectivity of action" discussed in chapter 1 (Hegel 1821: 120). Of
course, this balance cannot be assured by just *any* political community. Hegel
suggests that there may be certain exceptional cases where even adherence to
moral conscientiousness may be the best alternative:

> Only in ages when the actual world is a hollow, spiritless, and unsettled
> existence *(Existenz)* may the individual be permitted to flee from actuality
> and retreat into his inner life. (1821: 138A)[10]

This much of Hegel's assessment has been discussed at length and, left at
this, may appear relatively noncontroversial.[11] Still, certain key issues surrounding the relationship between Kantian and Hegelian ethics remain unresolved.
Even if the moral agent's judgment must be informed by the content of certain
social institutions and practices, it remains unclear exactly what the agent is to
make of this fact. By itself, this emphasis has often been thought to suggest a
certain conservative tendency in Hegel's view, enjoining the agent to "balance"
the demands of freedom and self-governance with the traditions of a community, thus making Hegel's account apparently ill-suited to the purposes of political liberation. Moreover, it remains to be seen how morality could function
as a dialectical starting point for the ethical life, as Hegel argues that it must
(cf. 1821: 57R, 135R). Although it seems clear that the rights of the individual
and the society might be at odds with one another, exactly how the ethical life
could dialectically "resolve" that tension remains obscure. Finally, it is critical to

explore the precise manner in which morality is to be embodied in the very institutions and practices that it would regulate. If Hegel is to sustain any kind of ethical realism, certain moral concepts must be able to operate independently of the concrete values of a community.

In his remarks to paragraph 57 in the *Philosophy of Right* (1821), Hegel takes up the relationship between the "ought-to-be" of universalist moral philosophy and his conception of *Sittlichkeit* in unusual detail. Using the example of slavery—his paradigmatic case of a flawed social practice—Hegel carries out a very brief but illuminating dialectical analysis of the various *ethical approaches* to the practice. His discussion follows the dialectical progression from so-called "empiricist" justifications of slavery, to "morality's" abstract condemnation of the practice, to the concrete embodiment of the human being's unfitness for slavery in a rational social order.[12] Unlike the account of "Lord and Bondsman" in the *Phenomenology of Spirit* (1807), which took up the phenomenon of slavery "internally," as it properly expressed a particular historical shape of human consciousness, Hegel's remarks here concern the problems confronting ethical assessments of the practice.[13] While the passage leaves critical aspects of the *transition* between morality and the ethical life unclear (a point I shall address in part in section 4), it nevertheless affords important clues toward an understanding of the place of moral universalism in Hegel's own approach to normativity.

Hegel begins by favorably contrasting Kantianism's absolute condemnation of slavery with various attempts to justify the practice by appeal to empirical considerations. In Hegel's view, all such appeals, whether to the enslavement's historical origins, the slaves' welfare, or even the slaves' willingness to submit to bondage, "depend on regarding man as a natural entity pure and simple, as an existent not in conformity with his concept." This analysis calls on his distinction between an entity's "actually existing" as the embodiment of its concept—the inner guiding principle of its activity—and its "merely existing" as an object for consciousness.[14]

The distinction between the mere existence of a shape of self-consciousness and that shape's *actual* existence—its existence according to the concept—plays an important role in Hegel's ethical thought. For self-consciousness actually to exist, it must embody a fully self-conscious grasp of universality. Realizing this state of affairs requires, at least minimally, that consciousness be able to assume a self-conscious grasp of its activity as its own. As discussed in chapter 1, such comprehension is impossible to the extent that one's agency is publicly identified as entirely alien to oneself, as in the activity of a slave. Though a human being can "merely exist" as a slave, this historical shape fails even minimally to meet the conditions of self-conscious agency, and so fails to be in keeping with the "concept."[15]

For Hegel, this failure becomes fully transparent with the actual historical eclipse of the shape of consciousness identified with master and slave, described in chapter 4 of the *Phenomenology of Spirit* (1807: 178-196).[16] In the latter account, the relationship of "Lord and Bondsman" fails adequately to embody the satisfaction of self-consciousness, is driven into contradiction, and so, goes under. Thus, in stating that the slave is not in keeping with its concept, Hegel means that it is not in keeping with a conception of humanity as the latter has emerged through the struggles of history. He does not mean that it fails to meet the demands of some abstract or formal standard, or at least not a standard that could have been known fully apart from its actual social embodiment. That slavery is inconsistent with the concept of the human being becomes clear only with that practice's actual failure in a historical system.

This point is even clearer in the Additions to the passage:

> Slavery occurs in the transitional phase between natural human existence and the truly ethical condition; it occurs in a world where a wrong is still right. Here, the wrong is *valid*, so the position it occupies is a necessary one. (Hegel 1821: 57A)

Hegel's use of "necessity" *(Notwendigkeit)* here should not be confused with the notion that slavery had to exist—that it could not have been otherwise—but rather that it was a real and concrete part of the system of needs *(Not)* characterizing a socio-economic whole. As such, its existence was embodied in the wants and needs of the agents of that culture as well. Under those historical conditions, the "wrongness" of slavery, its inconsistency with the freedom of the human person, remained an abstraction, an idea the "truth" of which was still in a latent or potential form. In a slave society the freedom of the individual is not fully realized, and the wrongness of slavery not yet "fully wrong."

These contingent historical conditions clearly do not hold for the reader of the *Philosophy of Right*, however, for whom the freedom of the individual has achieved historical recognition. The modern defender of slavery who would appeal simply to the existing condition of the slave (its capture in war, its material needs, etc.) to justify its enslavement, is to ignore the actual historical development of self-conscious human agency, and the "concept," i.e., the principle of freedom that this development has embodied. Thus, Hegel lauds the Kantian recognition of slavery as a violation of basic human rights (i.e., a failure to respect human beings as ends in themselves). By remaining faithful "to the *concept* of the human being as spirit, as something free *in itself,*" this perspective alone is the starting point for a genuine grasp of the right (1821: 57R). Hegel, however, qualifies his praise by adding that the moral point of view is "*only the starting point*" for the discovery of truth, indicating that something essential is lacking. He further explains this in his complex conclusion to the passage:

> [T]he claim that slavery is absolutely contrary to right . . . is one-sided inasmuch as it regards the human being as *by nature* free, or (and this amounts to the same thing) takes the concept as such, in its immediacy, not the Idea as the truth. . . . But that the objective spirit, the content of right should no longer be apprehended merely in its subjective concept, and consequently that the ineligibility of the human being in and for himself for slavery should no longer be apprehended merely as something which *ought* to be *(als ein bloßes Sollen),* is an insight which comes only when we recognize that the Idea of freedom is truly present only as *the state.* (1821, 57R)

If non-universalist accounts fail to honor the human being by attending only to its existing social determinations, Kantianism, by simply assuming that the human agent *is* free, ignores the equally pressing truth that a human being *cannot be free* in the absence of those contingent social conditions by which freedom is mediated. Thus, to conclude on this basis that a human being "ought not to be a slave" when a class of slaves does in fact exist, only deficiently honors the freedom of members of the slave class. In order to come to a better understanding of Hegel's rather subtle criticism here, it is useful to look more closely at some of the concepts employed in the passage.

Hegel states that the "ought" judgment "takes the concept as such in its immediacy, not the Idea as the truth." As noted in chapter 1, to take up a concept in its "immediacy," or as a "subjective concept," means to apprehend it in abstraction from the kind of community in which that concept would be actual, i.e., a community in which it would find mediation in concrete social practice.[17] Hence, the conditions to which Hegel is referring in the passage include (1) an existing practice of slavery, and (2) the failure of that practice to meet the standards of a formal criterion of morality.[18] In other words, the judgment must convey a conflict between the actual practices of a culture and the concept of a human being as the latter has been formally defined (e.g., as an end and not merely as a means). Such judgments are not without value, but because they are made in the absence of the social practices by which the state of affairs toward which they aim would be realized, they remain abstract. The concept of human freedom employed in a proposition such as "slavery ought not to exist" must be immediate or "subjective," in that it refers to a state of affairs that is not yet fully socially mediated, or "objective."

The "ought" judgment, because it both expresses a criticism of existing social reality and, at the same time, relies upon the content of that reality to make its charges meaningful, is limited in two important respects. In the first place, although such judgments may play a vital negative role in calling attention to the contradictions of a given social order, they must remain tied to that order in arriving at concrete injunctions.[19] If the moralist were to assert, for example, that the slaves ought to be free, she would be asserting that they ought to participate in the institutions and practices by which "freedom" is mediated in a slave society. Not only would the conception of freedom be a highly degraded one in such a social order (since, on Hegel's account, the "masters" in a slave system lack the recognition necessary for truly free agency),[20] but, to the extent that the ethical life in which the slaves would be permitted to participate was one for which their enslavement was the historical condition, it might be inadequate to embody their interests as members of a formerly enslaved class.[21]

Secondly, social systems of subordination such as slavery shape the needs and interests of society in such a manner that positive motivations toward enslavement may continue to exercise a hold over the agency of its classes. To the extent that moral prescriptions run counter to the actual institutions and practices of society, not only can this compromise the content of the prescriptions, but the will of the moral agent may be divided against itself. This criticism, it should be noted, derives much of its force from the characteristically Kantian concern for the condition of the individual's moral agency. Within a slave system, I may conclude that enslavement is unacceptable from the moral point of view and nevertheless have a real interest in reproducing the system through my action.[22] This could be either because I find myself in need of slave labor directly, or, more generally, because the satisfaction of certain of my basic desires (for food, housing, etc.) depends upon the functioning of a slave system.[23] So long as a society is materially dependent upon the labor of a slave class, all the accomplishments of persons within that society will embody, however remotely, the "truth" of that system.

This extends, of course, to the agency of the slaves themselves. For Hegel, the development of self-consciousness is contingent upon participation in those social practices by which self-conscious agency is embodied and brought to public recognition. Because slaves are excluded from such institutions or practices as education, ownership of property, suffrage, and meaningful labor, their capacity as genuinely free agents itself remains abstract and unrealized. Where the "actualization" of self-conscious agency must be embodied in the institutions and practices of a society, the absence of such embodiment results in the free agency of members of subordinated classes remaining potential and lacking the social recognition by which it might become actual. If we live in a society where our apprehension of the freedom of the human being is best expressed as an "ought to be," then the agency of all persons in that society remains in conflict, and the truth of the proposition that all persons are free remains only potential.

These limitations call attention to a further implication of Hegel's criticism of Kant. Because the moral agent must embody one of the shapes of self-conscious agency available in her culture, the judgment that she "ought" not to embody the values of a slave society need not imply that she "can" escape those values (either as a slave or as a non-slave) or, at least, that she can do so on her own. To the extent that the agent's freedom is the end of the moral life, and to the extent that such freedom can be realized only in a society where systematic relations of subordination do not govern our agency, an individual agent is not self-sufficient to bring about that end. Although a non-slave may succeed, to a greater or lesser degree, in *suppressing* morally objectionable action (e.g., by not keeping slaves, by trying not to benefit directly from slave labor, etc.), she cannot bring it about that slaves no longer exist, nor that her interests and desires are no longer embodied in such a system.[24] She cannot "transform" her agency such that the institution of slavery is not assumed in her own concrete interests or desires.[25] The transcendence of the divided condition of the will require a major alteration in the political structure of society.[26]

It is only when the agent is part of a community that embodies freedom in its actual institutions and practices that she can come to apprehend the concept of human freedom as *Idea*.[27] This permits a grasp of slavery's being "absolutely contrary to right," where that unfitness shapes the content of our own interests and desires and is not merely a moral demand imposed upon them. In such a community, public social practice (as embodied in the legal code and in economic relationships, for example) "negates" the form of agency whereby consciousness achieves satisfaction by enslaving another consciousness.[28] In this manner, the "truth" of a slave's freedom finds its embodiment, and the "Spiritually primitive" desire of one human being to enslave another is socially transformed.[29] In the absence of these conditions, freedom exists only as a state of affairs that ought to hold, and has not yet found its "objective" expression in the state. So long as cultural practice expresses the *fitness* of some human beings for subordination, the content of the proposition that all humans are free remains abstract and, in a concrete sense, untrue.[30]

It is clear then that the Hegelian focus upon the role of social institutions in informing the content of morality need not issue in a conservative ideology. In fact, it may serve to call attention to the insufficient development of key moral and political concepts as they exist in liberal society.[31] In the first place, Hegel insists that abstract concepts such as "freedom," "respect," and "person-hood" can have a tangible effect on social history, forcing the social orders that fail to embody them into chaos and revolution. Consistent with moral realism, Hegel recognizes the existence of what Peter Railton (1986) has termed "feed-back loops," through which moral norms can make their existence felt by the effects that they have on societies that fail officially to recognize their existence (in law and civil society) (192-194). On the other hand, stated propositionally in the form of abstract moral imperatives, these concepts remain critically underdetermined. Such imperatives may be taken in such a way as to be consistent with practices that systematically violate the interests of individuals of certain social classes.[32] If genuine universality exists only in a community in which the interests of all persons are actually embodied in public life, then achieving the universal may require the wholesale rethinking of our moral categories and how they are applied.

It must be added, however, that if the Hegelian emphasis on society need not entail a conservative approach in political philosophy, there is little question that Hegel himself often pushed it in just that direction. In part, this may be implicit in Hegel's conception of phenomenological description. Hegel intended such descriptions to replace the formalistic prescriptions of tradi-tional moral philosophy with descriptions of the unfolding of reason in his-tory.[33] To prescribe or to deduce in detail the movement of Spirit in developing new shapes of self-conscious agency would risk falling into the very formalism of which Hegel was critical.[34]

Even taking this methodological point into account, however, there are further problems. Hegel's explicitly political works take up the perspective of the governors of a state, rather than that of the diverse social movements by which the latter might find itself driven toward new and higher forms of uni-versality.[35] On this aspect of Hegel's mature political position, Seyla Benhabib (1986a) remarks:

> The irony of Hegel's theory of the state, disputed since the time of the Left Hegelians, cannot be overlooked. Here . . . the concrete universal is not *willed* by the citizens of the state, but is *administered* to them by a "universal class." (98)[36]

The unity which characterizes the ethical life of the Hegelian community, that embodies genuine universality seems unable to brook the passion and disrup-tiveness that marked the historical struggles by which it was brought about.

This underscores a critical difficulty in Hegel's description of the ethical life in Part III of the *Philosophy of Right* (1821). Hegel's attempt to describe a political order which at once embodies a concrete unity of diverse class interests and yet maintains the capacity to preserve itself against "illegitimate" challenges to social order, leads him to invest a universal class with the responsibility for preventing the formation of rabbles.[37] Unless the administrators of the state actually do stand at the "end of history" (and know it), however, they will be ill-placed to discern whether disruptive or subversive actions by certain classes are merely destructive, or the mark of an advance to a yet higher stage of the universal. As Hegel himself noted in the *Phenomenology* (1807), the fact that the law sees only "self-will and disobedience" in an action need not indicate that nothing more than that is at stake (466).[38]

Despite the "conservative" use to which Hegel put his theory in his later political writings, his conception of agency and the critique of Kantian morality that follows from it have implications that go well beyond the concerns of administering the state.[39] In particular, it suggests a link between our conception of universality and the collective development of agency that embraces certain important aspects of both classical liberal and communitarian theories, without being easily subsumed by either view. I shall now take up some of the implications of this link.

The Reconceptualization of the Universal

On Hegel's account, a meaningful conception of universality cannot avoid appeals to the institutions and practices of a particular social order. Concepts such as "equality" or "fairness" take on meaning in virtue of their specific function in regulating a given set of social relations. Because the ability of a particular set of institutions and practices to express adequately the self-consciousness of all its classes is subject to historical change, however, our conception of what constitutes universality may itself have to undergo alteration, or what I shall be calling "reconceptualization," with those changes. In this section, I shall detail the nature of such a process, contrasting it with mere rejection or overthrow of the moral categories. Although reconceptualization is not among Hegel's terms of art, I shall argue below that it may be understood to follow from certain parts of his doctrine of "concepts." Moreover, I hope to show that it can capture an important aspect of his understanding of the function of the categories of Kantian morality, categories that—as the discussion in the last section made clear—Hegel did not mean simply to abandon. In future chapters, I argue that something very much akin to reconceptualization is at work in feminist critiques of sexism.

As noted above, the use to which I am putting Hegel's doctrine of concepts, while it is suggested by some of his own examples in political philosophy, prescinds from the putative epistemological and metaphysical ends of his system. It is not my intention to use Hegel's dialectic of concepts to *justify* the emergence of any particular set of categories by demonstrating its logical relation to the final realization of Spirit at the End of History. The more modest claim that I am advancing here, and that I shall fill out in the succeeding chapters, is that Hegel's highly unorthodox doctrine of concepts may shed light on a basic problem in political theory. By providing a description of how the moral and political categories of Enlightenment thought appear to have both the capacity to guide (serve as a "starting point" for) and the need to be filled in by the content of particular social practices (their "emptiness"), Hegel developed a novel approach to the problem of political justification that avoids some of the critical pitfalls of both communitarianism and liberal proceduralism.[40]

This conceptual development of a criterion through a series of historical conflicts of meaning that reveal the implicit content of the criterion is, of course, central to Hegel's epistemology. For Hegel, "concept" does not merely designate a term that is applied to reality, but is that by which the underlying "necessity" of a reality is expressed. Because (1) we cannot come to a grasp of reality at all in the absence of certain concepts (1807: 110), and (2) these concepts may themselves be incoherent in their application to reality, it follows that this incoherence must move toward resolution in "higher" categories. These higher categories cannot simply replace the earlier ones, since they were indispensable in coming to a grasp of reality in the first place, but must incorporate them in a new synthesis.[41] For Hegel, ethical reality is similarly prey to contradiction in that certain categories are both indispensable to a conception of the right and subject to incoherence in their application to social reality. Hence, they too will be subject to reconceptualization in higher stages of universality.

This fundamental doctrine is manifest in certain of Hegel's remarks in the Introduction to the *Philosophy of History* (1837c):

> [An] ethical whole,[42] as such, is limited. It must have above it a higher universality, which makes it disunited in itself. The transition from one spiritual pattern to the next is just this, that the previous universal, through being thought (in terms of the higher universal), is abolished *(aufgehoben)* as a particular. (38)

A particular set of ethical conventions is always open to reinterpretations which may expose them in such a manner as to challenge or to alter their universality. By "being thought" in light of a new set of social relations, the demands of an old ethical order may be revealed as contradictory, or at least in conflict.[43] Consistent with his Logic, Hegel points out that this process of surpassing an old ethical order is not simply a matter of showing the old institutions and practices "wrong" and endorsing their replacement by a new set of institutions and practices that are "right," or justified. He goes on in the same passage to assert that the content of the higher form of universality is contained implicitly in the perspective that is overthrown:

> The later universal, so to speak, the next higher genus of the preceding species, is potentially but not yet actually present in the preceding one. This makes all existing reality unstable and disunited. (38)[44]

The dynamics of this dialectical process were in evidence in Hegel's descriptions of the surpassing of various orders in world history in the *Phenomenology of Spirit* (1807). In the account of the breakdown of the ancient order, discussed at length in chapter 1, Hegel's retelling of the events of *Antigone* displays the characteristic features of such a process. Antigone's charge against Creon takes shape against a structure of religious obligations that, along with (and previously in union with) the civil law, characterized the ethical life of Thebes. Although the specific use to which Antigone put these conventions was entirely novel (because it expressed a point of view that had not previously been put forward), it was not for that reason inaccessible once it had publicly emerged. Because the law of the gods and the familial obligations in which they were expressed were already recognized as legitimate, there was a clear ground for Antigone's action. This existing ground justified an action, however, that disrupted another principle—that of the unity of the divine and the human law in the life of the Theban state. More precisely, Creon's apparently lawful *act* was the occasion for a reaction that showed it to be an illegal act when taken from an equally legitimate point of view. Hence the tragic nature of the conflict.

In this description, the new "universal" toward which the tragic clash gestures is not simply inconsistent with the old obligations, but represents a reconceptualization of them. The emergence of a previously quiescent form of agency (i.e., that of Antigone in particular and women in general) has led to a diremption in a previously unified conception of ethical obligation.[45] The twin "ethical powers" of the divine and the human law are cut asunder when Creon, apparently innocently embodying the masculine agency of the human law, violates and awakens the divine law's feminine agency in Antigone (465). The rebellious agency of women displayed the old ethical unity to be at odds with itself, as it put forth as absolute sets of obligations to the gods and to the state that could be brought into conflict with one another.[46] The new (and ethically disastrous) "separation of powers," however, required the invocation of no new principles. Its appearance came with the exploitation the previously unexplored "potential" of the old law brought about by the effective emergence of the agency of a violated class.

Of course, the effectiveness of Antigone's feminine agency relied upon the social legitimacy of the point of view it embodied. Because women's agency embodied the divine law, Creon could not merely brush off Antigone's act as "only the self-will and disobedience of the individual" (1807: 466).[47] Moreover, in the modern world, ethical reconceptualization cannot take the form of an implicit division between the divine and human law. In Hegel's view, however, the abstract categories of universalist morality as they are embodied in the legal and ethical life of society may lend themselves to a similar reconceptualization. Because Hegel takes these universal categories and the moral principles derived from them to be abstract or "empty" in themselves, there can be no question of "morality" collapsing in quite the same manner as the ancient *Sittlichkeit*, with its determinate institutions and practices.[48] Nevertheless, as noted above, Hegel held that the particular embodiments of the moral categories were capable of producing conflicts in our conception of the right. These conflicts, when occasioned by a newly emergent form of agency, may serve as the mainspring in moving toward a new understanding of our ethical concepts. Such a reconceptualization could take place if a novel manner of adherence to the implicit constraints of a socially accepted formal criterion were to contradict the previously accepted meaning of that criterion.

Although, as noted already, Hegel's mature political writings had little concern for emphasizing the positive possibilities for emergent forms of social consciousness, some of his own remarks on the "penurious rabble" lend themselves to such an interpretation. With his observation that the poorest man in England "believes that he has rights," Hegel suggests a fundamental reconceptualization of the notion of rights as that category is read through the experience of a particular social class.[49] It is worth considering this in some detail.

Suppose, for example, that a particular society publicly maintains a political commitment to a concept of "natural rights," but one which does not encompass impoverishment as involving a claim against the state.[50] Suppose further that members of the impoverished class are, by reason of their poverty, effectively excluded from participation in the practices by which persons achieve public recognition as agents worthy of respect (e.g., engaging in the marketplace, becoming involved in civic activities, voting in elections, etc.). Although the plight of members of this class might be publicly recognized as unfortunate, pitiful, or perhaps indicative of laziness or irresponsibility on the part of individual members of the class, its political nature will remain unmediated and (thus) unrecognized.[51] Such a recognition would require, contrary to the publicly available conception of rights, a recognition that poverty is an actionable violation of self-conscious agency of members of the indigent class.

Were the political nature of such a condition actually to achieve effective social recognition (i.e., were the state to come to grasp poverty as a violation of the *rights* of members of the poor), this might involve reconceptualizing a historically mediated category of rights. In the first place, this kind of recognition would be impossible where no antecedent commitment to natural rights existed at all. The complaint by a disenfranchised class that its disenfranchisement constitutes a violation of basic claims that human beings have against the state is not possible in a social order that does not formally recognize the legitimacy of such claims. Still, the existence of such a formal commitment does not ensure the emergence of this complaint at any given point in time. To the extent that the conditions of poverty serve to exclude poor persons from those institutions and practices by which that understanding could be effectively mediated, such a reconceptualization may be rendered extremely difficult.[52] Unless the members of the impoverished class can begin effectively to express the nature of their subordination and thereby to impress the content of their violation on the state, that violation will fail to assume political significance.[53]

Secondly, to the extent that such an expression constitutes a genuine reconceptualization of a category, it must generate a conflict in the prevailing conception of the category. In the unsettling of the ancient order discussed above, such a conflict was manifest in a wholesale reversal of the meaning of an act—Creon's order passed from legal decree to "crime."[54] In a case of a putative right against impoverishment, once the public conception of rights comes to include a claim against the state for the *material* welfare of all persons, that conception may well function differently from the way it did when legal rights were not understood to encompass such claims. If, for example, the paradigmatic expression of rights in the society in question included that to the unlimited acquisition of private property, the kind of state redistribution of property that would be required to honor the rights of the poorest might well contradict such an understanding. Likewise, the activities of a bourgeois class in legally impoverishing a class through their acquisition of more and more property may well appear criminal in retrospect. Moreover, should the public recognition of such a right involve a rebellious destruction of property, then that too would likely challenge the old conception, and itself be met by accusations of lawless rabble-rousing by the guardians of the old order.[55] Of course, on Hegel's account it *is* lawless on the old conceptualization. Nevertheless, like Antigone's lawless act, it functions to reveal the lawlessness of the previous embodiment of the concept, and thus drives it on to a higher one.

If this is a genuine instance of dialectical reconceptualization, two further and highly controversial claims must hold: (1) that the rights that are being claimed by the impoverished class are truly an extension of the extant conception of natural rights, and not the creation of a new set of claims; (2) that the liberal conception of rights, and that of respect for persons in which it is grounded, is an indispensable category for making the kind of claim that is at stake here.[56] Given the hypothetical nature of the example, it would be pointless to attempt to show that such is the case here. Nevertheless, to the extent that this model of political development offers a conceptual framework in which a commitment to universal ethical categories is consistent with radical alterations in the meaning of those categories, it will be of considerable value in coming to an understanding of modern movements of political empowerment. While such movements have at least implicitly relied upon a set of liberal categories inherited from the Enlightenment in their critiques of oppression, they have also called attention to the manner in which those categories have been used effectively to thwart the development of disempowered groups.[57] To the extent that it makes sense to speak of the reconceptualization of universal categories, it is possible simultaneously to critique those categories, to engage in activities that may appear to be in violation of them, and yet to rely upon them in ethical analysis.[58] This will turn out to be of no small importance in coming to a grasp of a variety of issues in the feminist political critique with which I shall be concerned in the coming chapters.

Situating Impartiality

The manner in which Hegel's approach to the ethical life builds upon the Kantian model, while at the same time rejecting that we have procedural access to the moral point of view, underscores the complexity of the relationship between Kant's and Hegel's ethics. In section IV of chapter 2, after having discussed Hegel's critique of "formalism," I outlined some of the reasons that Hegel's notion of universality differs from that of impartiality, even at the end of history. Given the discussion of Hegelian reconceptualization here, it is possible to address the more general issue of how the abstract principles of Kantian morality can function within a Hegelian account of political change. In this final section, I shall argue that a Hegelian approach to impartiality may, at least in some circumstances, have strikingly "un-Kantian" implications as concerns the types of and motivations for political action. On the other hand, the manner in which Hegel maintains a certain kind of appeal to impartial principles in political criticism suggests that we might better understand Hegel's "conceptual" approach to political philosophy as a novel variation on the Kantian model than as an outright rejection of it.

In moving toward an understanding of precisely how a Hegelian approach to political change "situates" the moral point of view, it is useful to compare its notion of ethical reconceptualization with Kantian procedural justification. On the latter account, the agent employs a formal procedure to gain access to an impartial point of view for judging an action or set of actions. The moral agent acts rationally insofar as she conforms her action to judgments from that point of view. With regard to decisions concerning social action (the decision to engage in, to avoid engaging in, or to oppose action that is part of a social practice), the agent might ask, for example, whether or not a maxim to engage in, to avoid, or to oppose a given social practice is universalizable, i.e., whether or not it is consistent with treating all persons (oneself included) as ends and not merely as means.

As emphasized in chapter 2, however, Hegel does not think that the moral agent can answer such a question without invoking a socially particular set of background assumptions. Answers even to such basic questions as who counts as fully a person or what constitutes respect toward such a person, will vary with different kinds of social order. Returning to the example of the previous section, whether or not it is moral to engage in, or to resist, practices that have as their consequence the development of an impoverished class, will likely rest at least in part on whether or not poverty is apprehended as a violation of the agency of that class. Because the existence of such an apprehension depends upon the historical development of a society, there is no assurance that a maxim's apparent success or failure to meet the demands of a formal criterion actually reflects the demands of impartiality. Even if the truly "impartial" point of view could tell us how to act, the availability of such a view cannot be guaranteed procedurally.

Issues of access assume even greater significance in light of the fact that the development of universality may proceed through a thoroughgoing challenge to an existing social order. Although a challenge such as that described in the last section will implicitly rely upon the categories of the old political order (i.e., they may re-conceptualize the principles as discussed above), this process cannot be consciously *motivated* by respect for a set of moral principles. This is because a challenge to the most basic background assumptions that govern the application of a moral principle or set of principles in a society *ipso facto* challenges the conditions for access to the principle or set of principles in that society.

By claiming a right against poverty, for example, members of an impoverished class may effectively challenge the prerogative of individuals to the unrestricted ownership and acquisition of private property. If a category of rights has been historically mediated by the assertion of such bourgeois interests, however, claiming a right against impoverishment may appear, even to members of the class demanding it, as a rebellion against "rights" themselves.[59] Once again, because moral categories are meaningful only insofar as they embody specific background assumptions, challenges to those assumptions, even when they invoke a familiar principle or set of principles, may be indistinguishable (especially in the earliest stages of the challenge) from attacks on morality itself. Thus, if the development of the moral law in a particular social order demands such thoroughgoing challenges, an attitude of respect for the moral law in that society (i.e., the moral law as embodied in its institutions and practices) will not be "morally" desirable. Ironically, in some cases the kind of motivation needed to advance morality may appear entirely immoral and disrespectful toward its law.

It is also important to emphasize that the typical motivation in cases such as this will be "particular" in its focus and consciously eschew a stance of neutrality. As suggested above, the sort of motivation needed to expand the scope and content of a conception of rights may be the development of the *self*-interest of members of a class whose interests have failed to find expression in social practice. Before a poor individual could grasp her condition as reflective of injustice, for example, she would have to comprehend her own *agency* as violated by the conditions of that poverty. To come to such a grasp, however, she will have to take up a particular point of view with respect to the issues of poverty and wealth in her society—i.e., that of a reflective member of an impoverished class. Though this perspective is not "particular" in the sense of being merely *individually* self-serving (the sense with which Kant is most concerned in his discussion of "self-love"), neither does it aspire to impartiality in its assessments of the social order.[60] It seeks to articulate a perspective on a set of institutions and practices that have been denied, ignored, or discredited. This articulation aims (1) to develop the self-conscious agency of the impoverished class has been violated, and (2) to bring about effective recognition of that particular perspective on the society, and thereby to force a critical re-thinking of its notion of "impartiality."[61]

Of course, when the social conditions are not conducive to this kind of project (e.g. if indigent persons lack recognition as citizens at all), it may require extraordinary measures both to develop and effectively to assert the agency of a subordinated class. As I shall discuss in detail in the next chapter on "consciousness raising," the deliberate attempt to cultivate a suppressed form of agency may demand constructing separate communities within a given social whole. The alternative institutions and practices of these communities can then serve to mediate the interests of members of a subordinated class to themselves. Likewise, when it comes to asserting these interests within an order that ignores, denies, or discredits them, it may require the most aggressive means in order to break through the institutional denial.[62] Once again, to the extent that consciousness raising, and social action, succeeds in embodying the agency of the members of a socially subordinated class, the "justice" of that action will be accessible to impartial reflection in the society in question. The development of the conditions for such access, however, may require action contrary to both the spirit and the letter of a conception of impartiality as it exists at a given time.[63]

On a Hegelian account, then, we cannot rely upon the judgments following from a particular conception of the moral categories to bring about the political conditions under which the freedom of all persons is actual. While appeals to rights, or to the freedom and autonomy of individuals, do not cease to be operative in ethical and political criticism, access to the content of these categories is unavailable apart from the contingently available forms of agency by which they are embodied.[64] Hence, the appeal of a subordinated class to the extant conceptions of rights or justice does not simply "ground" the claims of a particular agent by purporting to adhere to the strictures of a formal criterion. It likewise alters the meaning of the criterion by making the novel kind of appeal that it does. Put in more Hegelian language, it might be stated that as self-conscious universality develops historically, it reconceptualizes universality.

This account of the development of self-conscious agency providing the content of the moral law complements the charge of emptiness discussed in the last chapter. For Hegel, as for Kant, the emptiness of a category need not indicate its uselessness.[65] Unlike Kant, however, Hegel cannot accept the formal injunctions of morality as "constraints" in the sense of procedurally accessible limits that can be applied to the content of a given social order. The "abstract universality" represented by the moral categories must be apprehended through the "particularity" of specific forms of agency, establishing the "dialectical" condition for genuine universality or "individuality" to emerge.

Returning to the case of abstract "rights," if these are to take on a genuinely universal meaning, they must be "thought" through the interests and desires characterizing a shape of consciousness. The Enlightenment *appeals* of the bourgeois class to the "Rights of Man," for example, served also to lend content to that category by conceiving it through the particular interests and desires of that class. It was thus that the category came to signal the rights of the "individual" against the threat of state tyranny. Likewise, the subsequent appeal of an impoverished class to the same category will serve to alter that content by seizing it through a different set of interests and desires.[66] With the social development of a new shape of self-conscious agency, the meaning of the ethical categories to which it appeals also assumes a new shape.

Thus, despite Hegel's rejection of an impartial perspective that is procedurally accessible, he does not deny that appeals to impartiality play an important functional role in the development of a conception of the ethical life.[67] Hegel can retain a role for the formal categories as constraints on political action, while at the same time insisting that they can be grasped only through their particular social embodiment. By developing the implications of this doctrine in terms of the administration of the "rational state," he likewise encourages a notoriously conservative reading of it. As I have suggested above, however, it is entirely consistent with this doctrine (and further suggested by Hegel's conception of collective agency) that movements of collective consciousness raising within a given social order may serve as the impetus to revolutionary "appeals" to familiar moral categories.[68] For Hegel, arriving at the *meaning* of the categories and thereby rescuing them from the perils of "emptiness" requires that we follow their historical emergence through the particular interests and desires of the classes of a given society. Because the emergence of those interests and desires cannot simply be taken for granted, neither can our access to the universal.[69] The development of the institutions and practices by which the agency of all social groups can be effectively embodied is nothing other than the necessary condition for coming to an adequate conception of universality.

I shall add detail to this contention in my "applications" in Part Two. Already, however, it should be clear that Hegel's rethinking of Kantian universality bears important similarities to certain versions of feminist "standpoint epistemology," and may be understood to provide an important grounding for it. In fact, the connection between Hegel and standpoint theory has not gone unnoticed, as evidenced by Sandra Harding's (1986) observation that "the *feminist standpoint* originates in Hegel's thinking about the relationship between the master and the slave" (26).[70] I shall take up the master-slave passage and some of its specific applications in Part 3 of the book. As I have argued in the last two chapters, however, some of Hegel's most salient points concerning the limitations of Kant's approach to universality point toward a re-valuing of particular points of view as a means for expanding moral knowledge. While

Hegel retains a commitment to universality, this is not lacking in feminist approaches as well. As Harding notes:

> The leading feminist theorists do not try to substitute one set of gender loyalties for the other—"woman-centered" for "man-centered" hypotheses. They try instead, to arrive at hypotheses that are free of gender loyalties. It is true that first we often have to formulate a "woman-centered" hypothesis in order even to comprehend a gender-free one. But the goal of feminist knowledge-seeking is to achieve theories that accurately represent women's activities as fully social, and social relations between the genders as a real— and explanatorily important—component in human history. (1986: 138)

Far from eschewing universality altogether, Harding's goals bespeak a concern for overcoming the false universality that has characterized those approaches that have failed to take account of their social and historical assumptions.[71]

Moreover, Hegel's historical realism explains how a point of view that challenges and destabilizes a conception of "objectivity" may nevertheless claim to be describing the real world. Because our capacity to challenge and destabilize the "universals" that describe reality has as its necessary condition an unstable, incoherent, and ultimately "partial" reality, a socially and politically disruptive point of view has its ground in the real world. On a Hegelian account, standpoint epistemology stands clear of the pitfalls of relativism inasmuch as its ability to challenge the old concepts is itself grounded in a world in transition. Helen Longino's defense of a "minimalist realism" takes a position remarkably similar to that of Hegel:

> Experience itself must be rethought as an interactive rather than a passive process . . . . [W]hat we experience at a given time and place can be described and measured in contextually fixed ways . . . . The view of experience and the constraints that it places on justifiable belief leads to a minimalist form of realism. There is a world independent of our senses with which those senses interact to produce our sensations and the regularities of our experience. There is something "out there" that imposes limits on what we can say about it . . . . The sorts of things we measure, however, will change as our needs, interests, and understanding change . . . . The reliability of [descriptive] systems lies not with their ability to transparently represent the natural world as it is "in itself" but in the fact that the gradations and changes in parameters of a system match gradations and changes in the natural world. (1990: 221-222)

For Hegel, the interactive process lies precisely with the concepts that, in their capacity to mediate the real world, likewise express changes in it with the process of reconceptualization.

Conclusion

In the course of the last two chapters, I have tried to draw out some of the implications of Hegel's complex assessment of Kantian moral philosophy. In chapter 2, I detailed Hegel's argument that meaningful *access* to the moral point of view requires a specific set of background assumptions. In this chapter, I have identified the interests and desires of particular social classes as a pivotal assumption at issue in arriving at a meaningful conception of the right. While Hegel agrees with Kant that a universal perspective is the proper point of departure for ethical justification, because access to that point of view must be mediated through the historical emergence of self-consciousness, it cannot assume the kind of regulative role it does in Kantian morality. Some of Hegel's most important criticisms of Kantian universalism—his rejection of morality as a formal criterion to be applied to action, his emphasis upon the development of the institutions and practices of society, and his focus upon "passion" as the mediator of the universal—derive from this basic point. Because these criticisms derive from a dispute regarding access to universality, and not from the rejection of universality itself as an abstract criterion of ethical justification, Hegel's ethics may be understood to fall within the broad sweep of "universalist" theories. It does so, however, without assuming that we have access to the full meaning of universality, at least before the end of history.

In the chapters to follow, I shall consider several different aspects of the feminist critique of traditional moral philosophy. If I am right, some of the most important articulations of this critique have taken a form strikingly similar to that of Hegel. In particular, feminist criticisms of sexism, on both the institutional and interpersonal levels, have both appealed to a universal conception of the right and, at the same time, transformed that conception in making the appeal that they have. While feminist critics have not generally eschewed universalist categories (i.e., their appeals have been to rights, freedom, etc.), neither have these critics found those categories entirely adequate for their critique—at least not when the criticisms were voiced initially. To the extent that the assumptions of gender (e.g., active masculine agents and passive feminine respondents) thoroughly pervade our historical grasp of a moral category, the attempt to extend that category's scope to include the interests and desires of women will occasion a fundamental disruption in meaning as well.

PART TWO

FEMINIST JUSTICE AND HISTORICAL REALISM

CONSCIOUSNESS-RAISING AND POLITICAL CRITIQUE
Reconceptualizing Universality

> *Kwame Nkrumah said, "Thought without action is empty and action without thoughts is blind." He says, "Revolutions are made by men who think as men of action and act as men of thought. These are the only people who make revolution."*
> —Stokely Carmichael
> *Akwesasne Notes* 1974

Suppose that the socially constitutive institutions and practices of a modern liberal society were to fail in consistently mediating the recognition of the self-conscious agency of members of a particular social class. Suppose further that this failure of recognition not only played a functional role in maintaining a social system that accorded various concrete privileges to those who were not members of this class, but that the institutional embodiment of the group's exclusion was so effective that identification with the group itself denoted the absence of fully self-conscious agency. Where background conditions such as these governed the application of that society's formal criteria for equality, it would not be surprising to find that even the most vigilant attempts to adhere to the strictures of the criterion were falling short, at least where the agency of members of the excluded class was at issue.

It is, however, precisely the kind of exclusion that characterizes the social status of the "other," and that has informed the critiques of a broad range of feminist theorists since de Beauvoir.[1] On these accounts, feminine agency, or "the feminine," not only has existed in the service of masculine interests, but has been socially defined *as* a peculiar lack of agency, as capable of acting only in the pursuit of masculine interests. Of course, much of the work of contemporary feminists has been directed toward changing that social definition, both by broadening the scope of opportunities for women and by rediscovering a true feminine agency that had been suppressed. In developing a critique of the dominant institutions and practices of society, however, feminists have faced a paradoxical task. On the one hand, coming to an understanding of the "objective wrongness" of women's condition seems to require an impartial or universal standpoint from which that wrongness could be accessible. On the other hand, to the extent that women's agency is socially degraded in the manner just described, the background assumptions necessary for such an impartial judgment of women's situation appear to be lacking. Either women can come to such an awareness of their oppression and the problem is not so intractable as some have claimed, or no such awareness is really possible.

In the last chapter, I discussed some of the implications of Hegel's critique of Kantianism's adherence to the "absolute freedom" of the morally autonomous agent. These represented developments of Hegel's basic insight that where the social embodiment of "freedom" has explicitly excluded classes of agents, the meaning of that concept when applied to members of those classes must remain abstract and not fully accessible to reflective thought *(Verstand)*. Hegel insists upon a distinction between abstract universality, on the one hand, and the social and historical conditions by which it must be mediated on the other.

In this chapter, I shall consider the Hegelian account developed in part 1 and its implications for the political practice of "consciousness raising." Drawing primarily upon the experiences of feminists in the early years of the "Second Wave," I shall argue that consciousness raising represents a non-procedural practical method for arriving at the content of norms under conditions of collective inaccessibility. While this method relies upon the regulative capacity of universal moral concepts as the latter have taken shape in an existing social order, it alters those concepts as it seeks to discern their meaning through a set of interests that do not find expression in that order. Unlike moral evaluation, it does not simply "apply" moral norms to the condition of women. It does not, for example, strive to take an impartial point of view with respect to phenomena such as rape, sexual assault, or harassment. Rather, by cultivating a sense of "righteous anger" surrounding such events, it articulates women's collective experience of those practices, and thereby brings one of the necessary conditions for developing a concrete awareness of their wrongness into being.

While the dynamic interaction between the collective anger of women and the evolution of ethical and political life reflects Hegel's description of the development of the universal through passion in the *Philosophy of History* (1837b), it likewise diverges from the latter account in two important respects. In the first place, it calls attention to the role of a movement of collective activism in developing universality. As noted in the last chapter, and as I shall discuss further in chapter 7, Hegel was generally suspicious of the creative potential of mass movements.[2] Secondly, because feminist consciousness raising, as well as the movements of race- and class-consciousness in which it is rooted, are explicitly concerned with the development of collective consciousness, its agency cannot take on the same kind of self-ignorance that characterized Hegel's world historical individuals. Though the latter serve to advance Spirit through their own passions, these individuals typically "have no consciousness of the Idea as such" (Hegel 1837c: 40). Though the persons in the examples of consciousness raising with which I shall be concerned are very passionately and personally engaged, and are far from having a clear "blueprint" for the future, they are likewise unquestionably motivated by a conscious collective concern for improving the condition of women.

It is precisely because consciousness raising involves both passionate expression and a concern for justice, however, that it may serve as a concrete example of how the advancement of the ethical life can take place without falling into either moralistic "formalism" or mere "feeling, heart, emotion, and inspiration" (1821: 21R). Hegel, of course, did not think that either of these could adequately meet the demands of the ethical life of a modern social order. As has already been noted, his attempt in the *Philosophy of Right* to mediate this conflict through the effective management of the rational state leaves it questionable how any meaningful social changes could take place. If Hegel's distinction between the formal demands of universality and the conditions of access to it offers a suggestive framework for understanding the balance between the political and the personal in consciousness raising, the practice of consciousness raising itself suggests a concrete model of how Hegelian mediation of the universal can take place. Its characteristic elements offer a model for the actualization of universality under conditions of self-ignorance that includes a positive role for the pursuit of particular interests without implying that "moral" considerations are entirely irrelevant to these interests, and that addresses the collective development of agency without the conservative implications of Hegel's state.

In the next section, I use examples from feminist consciousness raising to develop an outline of the basic normative structure of that practice. In the third section, I detail some of the difficulties associated with the attempt directly to apply a standard based on autonomous agency in certain important cases of women's subordination. In particular, I discuss the link between such attempts and the phenomenon of "victim blaming." In the next section, I show how the reconceptualization of a formal criterion in consciousness raising may serve not merely to alter the scope of application of such a criterion, but to alter its meaning in a substantial way. This will establish the ground for my discussion of the significance of such a reconceptualization for ethical agency in chapter 6.

Consciousness Raising as Critique

In developing an account of the normative implications of the practice of consciousness raising, it is important to be clear about which meaning of that phenomenon is at issue. In recent years, the term has come to stand for many different things, ranging from little more than disseminating information to the enacting of specific and complex sets of guidelines for meetings and discussions.[3] Likewise, the misunderstandings that developed out of the consciousness-raising sessions of largely white middle- and upper middle-class women in the United States has been the subject of much recent discussion in feminist theory.[4] In developing my arguments in this chapter, I shall be concerned with the practice of consciousness raising as it initially took shape in the feminist activism of the late nineteen sixties. Although this practice developed without a preordained agenda, in retrospect it may be understood to have been characterized by a specific set of aims and certain characteristic methods for achieving them. I shall not be claiming that the findings that arose in the context of that movement are infallible (as will become clearer, consciousness raising is necessarily a fallible method), or denying that these might themselves be subject to further "consciousness raising" that would challenge the unquestioned assumptions of relatively-well-off white women. Rather, I shall clarify the methods actually employed in the practice with a view toward assessing their significance in the context of universalist political justification.

Looking back on early feminist consciousness raising, it is possible to discern three general features of these very diverse groups. First, the groups were established expressly for the purpose of airing and critically discussing the interests of the women in the group, largely setting aside the broader concerns of political liberation. As I shall note below, this was essential in establishing the independence of the feminist movement from the broader aims of the political Left. Second, in pursuing this end, feminist consciousness-raising groups most often restricted their membership to women—a move that occasioned no small amount of dissention from former comrades. Third, these groups sought to articulate their discoveries about women's collective condition in the form of grievances against a male-dominated society. This feature distinguishes the concerns of the early movement from those of what have sometimes been characterized as "cultural feminists," for whom the development of a distinctly women's culture was dissociated from any explicit concern for criticizing the institutions and practices of patriarchal society.

The development of specifically feminist consciousness raising in the United States came in the midst of the broader civil rights and anti-Vietnam war organizing of the late nineteen sixties. In large numbers, women political activists judged that the status of both women's issues and women activists themselves in many groups, most notably the Student Non-violent Coordinating Committee (SNCC) and Students for a Democratic Society, was distinctly subordinate.[5] Although "women's liberation" was among the broad set of concerns of the radical Left from the mid-nineteen sixties, women's exclusion from the primary organizing activities of the major movements, and their being consigned to traditional feminine roles and activities, fed the belief that women's issues needed to be addressed separately.[6] From 1967 on, a variety of grassroots women's groups proceeded to splinter from the radical Left, rejecting the widespread assumption that women's oppression was merely "epiphenomenal," and thus to be eradicated as part of a broader revolution. Though the "separatism" that characterized these groups was originally a function of their nature as a protest against the male Left's disregard for women's issues, the positive results of gender-exclusive groups of women sharing their personal experiences of masculine domination was soon apparent.[7]

Under the influence of the Maoist models which were prevalent in many of the movements from which the consciousness-raising groups emerged, their analysis centered on the development and articulation of a previously suppressed point of view.[8] In pursuing this end, it was considered essential to cultivate an explicitly woman-centered perspective on the issues up for discussion. As I shall discuss at length in the next section, this cultivation of a distinct manner of perceiving the world—"creating its own way of seeing"[9]—proved essential not only in the *descriptions* of the issues that participants found most compelling, but in coming to an *evaluation* of their significance as well. As a matter of process, of course, the emergence of the issues was most often inseparable from an (at least implicit) negative evaluation of them. Women's descriptions of their experiences of household labor, everyday harassment, or violent abuse was charged with dissatisfaction and anger toward those phenomena. What distinguished consciousness raising from simple complaint, however, was the manner in which it cultivated and sharpened that negative evaluation by attempting to exclude those perspectives and perceptions that might blunt women's own unique appreciation of the phenomena.[10] It is worth considering the nature of this unapologetically "interested" approach both to describing and assessing women's issues in greater detail.

In the first place, the early feminist movement developed an understanding of the issues that were of greatest importance to women by encouraging women to articulate very personal and often seemingly trivial experiences of frustration in daily life. Though the experiences shared in these sessions sometimes did concern now familiar "women's issues" such as harassment, assault, and domestic violence, at their earliest stages their focus was more often on the myriad ways in which the everyday demands placed on women to look, act, and be a certain way constituted an unwanted imposition.[11] Participants in consciousness raising sought to reassure the women who voiced their feelings and experiences—in many instances for the first time—that they were not alone in these feelings and (thus) that their experiences were not trivial.[12] This validation of women's experience was more than an exercise in polemical partiality. It was grounded in the working assumption that women's own perceptions of masculine oppression had been so effectively suppressed that an attitude of partiality was necessary if they were to surface at all. As the experience of the civil rights movement had shown, where the institutions and practices of culture implicitly embody the oppressor's perspective on the oppressed, the expression of an oppressed group's point of view, when it challenges that perspective, will be both difficult and dangerous.[13] To the extent that the fear of occasioning ridicule or even violence for expressing such a challenge is internalized, the social conditions governing "ordinary" discourse may effectively silence the point of view of the oppressed altogether.[14] In the course of the movement, "a working assumption [became] a working discovery," as women's expressions of their experiences came to form the nucleus of a political movement (MacKinnon 1989: 86).

Because both internalized and explicit fear were among the key reasons for the failure of women to express their point of view in the first place, the absence of men from consciousness raising proved essential to its development.[15] To the extent that women were conditioned to seek male approval, or were prone to passivity in the presence of men, or were outright intimidated by the presence of men, a genuine articulation of their experience of oppression by men would be practically impossible.[16] It is important to notice that because these responses were most often taken to have been "internalized," the precise extent to which male exclusion would prove an asset to consciousness raising was not fully determinable in advance. Indeed, this proved to be a major point of contention where women attempted to form gender-exclusive groups for considering women's liberation in the context of other movements.[17] Once again, it was only by defiantly assuming that these conditions did hold, and by acting to exclude men on the basis of that assumption, that the scene was set for the assumption's verification. Once gender-exclusive groups dedicated to the articulation of a still unarticulated or poorly articulated way of perceiving were established and functioning, they did in fact serve to develop a heightened awareness of a set of issues shared by the members of the group.

As noted above, however, the partisanship toward women's perception did not end with the achievement of this heightened sense of a particular set of phenomena. In addition to their partisanship in developing an articulation of women's experience, participants in consciousness-raising groups sought consciously to *evaluate* the ethical significance of this experience with a bias toward women's experience. This is a significant point, and one that is worth taking up in greater detail. For it may not seem altogether clear why, once women's descriptions of their experiences were brought to awareness, they should not be subject to the same impartial assessments that any other descriptions would. Even if certain biased assumptions are among the conditions necessary for gaining access to certain features of a particular group's experience, this fact would not appear to warrant a biased approach to the ethical scrutiny of them.

Respect, Consent, and Blaming the Victim

The "Principles" (1969) of the Redstockings stated:

> We take the woman's side in everything. We ask not if something is "reform-ist," "radical," "revolutionary," or "moral." We ask, is it good for women or bad for women? (Morgan, ed. 1970: 583)[18]

Setting aside the reformist/revolutionary questions was central to the break with the Marxist Left, which took the concern for women's oppression to be subordinate to broader revolutionary aims. As the quote makes clear, however, consciousness raising also eschewed a "moral" or "impartial" point of view in developing its assessments, and made its assessments of phenomena in terms of their good or bad effects on women. To understand why feminists insisted on partisanship in their considered evaluations of the experiences that women shared, it is useful to begin by considering the consequences that might be occasioned by striving for "impartiality" in such a context.

In the first place, to the extent that violence played a part in women's oppression, they would share the lot common to most victims of violence in being psychologically disposed to assume undue responsibility for the violence that was done against them. This is part of a normal set of psychological responses to finding oneself a victim:

> At some point in their healthy coping processes, victims blame themselves in statements like "I shouldn't have left the door open" and "I shouldn't have gone for a walk by myself." In these usually erroneous statements, people are at-tempting to regain control over random events by blaming themselves rather than accepting the arbitrary chaos of violence . . . . We wonder, "why did this happen to me?" We search for an explanation, even a self-blaming one, that will restore control and order to our lives. (Schechter 1982: 18)

It may be objected, of course, that a truly impartial accounting of an agent's responsibility for a harm done to her would be able to identify and eliminate the "erroneous" propositions in her account. Even if this were so, however, the psychological disposition of the victim herself would place her in a poor position to carry out such an assessment on her own, especially in the period immediately following the offense. The state of denial that her victimization has occasioned may make it desirable for her to give herself "the benefit of the doubt" more than would ordinarily be the case if she is even to approach an objective assessment of the offense against her. Where victims strive simply to "be objective" with regard to their plight, they will be prone to diminish the extent to which their situation was actually out of their control.[19]

If self-blame presents evaluative difficulties for the individual victims of socially recognized criminal activity, those difficulties will be still further compounded where hidden relations of oppression are involved. This is because the epistemological situation of the members of the early consciousness-raising groups were far worse than that of "ordinary" victims. To gain a better sense of this, it may is useful to consider a concrete example. In a normative evaluation of the issue of the verbal harassment of women on the street or on the job, certain kinds of questions might seem normal for reaching an impartial judgment regarding a particular incident.[20] Once the victim had found a receptive atmosphere in which she could express her discomfort or intimidation in the face of the harassment, we might imagine her going on to evaluate the ethical responsibility that the perpetrator of the act should bear for that harm. She might ask such questions as, "Was what I was wearing, doing, or suggesting causally related to his behavior?" or "Did the perpetrator really mean the act that way (i.e., did he mean any harm)?" In other words, in aspiring to a more universal point of view, she may try to get beyond her own subjective appreciation of the harm, and to see the act in question from a different perspective. Even to consider questions such as these, however, might have posed very serious difficulties for the woman who asked them.

As already discussed, the question of how the appearance or behavior of the woman might have played a part in her subjection could easily play into the kind of self-blame that generally characterizes victims. Moreover, where harassment is part of a broader system of the oppression of one group by another, such a question would have even more treacherous implications. To the extent that the woman was part of a social order in which women *were* in the role of "sexual objects" for men—i.e., where their typical actions, speech, dress, and general bearing were publicly understood as invitations for sexual advances on the part of men—merely acting in that role (merely being a woman) *was* all that was required to occasion sexual advances on the part of men. While the victim in ordinary cases of robbery or simple assault may distort the actual conditions of the crime in assigning responsibility for the act to herself, the victim of sexual harassment need only be informed in her reflection by the prevailing assumptions regarding women in society to assign herself a role in her victimization. While the victim of harassment may also distort the account of the harm against herself, to the extent that she is part of a social order in which women are assigned the role of sexual objects, even an "undistorted" accounting of the facts would lead to the conclusion that she is, at least in part, responsible for her plight. The harm that consciousness raising brought to light would thus become a source of self-blame.

Likewise, in a social order characterized by the objectification of women, it is often the case, particularly in the early stages of feminist consciousness raising, that the harasser can honestly report that he did not consciously "mean" any harm in his act.[21] Though offense may have been *taken* at the act, given the prevalent social norms there was no *a priori* reason to think that the harasser consciously intended that outcome. It is perhaps interesting to note that the victim of a robbery would not come to a conclusion of quite this kind in assessing the intentions of a robber. Though she might be moved to ascribe more or less agent-responsibility by considering such factors as what the robber had in mind during the robbery, what motivated the robber to rob, or even whether or not the robber really wanted to rob, there is no question about the robber's *meaning* harm of some kind by robbing. Given the prevailing assumptions of our culture, there is little debate that one cannot effectively carry out a robbery without intending some harm. Where prevalent social norms permit the assumption that a man can sexually harass a woman and mean no harm, the opening exists not only for the victim to blame herself for the offense, but for her to conclude that nothing morally significant has occurred at all. In other words, contrary to the description that arose in consciousness raising, the victim may come to the belief that the offense she has taken at the act must be an overreaction after all.

This discussion sheds important light on exactly how an attempt to "be impartial" under conditions of oppression may actually result in being "partial" toward the oppressor. In the first place, because actions such as sexual harassment are the expressions of an oppressive relation of power between two groups, they embody the socially established capacity of the members of one group to objectify the members of the other. It is because men perceive women as the objects of sexual desire, *and* because men possess, or are perceived as possessing, the capacity to act on the basis of that perception, that harassment is experienced as a genuine harm, and not just as a nuisance.[22] Under these conditions, however, for a woman to attempt to take on the man's perception of harassment can only be, in some sense, to perceive herself as a sexual object. This means that among the requirements for an oppressed agent to take an impartial perspective with regard to her own oppression is, ironically, to perceive herself as an object, i.e., as one lacking any such capacity.[23] It was precisely by "taking the woman's side" that consciousness raising was able to avoid the (typical) kind of questioning that implicitly rejects women's agency as women altogether. By developing a practice that strategically ignored "the other side" in its assessments, consciousness raising permitted the articulation of a peculiarly feminine anger at those practices by which women are subjected to masculine power. In so doing, it set the stage for an entirely new evaluation of those practices in the society at large.

Partiality as a Means to the Universal

Consciousness raising's eschewal of impartiality is grounded in the assumption that, under conditions of oppression, the attempt by a member of an oppressed group to "give equal weight" to the oppressor's perception of an incident may serve only to heighten a sense of responsibility on the part of the oppressed person for that incident, or perhaps even to suggest that her perception of it as harmful was altogether misplaced. Either of these effects would likely thwart the development of the feelings of anger and outrage that could, in turn, serve as the mainspring for social change. Those moralists who have stressed the need to aspire to a "more universal" perspective in coming to an unbiased evaluation have largely ignored the possibility that a moral agent might be a member of an oppressed group. They have, in effect, assumed the perspective of the powerful. Kant aptly expresses this attitude in his remarks on "Enlightenment" in the third *Critique:*

> [It] indicates a man with a *broadened way of thinking* if he overrides the subjective conditions of his judgment, into which so many others are locked, as it were, and reflects on his own judgment from a *universal standpoint* (which he can only determine by transferring himself to the standpoint of others). (Kant 1790: 295)

As with other liberal thinkers, Kant takes the egoism of the self-interested individual to be the primary threat to moral order. While this may be true for those already possessed of social power—those whose interests are already mediated by the institutions and practices of society—this is not the case for members of all social groups.[24] Among deficiently recognized groups, the *lack* of any genuine "self-interest" may be one of the greatest impediments to justice.

On the other hand, it must not go unnoticed that these observations themselves assume normative significance only against a backdrop of concern that all points of view be respected. A demonstration that the moral psychology demanded by universalist procedures has never brought about genuine universality carries moral weight only for an agent who already grants a certain authority to a universal point of view.[25] Hence, the claim that the conditions of access to a truly universal point of view may require practices that do not consciously embrace impartiality as their direct aim need not count against impartiality as an abstract source of justification. What must be emphasized, rather, is that such an abstract ground is critically limited in lending concrete guidance for action—a point amply illustrated by the present discussion.[26] To the extent that issues such as rape, domestic violence, and sexual harassment have emerged as major "social problems," it is possible for the moral philosopher to look back on the early movements of consciousness raising that played a major role in that emergence and retrospectively to endorse their practice of "taking the woman's side." The impartial justification for the initial partisanship out of which the awareness of these issues emerged, however, was scarcely apparent at the time of the early feminist movements. Even if it could be argued that the practice of the oppressed "speaking bitterness" was (universally) justified by appeal to Maoist principles, the claim that women could properly be described as the victims of such oppression still lacked such a justification. As noted above, women's *suppressed* agency was a working assumption that found its validation through the "discoveries" to which it gave rise.

The manner in which consciousness raising simultaneously (1) develops the previously suppressed agency of a social class, and (2) appeals, at least implicitly, to abstract ethical moral norms in developing its grievances against society, strongly suggests the kind of reconceptualization of universality described in the last chapter. There, I defended a version of the Hegelian claim that the "moral point of view" can serve as an abstract starting point for fleshing out the actual social and psychological conditions that would embody the ethical life. Hegel criticized the Kantian claim that the task of ethics was complete when the moral agent could act on an abstract condemnation of slavery. Because the actual freedom of a slave cannot be mediated in a slave-dependent society, the meaning of the freedom of the slave, and hence of the attitudes and behaviors that are best suited to supporting that freedom, remain obscure. Though it is possible to utter the proposition "Slaves are free," to the extent that slaves are systematically excluded from the institutions that embody freedom for a society, and to the extent that the needs and interests of the classes of a society are satisfied by a slave system, the full meaning of that proposition can be neither known nor fully embraced by the persons of that society. Likewise, insofar as women are systematically excluded from the state and civil society, and insofar as the "needs" and "interests" of the society are met in the context of such a sexist system, the full meaning of "women's freedom" remains abstract, neither fully known nor embraced.

Because of this lack of specificity in historically unmediated concepts, the emergence of a new shape of consciousness may bring about a more or less thoroughgoing *re*-conceptualizing of an existing moral category such as "freedom." On Hegel's account, the expressive force of abstract moral categories derives from the ways in which those categories take shape within the institutions and practices they govern. This means that a major change in those institutions and practices (as might well be occasioned with the emergence of the agency of an oppressed class) will bring about an altered grasp of the categories as well. As the social conditions for a concept's public expression are transformed, the *meaning* of the concept is subject to an unpredictable transformation as well.[27]

Because feminist social critique is still in the process of calling attention to the myriad ways in which gendered assumptions inform our conception of morality, it is too early to know with any precision what all the implications of that critique may be. Already, however, it is possible to detect ways in which feminism could challenge the meaning of certain basic moral concepts. One such concept is that of "respect," and, in particular, the Kantian assumption that "consent" can serve as an adequate expression of it.[28] Of course, political criticisms of consent theory are not new.[29] Nevertheless, by revealing the ways in which society takes women's consent to certain acts to be both morally necessary and effectively meaningless, consciousness raising has suggested a thoroughgoing critique of consent as a measure of respect for persons. Moreover, to the extent that such a critique is warranted, it may have a profound effect on our grasp of the concept of "respect for persons" itself.

The criticism of consent came about as a result of consciousness raising surrounding heterosexual practices in general, and also their relationship to the status of rape in the law.[30] Although the subsequent feminist literature on this topic has been vast, for my purposes it is sufficient to focus on some of the implications of several of its most important (and least controversial) conclusions.[31] First of all, consciousness raising called attention to the fact that for women rape was not just an "isolated occurrence," but a terrorizing part of the landscape of everyday life. As Susan Griffin (1971) began her groundbreaking essay:

> I have never been free of the fear of rape. From a very early age I, like most women, have thought of rape as a part of my natural environment—something to be feared and prayed against like fire or lightning. I never asked why men raped; I simply thought it was one of the many mysteries of human nature. (313)[32]

As with all terrorism, that occasioned by rape serves to disempower its victims by making all action against it appear useless. The terror instilled by rape, however, is not simply that of a random and uncontrolled fate, but of one that effectively embodies the power of any man over any woman.[33] As Mehrhof and Kearon (1971) wrote:

> There are no actions or forms of behavior sufficient to avoid its danger. There is no sign that designates a rapist since each male is potentially one . . . . It is primarily a lesson for the whole class of women—a strange lesson in that it does not teach a form of behavior which will save women from it. *Rape teaches instead the objective, innate and unchanging subordination of women relative to men.* (230)[34]

Thus, the phenomenon of rape reveals itself not only as entailing certain risks for women, but (largely without their consciously being aware of it) as defining their condition vis-à-vis men.

This condition of fear takes on even greater significance when it is considered in the context of "ordinary" heterosexual relations in which the man takes on the role of initiator and the woman that of respondent. On the one hand, as many feminists have pointed out, women's refusal of sex is not taken as a genuine refusal but as an invitation for a more aggressive approach. This fact alone would be sufficient to render women's consent problematic.[35] To the extent that women's experience is characterized by fear of rape, however, that fear will serve further to compromise the conditions of consent for "ordinary" sex. As Catharine MacKinnon (1987) noted, "If you feel that you are going to be raped when you say no, how do you know that you really want sex when you say yes?" (83). Not only may women's acquiescence to sexual relations not accurately represent their feelings and desires, but their feelings and desires may themselves be expressive of the legitimate fear of rape that pervades women's experience.

That such a fear is legitimate is made manifest not only by the relative frequency of rape and sexual assault, but by the fact that the majority of those offenses are not legally actionable. From their earliest considerations of the issue, feminists have called attention to the manner in which the psychological and sociological impediments to consent find institutional embodiment in the laws concerning rape and sexual assault. The absence of a category of "marital rape" meant that women's right of consent over the sexual use of her body could legally be relinquished to a particular man.[36] Moreover, the extraordinary difficulties for the woman who would attempt to prosecute her assailant in rape and sexual assault cases revealed the extent to which women's right of "sexual consent" was abstract at best. The manner in which rape trials involved a critical reversal of certain basic assumptions regarding the accuser and the accused, the virtual impossibility of obtaining convictions against any man with whom the survivor was acquainted, and the rigid requirements for "proof" of actual penetration and force all contributed the realization among women that "Rape is only slightly forbidden fruit."[37] Consciousness raising revealed that it was not women's experience of violation and humiliation that defined the crime of rape, but the proof that the access was not one to which the man was entitled.[38]

Obviously, this is a very quick reading of an extensive, complex, and often controversial critique of consent as the boundary between rape and ordinary heterosexual relations. What is important from an ethical point of view, however, is that insofar as these descriptions even begin accurately to express women's long-suppressed experience of rape, they cannot but call into question the capacity of the criterion of "consent" to embody the violation of respect for women that the prevailing sexual practices occasioned. To be the proper agent of consent, a person must be possessed of a certain "domain" over which she maintains control.[39] An agent cannot properly consent to an action that falls outside such a domain, and anything that falls within such a domain cannot be the proper object of another's action in the absence of her consent. Women's experience of rape, however, reveals that the possession of their bodies as *their* domain cannot simply be assumed.[40] The actual social practices and legal institutions surrounding sexual access do not define a woman's body as falling within her proper domain, at least in any consistent fashion.[41] As the condition of Hegelian slavery was marked by the slave's labor belonging to another class, feminine subordination is characterized by a woman's body belonging to another class.[42] Likewise, as the "ineligibility" of the human being for slavery remained abstract so long as it was merely an "ought," so the requirement of respect for all persons remains an empty ideal in a culture where rape is not prohibited but "regulated."[43]

The Kantian may object, however, that what has been stated so far does not so much challenge the traditional concept of consent as it shows that consent has not been sufficiently honored in the case of women's bodily integrity. Ordinarily, obtaining consent under conditions of terror or duress serves to vitiate its moral and legal force. To the extent that this kind of terror or duress is a part of, or a frequent part of, women's experience, then it would seem clear, upon impartial reflection, that consent alone is insufficient to ensure that a sexual relationship between a man and a woman is really free. As Onora O'Neill (1989) has argued, there is no reason that an impartial principle of respect for persons cannot take into account instances of systematic or "unintentional" disrespect toward members of oppressed classes.[44] It is only when the true nature of respect is incorrectly grasped, i.e., if a socially or materially contingent capacity for consent is simply assumed to exist, that problems of the kind described here may ensue. For her, the capacity of an agent to give or refuse consent with regard to actions affecting her domain remains at least one distinguishing mark of personhood.

While few feminists would dispute the claim that women are not respected as persons under sexist conditions, however, there are several considerations that might lead them to eschew a "principle of respect" as that would be embodied in the context of contemporary Western institutions and practices. While an impartial principle of respect for persons may have the capacity to *account for* institutional forms of disrespect once they have been exposed, under conditions of inequality such an accounting after the fact may not be the only or the most important point at issue. Moreover, when a principle has historically failed to embody the experience of women as persons, it may require a more thorough-going rethinking than Kantians such as O'Neill suggest.

In the first place, in determining whether or not the conditions as they have been described by feminists "really do hold," it may well be necessary to look beyond the socially accepted criteria of respect for persons. As should be clear from the discussion above, until very recently the assumptions informing our notion of "respect" permitted very different standards of application for men and for women. Under such conditions, gaining access to the failure of respect embodied even in such actions as a husband demanding sex from his wife or a man raping a woman who has "consented" to go on a date with him may require paying special attention to the "woman's side" in the matter. When the victim has been socialized and/or brutalized into silence, it may require more than an attitude of impartial respect toward the disputing parties to arrive at the truth. Moreover, as consciousness raising has demonstrated, the social transparency of the socialization and brutalization may itself require an attitude of partiality.

In addition to the blindness to oppression that may be brought about by adherence to socially accepted criteria of respect for persons, such adherence

may also occasion the ascription of moral and legal responsibility to the oppressed. This is well documented in the case of contemporary[45] rape trials. To
the extent that a link is generally acknowledged to exist between an agent's
worthiness of respect and her capacity to consent or refuse consent to actions
affecting her domain, this will be assumed to apply to the social situation of
women. If the agent really did perceive an act as a violation of her person, then
it would be reasonable to expect that the agent would display appropriate
resistance to that act, and would not behave in such a manner that her resistance could be understood as consent.[46] Such expectations are reasonable,
however, only if it can be assumed that the victim of a violent act is part of a
social order in which she does experience herself as an agent worthy of respect,
i.e., one in which that agency is itself consistently respected. Among the
minimal conditions for such a self-concept is that the agent not live in con-
tinuous fear of legally unactionable violation at the hands of members of a
different class. Under conditions of fear and domination, agents *cannot* reasonably be expected to demonstrate the behaviors of "free and equal" human
beings as those behaviors have been defined by the dominant classes. An agent
under conditions of victimization will act, with more or less success, in such a
manner as to survive those conditions.[47]

Hegel's remarks with respect to slavery are particularly relevant here. If
women *were* respected as persons in the way that men are in actual social
practice, then rape would not be the pervasive crime against women that it is.[48]
Yet, because rape is an ever-present reality for women, and because the legitimate fear of rape conditions women's sexual responses to men, an individual
woman's behavior in the event of rape is not likely to resemble closely that of
the self-respecting male agent. On the one hand, her fear may effectively
suppress her resistance. Even more importantly, however, to the extent that
actual rape and the fear of rape has conditioned women's sexual responses to
men, this will pose critical difficulties in distinguishing between a woman's
response to rape and her response to "consensual sex." To make such a distinction may well require very special attention to, and even cultivation of the
victim's perspective of the action against her. To the extent that rape as a
practice is politically effective, it serves in fact to deprive members of the raped
class of the social and psychological conditions necessary for genuine self-respect.[49] To hold members of that class up to the moral and legal standards of
respect under these conditions runs the risk of effectively reproaching them for
the violation they have suffered, and thereby repeating the violation. To treat
the merely abstractly free agent with "respect" may help to ensure that her
actual freedom remains unrealized.[50]

Now it may be countered that calling attention either to the peculiar conditions that may be necessary for coming to an awareness of oppression or to the victim blaming that may result from simply assuming that the social and material conditions for meaningful consent actually exist rather misses the point. The Kantian, after all, could grant that the manner in which Kant's and others' universalism ignored these conditions was of no small consequence, and that a critique of oppression is quite correct and insightful in condemning such ignorance. This would only show, however, that past procedural attempts to apply a principle of respect have in fact failed to do so. Moreover, the justification for the condemnation of these attempts follows from the principle of respect that they, due to ineptitude and/or malice, failed adequately to embody.[51] There need be no question here, in other words, of a transformation or a reconceptualization of our *concepts* of respect or consent, but rather a forceful case for developing a careful account of how they are best applied.

To construe the feminist critique of consent as stopping with the demand that the same principles that have been extended to men also be extended to women, however, assumes that such an extension can be effected without altering our understanding of those principles. In fact, the feminist critique, to the extent that it seeks to express the actual interests of women, cannot stop with the negative claim that women's consent has not been respected. If having a "domain" and possessing the social capacity to consent or fail to consent to others' transgressions against it are identical with, or are a distinguishing mark of, personhood, then it would follow that women have not "actually" been persons at all.[52] Among other things, such a conclusion runs contrary to the discovery in consciousness raising that women could gain a sense of personhood and self-respect out of their shared experience *of* oppression. Women were not merely victims but survivors, whose sense of self had developed, in however difficult and obscure a fashion, in, and to some extent through, a set of institutions and practices in which their agency as persons was not "respected" in any conventional sense.[53] If feminists can meaningfully make the charge that moral categories such as consent have failed to embody *their interests*,[54] then those interests must have found expression through some other means. If women have lacked the control over access to their bodies that would make their "consent" meaningful in society at large, and if they have nevertheless also been "persons," then it is not the case that an agent's personhood relies upon her capacity to consent. Although patriarchal society's systematic failure to accord women the recognition it does to masculine agents has constituted an oppressive situation for women, it has not in fact deprived women of their personhood altogether.

To the extent that members of an oppressed class have the capacity to come to self-consciousness as persons *and* as members of an oppressed class, it follows that the dominant conceptions of persons and respect for them do not embrace all the possibilities.[55] Women have remained agents, albeit subordinated ones, in their social roles as mothers, sisters, workers, and, of course, as the survivors of sexist society. The fact that consent has been socially meaningless for them thus has more than a negative significance. It may be for this reason, in large part, that feminist ethics has tended to refocus moral discourse away from traditional notions such as consent and toward a different set of concepts that express the care and mutuality no less than the antagonism and anger toward oppression that women have experienced in their peculiar roles as moral agents. Concepts such as these may well lend expression to a form of respect that transcends the boundaries of consent as patriarchal society has known it. As the self-development of the slaves in Hegel's parable of "Lordship and Bondage" in the *Phenomenology of Spirit* led to a breakdown in the old ways of the masters as well, so the development of the feminine cannot leave the masculine and its ethical world unchanged.

Nevertheless, as I shall detail in part 3 below, this last point will occasion no small amount of difficulty when it comes to distinguishing the aspects of women's agency that are simply suppressed from those that represent a genuine possibility for an alternative perspective.[56] To the extent that the practices that have embodied a group's agency have lacked the recognition accorded to the practices of dominant groups, asserting "difference" risks reinforcing oppressive social structures. On the other hand, by endorsing the simple extension of the prevailing grasp of concepts such as "consent," feminists may devalue women's own peculiar experience of personhood and thwart the possibilities for developing a more embracing and "universal" conception of respect for persons.[57] Because the full nature of women's agency and its implications for reconceptualizing our moral categories remains obscure within the institutions and practices of sexist society, the precise shape of that new conception must remain unclear.

Conclusions

Examining the reasons for the early consciousness-raising groups' eschewal of an attitude of impartiality in their evaluations affords important insights concerning the development of agency under conditions of oppression. Because women's perception of their situation remained socially unmediated, the actual existence of an impartial point of view with respect to their oppression could not be assumed. The fact that human beings are capable of being subordinated at all is expressive of a social order in which such a relationship has a certain "validity" (Hegel 1821: 57R). Hence, the truth of the proposition "human beings ought to be respected" remains unmediated and, at best, deficiently understood. Moreover, at least some attempts to treat members of different classes as simply "free and equal," and therefore as not deserving of any special consideration, may serve to reinforce existing relations of power and to thwart the emergence of grievances against the existing order. To paraphrase Hegel (in a way that he would doubtless not appreciate), unless and until women's absolute unfitness for rape, assault, and sexual harassment is no longer apprehended as a mere "ought to be," the freedom of women *and men* will remain abstract and elusive.

The practice of consciousness raising as it developed in the late sixties, however, adds a crucial dimension to the Hegelian criticism of the "moral point of view," one that eludes Hegel due to his characteristic mistrust of the masses. Here, we find an example of an integrally dispossessed social class developing an *alternative* set of practices within an existing social order through which its agency might come to expression. This is a possibility that Hegel could never have envisioned given his project of thwarting rabble-rousing demands for "equality."[58] The early feminists of the Second Wave, in accord with Hegel's own criticisms of liberal equality, recognized the limitations of the existing expression of "universality" as it pertained to the condition of women. Their response to this, however, was to attempt to develop a community in which certain forms of agency that went unrecognized in the larger society might develop and flourish. Although feminists were in no position to enforce an instantaneous change on the existing social order, neither were they restricted to "empty" demands for abstract equality.

In this sense, the practice of feminist consciousness raising suggests an alternative to both the moral self-transparency of Kantianism and the self-opacity suggested in Hegel's account of world-historical agency. While consciousness raising displays how a particular interest may be "inseparable from the actualization of the universal" (Hegel 1837c: 43), the motivation for developing that interest is far removed from the essentially blind "passions, private aims, and . . . selfish desires" that characterized Hegel's world historical individuals (26). While consciousness raising did develop a very particular set of interests, its aims in doing so were to foment social change, and to advance the recognition and power of women in society. Of course, as Allen Wood has pointed out, nothing in Hegel's account *requires* that agents of historical change have absolutely no idea what they are up to.[59] Nevertheless, his descriptions of the movers of history in the *Philosophy of History* clearly emphasize their blindness as to the momentous significance of their actions. By contrast, the aim of overcoming "oppression" was never far from the program of the early consciousness raising organizers, even where conventional approaches to this end were rejected. In this sense, feminists may be understood to have taken seriously Hegel's dictum that in the post-Enlightenment world the moral point of view can function as a "starting point"—and no more than a starting point—toward liberation.

If we are to do justice to a Kantian conception of justification, however, it is not sufficient to stop with the question of universalism. As I have noted previously, the Kantian concern for universalism derives from a still deeper commitment to the principle of autonomy. To the extent that our conception of universalism in morality is transformed, the conception of rational agency which it is supposed to govern must also be altered. In the next chapter, I shall take up this question with reference to the set of criticisms directed against sexist *agents* in consciousness raising. As I hope to show, the implications for conventional morality are no less important or striking there.

IGNORANCE, OPPRESSION, AND BLAME
Political Critique and Individual Reproach

> *"Pornography is the theory and rape is the practice"* —
> *learning to understand the truth of that statement* —
> *and to understand it personally, with respect to one's*
> *own life* — *is a political-ethical necessity. I believe*
> *that, for men: if men do not grasp that in themselves,*
> *then I think the social structure of sexual oppression*
> *is still abstract for them and that feminism is beyond*
> *them, out there, just an object again.*
>
> —Stephen Heath
> "Male Feminism"

Some of the same tensions that characterize the transformative appeal to universality in feminist political criticism carry over to its criticisms of the agency of sexists—in particular that of sexist men. While criticisms of this kind most often assume the capacity of the offending agents to judge their actions impartially and to act on the basis of those judgments, they likewise imply a serious deficiency in the prevailing background assumptions governing men in their ethical judgments and actions. Inasmuch as Hegel sought to combine a recognition of the central importance of social institutions and practices with Kant's distinctive concern for the autonomy of the rational agent, it would seem promising to reexamine his ethical thought with a view toward this issue. This is especially so in that, as discussed in chapter 1, Hegel's commitment to universality and its expression in rational agency does not exclude the possibility of an agent's being an exceptionally poor judge with respect to her actions, at least at certain pivotal moments in world history.

Feminist criticism of the acts of sexist men, at least when it is stated in its strongest forms, involves two critical claims. In the first place, it asserts that an action is part of a practice or set of practices that, under some description, is oppressive to women. Secondly, it assumes that the description under which the practice or set of practices is oppressive, is more or less inaccessible in sexist culture. Despite the latter assumption, however, the sexist agent is held personally responsible for sexist action, such that his agency can be called into question for it. When acting in this way, he is a *sexist*.[1] Such criticism of the offender's ethical agency may well appear inconsistent with the assumption that his act is not condemned, and may be even socially acceptable, in sexist culture. To the extent that he genuinely lacked reflective access to the description under which the practice was objectionable, it seems wrong to call his *agency* into question. Though his ignorance may not exonerate him of all responsibility for the effects of his action, reproaches against his willing appear unjustified.

Assuming that this strong articulation of feminist criticism is important (and not mere confusion), it is necessary to account for its apparent inconsistency. There are two obvious routes that such an account could take. First, it could maintain the blameworthiness of the agent by weakening the claim about social practices. Perhaps the extent of their influence is not sufficient to close the agent off from the relevant descriptions of his act. Marilyn Frye (1983), for example, has argued that oppressive action involves a kind of inattention to the plight of others that is morally culpable. To soften the role of social forces in this manner, however, occasions difficulties of its own. Even if it were possible to resolve the difficult question as to when an agent is sufficiently free from social "influence" that his agency is not at stake, by reserving the ascription of responsibility to the individual agent, it may seem that feminism's characteristic appeal to the power of oppressive *social* structures would be lost. Moreover, the assertion that most sexist agents have had anything like immediate access to feminist descriptions of their acts appears patently false. Indeed, the claim of the agent that he "didn't know what he was doing" (at least until after it was pointed out to him) has been perhaps the most plausible and effective male response to such criticism. If nothing else, it would seem that strongly articulated feminist critiques of sexist action make assertions that are less than obvious to the offending agent.[2]

In light of these objections, it is tempting to account for the apparent inconsistency by moving in the opposite direction and weakening the claim for individual responsibility. Perhaps these apparent ascriptions of responsibility are not motivated by a genuine belief that the sexist agent is responsible for his actions, but out of concern for the consequences that might accompany a failure to hold the agent responsible for his acts. This would be consistent, of course, with a consequentialist account of the critique, where the ultimate motivation for ascriptions of responsibility is driven by such concerns. Cheshire Calhoun (1989) has argued that it is not necessary to accept a full-blooded consequentialist account of blaming to weaken the force of feminist ascriptions of individual responsibility in these cases. By exonerating the agency of the sexist, however, it may appear that feminist ascriptions of responsibility are somehow disingenuous.[3] Feminists do not *really* mean to assail the character of the sexist agent, despite the tone of their rhetoric. Although I shall have much more to say about this strategy for salvaging feminist criticism in what follows, it would appear, at least *prima facie*, to put forward a claim about the intentions of that criticism which many feminists would not accept.

If making feminist criticism consistent by weakening one of its strong claims occasions serious difficulties, then it would appear that, to the extent that the strongest form of feminist criticism is worth defending, a different approach is needed. In this chapter I shall return to the Hegelian conception of agency developed in part 1 to challenge traditional objections to the conjunction of the claims. Most importantly, Hegel's historicizing of the moral autonomy of the agent entails that, under some conditions, an agent may be subject to reproach from certain parties against his agency for the harm associated with the performance an action, where knowledge of such harm is available only under a description to which he does not have immediate reflective access. By conceiving of agent-responsibility as a capacity that unfolds in the context of social relations over time, Hegel's conception permits critiques of ethically deficient *agency* (and not only actions) on the basis of facts (including ethical facts) to which an agent lacked reasonable access at the time of the act. By taking up this issue and its significance for feminist criticisms of sexist agency, I hope to shed light on certain otherwise unclear aspects of Hegel's approach to agent-responsibility and its relation to society and history.

In the next section, I shall discuss and criticize Calhoun's strategy for addressing this question by weakening the claim about agent-responsibility in some detail. Because the agents in oppressive systems do often appear to have been non-culpably ignorant of the wrongness of their acts, this strategy has a certain attractiveness. I then argue for an alternative explanation for feminist ascriptions of agent responsibility, tying those ascriptions to the feminist challenge to the prevailing set of normative assumptions for applying impartial moral standards in a society. Finally, I discuss how such an understanding of feminist critiques of masculine agency is consistent with the Hegelian conception of ethical agency developed in previous chapters, and also how it may serve to illuminate how Hegel's commitment to the primacy of institutions and practices can be squared with his attempt to retrieve Kant's central concern with rational agency.

Before turning to my discussion here, I should emphasize that I am specifically concerned in this chapter with feminist criticism of *men's* sexist agency. Clearly, this does not encompass a range of other feminist criticisms, which may be directed either toward the sexism of institutions and practices without reference to agency or toward the sexism inherent in certain actions of women. Because feminist critique finds its basis in the development of the collective agency of women (as argued in chapter 4) and the concomitant expression of a women's point of view with respect to the institutions and practices of a society, however, it may carry with it an implicit criticism of the men who have benefitted from the apparent absence of that point of view. If practices associated with the traditional marriage bond, the use of male-normative language, or pornographic representation embody, in some sense, the subordination of women, then the male agents who engage in such practices are, perhaps ignorantly, engaging in subordination that benefits them.[4] It is the special set of normative problems surrounding agency of this kind that will be my focus here.

Ignorance, Responsibility, and Reproach

In "Responsibility and Reproach" (1989), Calhoun takes up some important and difficult normative questions concerning the distinction between ordinary instances of wrongdoing and cases of oppression. In particular, she attempts a justification of what she takes to be feminist "moral reproach" against oppressive acts that are sanctioned by an ongoing social practice.[5] Because feminist criticism of activities such as the use of sexist language, engagement in traditional courtship and dating rituals, and even the pursuit of certain kinds of scientific research[6] clearly makes appeal to a perspective not ordinarily available to the agents being criticized, it does not appear reasonable to reproach the agency of the men who are engaged in them. Calhoun endeavors to make sense of these critiques by appealing to the peculiarity of the circumstances, the "moral context," in which they arise. She argues that while "normal moral contexts" permit moral ignorance to be taken into account as a factor in exculpating an agent from blame, feminist criticism occasions an "abnormal" context in which ignorance cannot be excused in this way.

Calhoun defines normal moral contexts as those in which moral knowledge is "transparent" in the sense of being sufficiently public and shared that "most rational, reflective people could come to correct judgments about which courses of action would be right, wrong, or controversial" (395). In the normal context, we consider all but the most exceptional of agents responsible for their immoral actions, since we can rely on the moral knowledge of rational agents to guide their judgments. In abnormal contexts, however, this reliability is lacking:

> Abnormal moral contexts arise at the frontiers of moral knowledge when a subgroup of society (for instance, bioethicists or business ethicists) makes advances in moral knowledge faster than they can be disseminated to and assimilated by the general public and subgroups at special moral risk (e.g.

physicians and corporate executives). As a result, the rightness or wrongness
of certain courses of action (for instance, routine involuntary sterilization of
the mentally retarded) are, for a time transparent only to the knowledge-acquiring subgroup but "opaque" to outsiders. (396)

Moral ignorance becomes the "norm" in the abnormal context because most
persons in a society will fall outside the "knowledge-acquiring subgroup."
Likewise, the "opacity" of moral norms seems to exculpate the agents most
likely to be in violation of them.[7] If the physician is not up on the latest moral
"advances," she may, for instance, be carrying out sterilizations on developmentally disabled patients without their consent, all the while being unaware
of the wrongness of these acts.

Calhoun argues that feminist criticism of sexism takes place in just such
an abnormal context. Since the critique "has made only limited inroads on
popular consciousness," those agents guilty of sexist acts may well appear not
to be *blameworthy* for their actions, as they would be in the normal context
(396). When a teacher's use of sexist language is first pointed out to him, for
example, he may truthfully claim ignorance regarding the moral implications
of his act. To the accusation that his use of male pronouns neutrally is sexist,
he may correctly report that he believed at the time that he was only employing proper English grammar and, further, may insist that English grammar is
not, of itself, sexist. Although Calhoun thinks that some feminist moral criticisms have filtered into popular consciousness ("the wrongness of discrimina-
tory hiring, sexual harassment, and marital rape"), the context of a wide range
of actions sometimes labelled sexist, including the use of sexist language, remains abnormal (396). In the latter cases, moral ignorance derives from social
determinants (such as language and custom) rather than conscious motivations
of the individual agent.[8] Insofar the agent's ignorance of the moral wrongness
of his act is in no way culpable, blaming, or moral reproach for the act does
not seem warranted.

Despite the absence of what we would normally consider blameworthy
behavior in these cases, Calhoun argues that moral reproach may be justifiable
just because the context of the act is abnormal. In such contexts, Calhoun argues
that focusing on the social determinants of moral ignorance has the effect not
only of freeing the agent in question from blame, but of sanctioning his action
(400). Where the object of moral critique is at least in part to *educate* the public
with regard to advances in moral knowledge, it must be established that action
consistent with that knowledge is not in any way heroic or supererogatory (as it
might well appear were one to emphasize the actual social odds against a competent moral agent's so acting) but simply obligatory (403). The point is not to

heap praise on "non-sexist men" but to establish the *prima facie* wrongness of sexist acts. This point will be lost where the agency of sexists (as opposed to ordinary wrongdoers) is exonerated on the basis of social considerations.

By drawing attention away from social determinants and focusing it upon the wrongness of the action, the agent's responsibility as an individual comes to the fore. This may seem to detract too much from the social conditions that made the act in fact all too ordinary. Still, to the extent that moral reproach serves to publicize heretofore unknown moral standards, to convey their obligatory force on all agents, and to reinforce the moral autonomy of the individual in following such standards, ascription of responsibility is justified. Calhoun concludes that, "In abnormal contexts, it may be reasonable to reproach moral failings even when individuals are not blameworthy" (405). Agent-reproach against sexist men is justified as a means of publicizing the wrongness of their actions.

I shall argue in the sections to follow that conceiving of ethical responsibility as a socially and historically emergent capacity affords a better understanding of the nature of sexist action than Calhoun's ahistorical reading. Even if Calhoun's account of sexist action were correct, however, it is not clear that undeserved blame is suited for publicizing its wrongness. It is not obvious how moral reproach against individuals who violate the as yet unassimilated moral norms will serve to disseminate the "advances in moral knowledge" of a particular subgroup—even when the offending individuals are members of groups "at special moral risk." It is scarcely apparent, for example, that it is reasonable to *blame* physicians for failing to abide by a moral injunction against routinely sterilizing developmentally disabled patients, where it is also assumed that the physicians were entirely unaware of the facts necessary for reaching that judgment.[9] Even if members of a moral vanguard were justified in vociferously educating the public as to the nature of these facts, including actions to condemn the practice by whatever means were effective, moral reproach against individual physicians would not appear to be efficacious in bringing about this end. Assuming that the physicians' ignorance concerned facts that were not accessible by ordinary means, and that moral principles were not at issue, ascribing blame would be misplaced and could well occasion counterproductive reactions against feminist critics. To the extent that these physicians truly were competent moral agents, a clear public statement that their action was wrong, and that they *would* have been subject to moral reproach *had* they been fully informed would seem to be the proper admonishment.

At least some of the confusion here may derive from Calhoun's use of the term "moral ignorance." If it were the case that sexist agents were ignorant not only of moral *facts,* but of moral *principles,* then reproach might seem warranted. It has traditionally been held that while blame is justified against an agent who is ignorant of moral principles, it is not against one who is unaware of particular facts regarding a case.[10] Such an ignorance of principle might be implied by Calhoun's interesting claim that feminists "reconstruct moral reasoning" to the point of developing alternative moral theories, and thus bring about a need for wholesale "moral reeducation" (397–398). This could be taken to suggest that non-feminists are ignorant of relevant moral principles, and thus in need of moral education in a sense not unlike that of young children. As I shall discuss in greater detail below, we do find it necessary to treat small children as if they were aware of principles that they in fact are not, in order to develop a sense of ethical agency in them.[11] As the bearers of potential but still "unactualized" universal agency, they are not simply irresponsible and should not be treated as such.

Calhoun, however, assumes that both the feminists and the sexist agents of whom they are critical share unconstrained access to moral principles and differ only in the facts to which they are privy. Feminist "expertise" concerns knowledge of certain peculiar facts relevant to the application of existing principles, and not knowledge of basic moral principles themselves. Precisely because of this, however, it is difficult to see why sexist agents would take their actions to be *excused* when the social conditions that clouded their understanding of those actions were simply explained to them. To the extent that the offending agents have the capacity to take on the moral point of view and thereby to "rise above childhood conditioning," blame would seem both unnecessary and misplaced (398).

In the remainder of this chapter, I hope to show that while Calhoun is right to stress the importance of "reproach" in feminist criticism of men's sexist actions, the warrant for this reproach in criticizing sexism derives from the fact that feminists are seeking to transform our understanding of moral principles themselves. They are not merely calling attention to a new set of "facts" to which an extant and universally accessible set of principles must be "applied." Although feminist criticism does not purport to offer new moral principles, by reconceptualizing certain basic categories of the old ones in light of a previously repressed agency, feminist critics occasion the need for, and are in a unique position to effect, a thoroughgoing ethical re-education of society. To put it in more "Hegelian" terms, while sexist agents had access to the abstract "principles" that they violated at the time of their acts, they did not at that time have access to the transformed awareness of those principles to which feminism gave rise. This means that while sexist agents are not "blameworthy" in the way that they would be had they been fully cognizant of the wrong they performed, neither are they exculpated from reproach on account of their ignorance. Rather, as ethical subjects whose awareness is capable of a transformation in which their responsibility could become newly appreciated, they are also subject to blame (or praise) in light of that transformation.

Sexist Agency and Intention

To get a clearer sense of the kind of responsibility that is at issue here, it is useful to consider the precise manner in which a sexist agent can be ignorant of the nature of his action. Calhoun cites Ruth Bleier's (1986) charge that scientists who "objectively" document and report on women's "deficiency in visuo-spatial skills" are guilty of reinforcing social stereotypes that women are innately deficient in these areas, such that "no amount of education or social change can abolish this biological gap" (Calhoun 1989: 391). Moreover, Bleier claims that these scientists cannot legitimately claim that they are unaware of these implications:

> It is disingenuous for scientists to pretend ignorance of their readers' beliefs and expectations and unethical to disclaim responsibility for the effects of their work and for the presumed misinterpretations of their 'pure' texts. (391)

Bleier admits that the thought process involved in the scientists' actions may be "unreflective." Nevertheless, she insists on their moral responsibility and the illegitimacy of any appeals to ignorance in defending the agency of the scientists.

Although Calhoun too is critical of the scientists' actions as they affect women, she finds this last move simply wrongheaded. Because the scientists' involvement in sexist structures is unreflective, and also because "the practice of science requires not reflecting on normative implications," Bleier's attributions of agency to the researchers simply cannot stick (Calhoun: 391).[12] In making their reports, the scientists are not "pretending" ignorance at all, but are genuinely in the grip of social structures beyond their control. Calhoun contends that even if Bleier's possession of special feminist "moral knowledge" entitles her to criticize the effects of the scientists' actions, it cannot warrant impugning their moral agency in bringing about those effects. Of course, Calhoun defends the "unwarranted" moral reproach here by appeal to the moral context. Still, because she holds that feminists have no special insight into the agency of sexists, the only possible justification for feminist moral reproach is a consequentialist one that actually exonerates the offenders' agency.

Is this the only alternative, however? Need it be mere confusion to ascribe sexist *agency* where the alleged sexism of an act can be grasped only from a feminist point of view to which the agent lacked reflective access? This would not be the case if it could be shown that male ignorance of the sexism at issue were somehow culpable. Marilyn Frye (1983) has argued that in the analogous case of racist ignorance, the failure of many whites to take note of the role that their actions play in an oppressive system "is not a passive state" but represents "a complex result of many acts and many negligences" (118).[13] She contends that much of the ignorance of whites with respect to the black experience of slavery and segregation has been due not so much to their lack of access to that experience as to their actively closing themselves off from it. In Ralph Ellison's *The Invisible Man*, for example, Frye argues that the "invisibility" of the black man is occasioned by a "dense veil made up of lies the white men tell each other about Black men" (119). The ease with which the white men can ignore is not the consequence of a passive condition, but one of their repeated lying.[14]

Even if some kinds of oppressive ignorance are culpable in the manner that Frye suggests, however, it would not appear that the ignorance involved in the actions of Bleier's scientist could be so characterized. When ignorance is culpable, it is usually attributable to some kind of negligence on the part of the offending agent. If, for example, the sexist effects of the scientists' studies were foreseeable collateral consequences of their intended effects (for Calhoun, the advancement of scientific inquiry), then it might make sense to hold the scientists morally responsible for them. In Bleier's construction of the example, however, there is no reason to assume that any collateral unintended sexist effects were foreseen by, or perhaps even foreseeable to the scientists.[15] Prior to feminist criticism, extant social norms rendered the sexism invisible. Likewise, this kind of invisibility seems to rule out any charge of recklessness or culpable indifference on the scientists' part. Where the extraordinary medium of feminist consciousness raising or something akin to it is the necessary condition for making the sexist consequences of their research apparent, it cannot be expected that the researchers would be aware of them.[16]

It might be thought, however, that even if male sexist agents cannot reasonably be expected to come to an awareness of the wrongness of their acts on their own, they nevertheless incur moral reproach by virtue of sharing in the collective benefits brought about by their ignorant acts.[17] If I use masculine pronouns neutrally, for example, then my individual action embodies a collective linguistic practice, the consequence of which is the identification of human beings with men and the invisibility of women. This kind of action has two distinct effects. In the first place, because I am a man, I share in whatever benefits accrue to men and their interests *qua* men from that practice. Secondly, and even more insidiously, my engagement in the practice may serve to reinforce my ignorance of its effects. Where a social practice serves to subordinate one group to another, and where this subordination is not publicly acknowledged, ignorantly engaging in the practice may actually contribute to the ignorance by stripping members of the subordinated group of the social means for challenging it.[18] If, for example, one of the effects of using male-normative language is psychologically to reinforce silent and submissive behaviors among women, then by using such language I abet one of the conditions that keeps the deleterious effects of my action hidden from me. I effectively silence the voices of women that may be necessary for my coming to awareness of the objectionable consequences of my act.[19]

Even if the collective implication of oppressive practices serves to benefit oppressors, or to shield them from the objectionable nature of those practices, however, it may yet seem that this is not obviously relevant as concerns the culpability of these men's ignorance. From the fact that an agent benefits from an objectionable practice, it does not follow that he is blameworthy for so benefitting unless he has reasonable access to the objectionable nature of the practice. Suppose, for example, that an agent benefits socially and economically by being a very effective fund raiser for an ostensibly charitable organization which, unbeknownst to all but a small subgroup in the organization, serves also as a front group for raising money for certain right-wing death squads in the Central America. Assuming that the agent is not a member of this subgroup, that the activity is very effectively hidden (perhaps due in part to large payoffs to those who might expose it), and that the agent is motivated by no ill intentions in her own activity, it would seem entirely wrong to *blame* her for her ignorance. If she truly lacks all reasonable access to those facts that would reveal her fund raising as participation in a corrupt and oppressive organizational practice, any reproach against her agency is misplaced. Moreover, the fact that the effectiveness of her fund raising may be a contributing factor to her ignorance of the situation would seem to be of no moral relevance.

Of course, there are some contexts in which ignorance is simply no excuse, such as that of the law. A motorist's ignorance of a traffic law, for example, does not normally exculpate her from legal responsibility for her violation of that law. Calhoun in fact takes feminist indictments to be akin to legal charges, there being "little point in having either system of obligations if people can easily avoid the sanctions against nonconformity by pleading ignorance" (396). It is questionable, however, that such an analogy is a useful, or even an appropriate one here. In the first place, the ascription of legal responsibility assumes certain publicity conditions with respect to the law. Yet it is responsibility under conditions of "non-publicity" that is at issue in feminist critiques of sexism. Secondly, at least on conventional accounts, *legal* culpability does not entail *moral* culpability when the agent truly could not be expected to know the content of the law.[20] To place feminist intolerance of excuse on the same level as that of the law concedes, in effect, that the sexist agent is not really deserving of reproach—at least not reproach against his agency. The reasons for ascribing responsibility are external to his thoughtfulness as a moral agent. Yet it is exactly men's agency—their agency *as men*—that many feminists are calling into question in reproaching them.

If the ignorance involved in engaging in such acts as unreflectively pursuing in sexist research or naively using sexist language is not culpable, and if feminist reproach is not simply confused, then the ignorance involved in sexist action must at least be significantly distinct from familiar instances of non-culpable ignorance. In a typical case, such ignorance involves an agent *(A)* ostensibly committed to an ethical principle or set of principles *(P)*, but whose ignorance of certain facts leads her unwittingly to violate *P*.[21] Moreover, the circumstances occasioning *A*'s ignorance are such that it would be unreasonable to expect that *A* should, or perhaps even could, have been aware of the relevant facts at the time of her action. Although *A* would not have violated *P* had she been aware of all the relevant facts, some set of circumstances that she played no conscious role in bringing about or supporting caused her to be unaware of those facts.

Suppose, for example, that I adhere to a principle of respect for persons that includes an injunction against unnecessarily inflicting pain and suffering on others. One day, while I am stopped at a red light on my way to work, a small child accidentally becomes caught on the rear bumper of the truck I am driving. Ignorant of this, I drive on down the street, dragging the child along and causing it great suffering before becoming aware of what has happened. (Suppose further that I am in no way reckless or negligent, nor did I have any good reason to foresee such an accident.) Given this construction of the example, it would be mistaken to impugn my agency on the basis of what happened to the child. I was engaged in an activity (driving to work) which, under ordinary conditions, involves no violation of an ethical principle of avoiding the infliction of unnecessary pain and suffering on others *(P)* to which I subscribe. So long as I was genuinely ignorant of the very peculiar set of circumstances that occasioned the violation of *P*, I cannot be held blameworthy for the act.[22]

The sexist acts of men would appear to differ in at least one important respect from an act such as that just described, in that ignorance of sexism does not ordinarily concern an unusual set of conditions that renders participation in an otherwise morally neutral practice (such as driving to work) an occasion for harm. Rather, the ignorance concerns the description of an action as somehow participating in or embodying an objectionable practice, where the agent lacks reflective access to the point of view from which the action can be grasped as part of that objectionable practice. It is when the agent grasps, for example, the role that using male-normative language *ordinarily* plays in a wider system of subordination that the wrongness of this usage becomes apparent. The ignorance of the agent is not occasioned by the opacity of a fact or set of facts that renders his participation in a practice problematic in a singular instance (such as in the driving example), but by his lacking access to the relevant social meaning of the action itself.

It is not clear, however, that opacity of social meaning as such warrants reproach against an agent. Suppose, for example, that *A*, a person ignorant of the political practices prevalent in Nazi Germany, were to walk into a crowd listening to a speech by the Führer in 1939.[23] Suppose further that upon hearing a particularly antisemitic comment and correctly taking it as a violation of her commitment to *P*, *A* thrusts her right arm into the air, intending a gesture of protest toward the comment. Contrary to her intention, however, the thrust of the arm is understood by the crowd as a salute, honoring the remark. Should a witness later question her commitment to *P* on the basis of this action, presumably she could defeat the charge by invoking her genuine ignorance of the fact that the thrust of her arm would be interpreted as a salute. To the extent that she did not have access to the description of her action under which it was a violation of *P*, it would be wrong to reproach her agency.[24]

What is peculiar about this kind of example, however (aside from the unlikely historical scenario in this particular case), is that *A*'s error concerns the expression of a moral principle in an alien social setting. Because the example places *A* outside her own set of practices, her awareness of how to effectively express her commitment to *P* through her behavior is deficient.[25] In order to act on a moral principle, an agent must have access not only to the abstract principle but to a set of socially specific background assumptions—assumptions that include, critically, the behavioral norms for expressing praise, blame, dissatisfaction, and so on. When "transplanted" into an alien set of practices, an agent will lack a full awareness of such norms, and thus may be subject to errors regarding the social implications of her behavior. It is in light of *this* ignorance that we would think it wrong to reproach the agency of *A* in such a case.

Now it may be thought that a similar set of circumstances exists in cases of sexist agency, in that feminist reproaches against men do seem to impose an "alien" set of assumptions on masculine behaviors. Certain behaviors which may not previously have been thought unethical at all, such as the linguistic use of the masculine as "neutral," are subjected to ethical critique in the light of a revised set of assumptions. The analogy here, however, must not be drawn too closely. Whereas the "assumptions" at issue in the case of the woman in the Nazi crowd concerned social norms for the expression of praise and blame, feminist critique (as discussed in the last two chapters) sometimes focuses upon more critical assumptions, such as who are to count as "agents" at all. It is one thing to be ignorant of the social norms that cause one's action to be erroneously received as a violation of a principle to which one ostensibly adheres, and quite another to be ignorant of the action's being a violation of principle when one is aware of those norms.

When the feminist criticizes the behavior of the male sexist agent within her own culture, her expectations for him generally reflect a shared set of behavioral norms. To take one of Calhoun's examples, when Western feminists first argued for the existence of "marital rape," they did claim that a behavior not generally subjected to critical scrutiny before was reproachable.[26] Nevertheless, the claim that a married woman's subjection to the sexual desires of her husband, regardless of her consent, constitutes a violation of her rights as a person (or some similar claim) appealed neither to principles nor to behavioral norms for the expression of those principles that were outside the accepted range of cultural practices. The same could be said of the appeal to principle and social norms involved in less dramatic cases, such as the claim that traditional uses of male-neutral and male-normative language serves to exclude women from the publicly acknowledged sphere of human agency and to foster deleterious developmental effects on women. Once again, the bulk of the controversy surrounding the arguments derived from feminist consciousness raising has concerned neither the novelty of the principles nor the alien social norms upon which the arguments rely, but their implicit charge that women have not consistently counted as autonomous agents in the ethical calculus of Western cultures.

It is this element of feminist consciousness raising that makes it seem odd to say that men had no *reason* to be aware of women's oppression until it was pointed out to them. Given the principles to which they claimed to adhere, and the shared cultural norms for adhering to those principles in other contexts (i.e., contexts where other men as opposed to women are the agents in question), the wrongness of the practices in question ought to have been more or less obvious. On a wide range of issues, men have, albeit without bringing it to consciousness, employed a kind of double standard in their moral thinking where women have not counted as "persons" in any consistent way. As Simone de Beauvoir (1980) put it in *The Second Sex:*

> Man gladly accepts as his authority Hegel's idea according to which the citizen acquires his ethical dignity in transcending himself toward the universal, but as a private individual he has a right to pleasure and desire. His relations with woman, then, lie in a contingent region, *where morality no longer applies,* where conduct is a matter of indifference . . . . His wife is often astonished . . . at the contrast between the lofty tone of his public utterances and behavior, and "his persevering intentions in the dark." (613) (Italics mine)

One of the central reasons that reproach from feminist perspectives can "stick" and cannot simply be brushed off as an inappropriate or bizarre point of view is that it calls attention to facts that, seemingly, *should* have been obvious all along but that, for some reason, were not.

This is not to say, however, that it would have been reasonable to expect the men whose agency is under attack to have developed such perspectives on their actions entirely on the basis of their own reflection. It was only in the wake of the feminist reconceptualization of certain ethical principles (i.e., in the wake of consciousness raising as discussed above) that the cultural mediation of the wrongness of sexism became generally accessible. As the previously suppressed voice of women rose through various cultural media (such as novels and films), as well as through the legal and educational structures of society, a "universal" grasp of the scope of sexism's violation of those principles became "actual." This means that, contrary to a familiar Kantian platitude, the fact that men *should* have known that their actions embodied an oppressive relationship (given the principles and norms of their culture) does not entail that men realistically *could* have known this in the absence of the historical movement of feminist consciousness raising. In this sense, the reproach against men's agency implied in certain strong forms of feminist criticism differs in an important respect from ordinary moral reproach. In the latter case, an agent can be held *blameworthy* only for those actions that she could reasonably be expected to subject to moral scrutiny (e.g., to subject to a procedural test such as that of the categorical imperative). Once again, because, in at least some cases, knowledge of the objectionable nature of the actions in question is within the range of reasonable expectation only after consciousness raising has appeared on the scene, it seems that men cannot be expected to have taken it into account before that appearance.

Hence the kinds of feminist criticism of sexism under discussion here do fall outside the usual categories of moral culpability. Because the ignorance that is at stake in cases of male sexist action is neither that of particular facts, in which case men would not be reproachable at all, nor, strictly speaking, that of moral principles, in which case the agents would be blameworthy *simpliciter,* it occupies a distinct category as concerns reproach. In this instance, the agents under criticism are ignorant of a key background assumption necessary for the application of the principles they hold. In a critical sense, they are ignorant of how to treat a class of persons with the respect due to moral agents.[27] On the one hand, men have been able unthinkingly to engage in a wide range of social practices which, through exclusion, marginalization, objectification, or brutalization have effectively closed women off from the social means for embodying their agency. This would appear to bespeak a simple failure to recognize that women are moral agents at all. On the other hand, as discussed in chapter 4, they have as a matter of course expected women to accept the *responsibility* of such agents in dealing with specific incidents of sexist oppression (rape, harassment, etc.).[28] Such a complex and duplicitous mode of application is possible precisely because the abstract concept of respect for persons is "empty," i.e., admitting of an indeterminate range of applications depending upon the interests that inform it. As discussed in chapter 4, it may be only when feminist consciousness raising creates an alternative set of practices that the objectionable nature of these applications becomes apparent.

Nevertheless, because the judgments arising in the context of consciousness raising do assume the abstract principles and norms of the wider society, once they are socially "mediated," the kind of violations to which they call attention may well appear so obvious that even the guilty agents themselves may scarcely believe the embarrassing fact that such gross "errors" with regard to the application of principle could be possible. Most men in Western societies, after all, would claim to be committed to the very principles that are being used against them. The "unbelievability" of the infractions manifests itself psychologically in various forms of masculine denial. Such denial, however, is not without social and political significance. As I discuss below, on a Hegelian account "denial" may mark not merely a kind of self-deception, but a form of epistemic access under conditions of socially and historically emergent agency.[29] If a sexist agent believed that he was acting in accord with the demands of morality in engaging in certain behaviors toward women, and if the emergence of a feminist perspective revealed those behaviors to be obviously immoral, the sexist agent might feel a moral imperative to deny his sexism. It might seem that he would not be respecting *himself* as a person to capitulate to such a critique. Indeed, in one sense he would be right because, as I shall discuss below, the ignorance under which he labored was akin to that of a small child. On this account, the member of a powerful class who acts on principles that are informed by the assumptions of an oppressive system takes on the risk of being legitimately subjected to this kind of "disrespectful" treatment should those assumptions come to light. If the socially mediated ethical principles of a sexist society can fail to respect the agency of women, then the kind of "self-respect" that they afford men will be perilous as well.[30]

Sexist Agency, Morality, and Self-Ignorance

If this analysis is correct, the criticisms of agency levelled by some feminists against sexist agents is not confused or unintelligible, but follow from the challenge to the background assumptions for applying the moral point of view implied in feminist political criticism. Because the norms of conventional morality—including norms for the ascription of agent-responsibility—assume that the social conditions for moral criticism remain in place, they do not take account of the implications of the kind of social criticism that these feminists have levelled. Such norms fail to accommodate the possibility of global historical shifts in the meaning of actions within a society. Under such conditions, the very state of an agent's willing, and hence her susceptibility to agent-centered criticism, may be inaccessible to her at the time of her act.

Of course, as discussed in part 1, Hegel's account of the social and historical embodiment of the moral life calls attention to the dramatic revelations of agency occasioned by such historical moments. At certain key "transitional" stages in the history of consciousness, an agent may find herself in a poor position to assess the normative significance of her acts on her own. Hence, it comes as little surprise that an agent might find her willing unexpectedly revealed to be worthy of reproach (or praise, for that matter). A Hegelian reading of the feminist critique of sexist agency is useful in light of the framework it offers for grasping what is at issue in certain kinds of feminist social criticism, and for the clarity it can lend to certain obscure and interesting aspects of Hegel's work. By coherently extending a critique of social structures to a criticism of agency, feminist agent-criticism offers a concrete illustration of how a commitment to historical realism may be linked to concerns regarding the autonomy of the agent. In the remainder of this chapter, I shall explore how Hegel and feminists have developed a concern for autonomy in the context of a political theory in which the historical emergence and development of institutions and practices assume primacy.

In the first place, as I noted in chapter 1, Hegel's "right of intention" constitutes an endorsement of Kant's central contention that the agent's own sense of what she is doing is decisive in the determination of right action. Like most deontologists, Hegel assigns a central place for the agent's "subjective" meaning in determining the rightness or wrongness of an act. Unlike conventional deontologists, however, Hegel does not link the claim that the agent's intention is determinative in ethical judgment with the distinct claim that a moral agent possesses a capacity to gain *access* to that intention on her own. Hegel distinguishes his position from that of deontologists such as Kant by arguing that an agent's intention is inseparable from the reception of her act by others in a community, i.e., a group united through a concrete historical set of institutions and practices. While this condition may not pose any particular problem for deontologists in times of institutional stability (i.e., times when an agent's assessment of her action will more or less simply mirror that of the community), Hegel sees it as occasion for tragic clashes in times of historical transition, when the social meanings of actions are themselves in flux.

This, of course, was centrally at issue in Hegel's reading of *Antigone*, discussed at length in chapter 1. There, Hegel presented a scenario where the revolutionary meaning of Creon's decree was accessible only in the wake of its tragic consequences. On a standard deontological account, so long as an agent in Creon's place were to subject her proposed action to impartial assessment and then to act on the basis of that assessment, her agency would be safeguarded and her action "right." This judgment would differ from that of a consequentialist who, by contrast, could not make a determination of the rightness of the act without reference to the state of affairs that its performance occasioned. Hegel agrees with the deontologist that it is the condition of the agent's willing that is determinative in assessments of the right, but rejects the contention that this condition can be "guaranteed" by the individual moral agent's adherence to a formal procedure. In Creon's case, the agent discovered not merely that he had made a mistake in assessing the consequences of his action, but that his agency was itself inescapably impugned by virtue of those consequences.[31] Moreover, this was due to no flaw in his reflection before the act. Rather, Creon's action (of which his intention was an inseparable part) played a critical role in altering the institutions and practices in the context of which that action took on its *meaning*.[32] When an action serves as the vehicle for transforming its own meaning within the community, the agent's sense of what she was doing will also be subject to transformation.[33]

At least in its earliest stages, effective feminist consciousness raising brings about a social context in which the male sexist agent finds his action occasioning an unexpected hostile reaction that transforms the action's meaning. By publicly asserting the previously unarticulated or suppressed point of view of women with respect to an act or set of acts, consciousness raising alters the background assumptions for the application of moral principles with regard to that act or set of acts. Under such conditions, the agent finds his action to be a violation of moral principles to which he ostensibly adhered, and one from which he cannot exculpate his agency without repudiating his principles.[34] For a male agent to claim, for example, that he had never noticed the violence done to his wife by his exercising—or perhaps even his legally holding—a right to sexual access in their marriage seems, in the wake of feminist criticism, to betray a seriously deficient understanding of a principle of respect for persons. Nevertheless, he may also legitimately claim that apart from the historically emergent agency of women in consciousness raising, he could not have achieved this kind of awareness.

This aspect of feminist criticism of masculine agency makes it somewhat akin to the social dynamics operative in the ethical education of small children. In these cases also, an action is the occasion for a positive or negative reaction which determines the normative significance of the act for the agent. In a culture such as our own, for example, if a two-year-old received a toy as a gift, a parent might instruct the child to say "thank you." Should the child refuse, or perhaps try to run away with the toy, she might well suffer reproach for such behavior. In such a case, the child finds herself engaged in a social activity the social meaning of which calls for specific behaviors and attitudes (i.e., those expressing gratitude) of which she is initially unaware. Her "merely existing" capacity to assume these behaviors and attitudes cannot become "actual" except through the reactions of significant adults who possess the standing to treat her as a participant in the practice. In Hegel's terms, her immediate ability to understand her action, e.g., to grasp her violation of a norm when she runs away with the gift, is mediated through the reproach of a parent who is familiar with the practice. In this way, the meaning of her acts, even as they initially take shape in her own awareness, express the norms of a culture as these have been mediated in the responses of certain others to those acts.

Of course, in instances of sexist agency such as those discussed above, the agent is not ignorant of the abstract "formal" content of his moral principle, as is the case with small children. Nevertheless, as discussed in chapter 2, in the absence of the socially and historically specific background assumptions for the application of principles, this formal knowledge is underdetermined. As the assumptions that lend content to moral principles shift socially and historically, the morally conscientious agent may be subject to much the same disturbances of conscience as those that regularly afflict the small child. To be rightfully reproached (i.e., to be reproached by an agent with the standing to do so) for his ignorance of the wrong occasioned in an act reveals the masculine agent's knowledge of principle to have been embarrassingly deficient, even if his formal capacity to have self-reflectively subjected his judgments and actions to scrutiny is not in question.

Because adult agents are not children, and thus are not generally accepting of reproach for an act where they lacked a reflectively accessible reason for refraining from the act, however, they are not usually disposed toward embracing such criticism. The conventional assumption that agent-reproach is justified only if the agent does possess such a reason underpins the familiar masculine attitude of "defensiveness" which is typical in the face of feminist criticisms. If, for example, a male agent could not reasonably have been expected to know that using masculine neutral and masculine normative language embodied an oppressive system prior to his awareness of feminist criticism, then how could he be legitimately labelled a *sexist* (where that impugns one's agency) for so using language. The man may feel that his personhood is not being respected if his capacity as a moral agent is called into question in such a case. On a Hegelian account, however, the fact that one is not strictly blameworthy for an act does not entail that her agency may not be at stake in that act. On the contrary, to exculpate one's agency on such grounds would itself fail to respect the "rational" capacity to assume responsibility as an individual for the meanings of one's actions as they are reflected in society.[35]

It should be added, however, that the kind of defensiveness that characterizes male responses to charges of sexism differs in at least one critical respect from the typical form of "tragic agency" which the above descriptions might be taken to suggest. In the case of tragic figures such as Oedipus, the agent comes to accept responsibility for consequences of an act without regard for purpose or intention at all.[36] Hence, the question of whether or not the agent had a principled reason to refrain from acting simply does not arise. As noted above, such a crude embrace of the consequences of one's act is consistent neither with the assertion of feminists that the male agent's intention *is* critically at stake nor with Hegel's qualified endorsement of the historical advance over the ancient world and its ethical order represented by Kantian morality.[37] The male agent experiences his responsibility either as an object of rejection and denial or of embarrassed acceptance, and not as tragic fate, precisely because his ethical responsibility is predicated not only upon his ability to embrace the meanings of his acts, but upon an acknowledged capacity to act on the basis of principle. Because that capacity can be meaningfully exercised only in the context of the shifting and unpredictable practices of a given social order, however, it cannot shield the agent's willing from unforeseeable social judgments. "In their actions, human beings are necessarily involved in externality" (Hegel 1821: 119A).

All of this assumes, of course, that feminist ascriptions of agent-responsibility will be taken seriously by men in the first place. Unlike the past characters and events of Hegel's narrative "chronology" in the *Phenomenology of Spirit*, feminist criticism represents a dynamic and unfinished challenge to an existing order. As discussed at length in chapter 4, feminist interpretations of male action have not, or at least have not yet, achieved anything resembling "objective" status in our society. Moreover, because the social position of men vis-à-vis women under sexism permits them systematically to disregard women's assertions, those women who have attempted to reproach men for their actions have met with effective resistance to their claims. Ironically, they have found themselves treated as children "talking back" (to use bell hooks's apt phrase) and taking on the risk of being treated as somehow emotionally unstable if not insane or even a criminal.[38]

On a Hegelian account of ethical agency, however, feminist reproach of men's sexist agency occupies a pivotal place in the transition toward a new set of social meanings. Challenging men's intentions when they (however unreflectively) engage in sexist practices defiantly asserts that the assumptions that have permitted the wrongness of such practices to go unnoticed are themselves unacceptable. The defensive reactions that such assertions occasion are in proportion to men's rejection of women's point of view as the agents who are victimized by the practices in question. On the other hand, the extent to which such reproach does succeed in compelling men to rethink the nature of their actions in light of the principles to which they claim to adhere marks the extent of feminism's success in altering sexist assumptions.

Conclusion

Hegel's developmental account of ethical responsibility is a useful tool in explaining criticisms that extend to the agency of ignorantly sexist men, even where such criticism must appeal to a particular conception of ethical principles that was unavailable to the agent at the time of his act. To the extent that feminist critique has been effective in making its case, men's "formal" access to principle has shown itself to be historically inadequate, an inadequacy for which men, as rational agents, must answer. As with some of the tragic actors of the *Phenomenology of Spirit,* a set of acts has set in motion an epic change in the relations of the social world. This change, moreover, has resulted in a transformed appreciation of the ethical nature of the actions by which it was occasioned—even for the agent who reflects upon the condition of his own willing in those acts. For feminist criticisms of the kind taken up here, as for Hegel, the agent cannot escape responsibility for the transformed meaning of his act.

FEMINIST ETHICS AND
CRITIQUES OF RATIONALITY

> *Just as the will may be divided against itself as a
> "savage," when natural drives are allowed to over-
> whelm reason, so the will is torn asunder as a "bar-
> barian" when principle tramples the sensuous.*
> —Friedrich Schiller
> *On The Aesthetic Education of Man*

> *One who loves is not selfless either. If the loving eye
> is in any sense disinterested, it is not that the seer
> has lost herself, has no interests, or ignores or denies
> her interests. . . . What is the case surely is that un-
> like the slave or the master, the loving perceiver can
> see without the presupposition that the other poses a
> constant threat or that the other exists for the seer's
> service.*
> —Marilyn Frye
> *The Politics of Reality*

Up to this point, I have attempted to establish a link between some of the
central concerns of Hegel's ethical thought and feminist social criticism primarily by means of Hegel's critique of Kant's universalist conception of justification. It is important to note, however, that in socially and historically
contextualizing Kantian morality Hegel also intended to provide an alternative
to Kant's moral psychology. In particular, he sought to overcome the duality
between reason and feeling, where moral motivation is entirely independent of
the drives of sensuous nature. Inasmuch as the moral and epistemological
"rehabilitation" of the emotions has played a central part in feminist ethics, this
too may be a promising site for exploring the links between Hegelian and
feminist thought.[1] The manner in which feminist ethicists have been critical
of the general downgrading of feeling and emotional response as a source of
insight having moral significance bears an important similarity to some of
Hegel's criticisms of Kantian moral psychology.

Still, placing Hegel in the context of this debate is more complex than it
might first appear. Although Annette Baier (1987) has suggested that Hegel's
criticism of Kantian reason makes his ethical philosophy interesting from a
feminist point of view, Lawrence Blum (1982) has argued that the centrality
of "reason" in Hegel's ethical and political thought sets him against the main-

99

stream of feminist ethics. In this chapter, I consider Hegel's ethics of reason in the context of certain influential feminist attempts to restore a central place for the emotions within ethics. I argue that Hegel's approach, while it begins from the Kantian project of grounding morality in reason, nevertheless broadens reason so as to encompass many of the most important concerns expressed by feminist critics. Moreover, because Hegel suggests a way of critically building upon rather than abandoning his Kantian "starting point," he does not fall prey to the sorts of difficulties that beset ethical theories that call for a simpler return to the partiality of feeling and care.

It is not my intention in this chapter to argue that Hegel's approach to reason can encompass the entirety of the feminist critique of traditional ethical theory. Not only do certain elements of that critique go well beyond anything in Hegel's thought, but the critique itself is so broad and diverse that it must defy any attempt to embrace it. Likewise, as I shall specify in greater detail in section 4, I do not mean to imply that Hegel would himself have agreed with this manner of employing his conceptual apparatus. Still, to the extent that overcoming the dualisms of Kantian morality was central to Hegel's ethical project, his motivation was akin to that of some recent feminist ethicists. In section 2, I consider some general aspects of recent feminist criticisms of "rationalism" and compare them to Hegel's critique of Kantian rationalism. In section 3, I take up Lawrence Blum's charge that Hegel is a moral rationalist in the traditional sense, and show that Blum's reading cannot be sustained. In section 4, I consider both the strengths and the limitations of Hegel's approach when taken in the context of feminist ethics. I conclude that while Hegel's approach is subject to some of the most important feminist criticisms of rationalism, he nevertheless provides a useful framework for integrating the concerns of universalist and care-based ethics.

The Emotions as a Source of Moral Knowledge

The devaluation or even the outright dismissal of feeling as a source of moral justification has been at the heart of a number of feminist critiques of moral philosophy. Perhaps the earliest and most influential such critic was Carol Gilligan (1982), with her charge that Lawrence Kohlberg's developmental approach to moral education failed to take account of the moral development of women. Specifically, Gilligan argued that by assuming that the rationalistic orientation of Kantian autonomy was the highest stage of moral development, Kohlberg ignored the manner in which women characteristically develop an alternative, and equally advanced, ethics of "care."[2] It would be a mistake, however, to identify all feminist arguments against "rationalist" approaches in moral and political philosophy as simply an endorsement of "care" over against "justice." The deeper issue that draws many of these accounts together concerns the place of feeling and emotional sensibility—the "sensuous side" of human existence—in ethical and political theory.[3]

In her essay "Love and Knowledge: Emotion in Western Epistemology," Alison Jaggar (1989) outlines some of the most important points raised by feminist theorists concerning the treatment of the emotions in Western philosophy. Although Jaggar's critique of "rationalist epistemology" is not specifically directed toward normative theories of justification, the points that she develops parallel many of those raised by critics of moral rationalism. Jaggar focuses her criticisms on positivist accounts that conceive of emotion as a purely involuntary sensation or even a behavior associated with a particular feeling. Following Elizabeth Spelman (1989), she dubs this the "Dumb View" of emotions. On such a view, emotions are immediate sensations or observable reactive behaviors that are devoid of all cognitive content. Jaggar points out that such a view is subject to obvious objections. In the first place, the same objective response and even the same sensation may be associated with different emotions at different times. Likewise, the view of emotions as mere sensation renders such phenomena as non-conscious emotional states or "being out of touch" with one's emotions incoherent. Finally, such a view fails to account for the way in which emotions are "dispositional rather than episodic" (1989:133). Emotions such as sadness, fear, outrage, or jealousy may exist even in the absence of the immediate feelings or observable behaviors typically associated with those emotions.

Jaggar extends her criticism to so-called "cognitivist" accounts of emotions as well. On these accounts, emotional states are held to possess a cognitive component in addition to the sensuous or behavioral one. Although cognitivism makes significant advances over the glaring inadequacies of positivism, Jaggar argues that the cognitivist account remains wedded to certain questionable aspects of the earlier view. Specifically, by dividing the emotions into two "components"—affective and cognitive—Jaggar contends that cognitivists "unwittingly perpetuate the positivist distinction between the . . . objective world of verifiable calculations, observations, and facts, and the individual, private, subjective world of idiosyncratic feelings" (134). Moreover, because cognitivists restrict an active intentional aspect of emotion to its specifically *cognitive* component, the rationalist devaluation of feeling remains. Now it is within an emotion that its "feeling" component is passive and in need of direction.

Jaggar explains that theories of emotion take on particular significance for feminist theory (and for oppression theory more generally) in that white males have identified themselves with the role of the "rational man," while seeing certain socially marginalized groups and especially women as guided by emotions. The devaluation of feeling and emotion, and the simultaneous imperative to bring them under the "reign of reason" has thus been taken as a reason for the control of women and other oppressed groups by the regime of white men (141). Hence the development of a richer philosophical conception of the emotions and their function has political as well as theoretical importance. Jaggar provides several conditions for such an enriched conception.

In the first place, such a theory would have to get beyond the notion that emotions are "involuntary." Inasmuch as emotional life involves the scripted performance of certain socially constructed and accepted emotions, and inasmuch as the latter tend to serve functional roles for society and the individual, "the action/passion dichotomy is too simple" (136). Emotions need to be recognized for their authentically *conceptual* content, that which enables them to play the socially functional role that they do. Adequately accounting for the manner in which emotions can function in an evaluative role is possible only if emotions are concept or rule governed in themselves, and not merely "reined in" by rational control (137).

Secondly, a theory or conception of the emotions would have to recognize and account for their role as the spur to politically liberatory action. As Jaggar points outs:

> People who experience conceptually unacceptable, what I call "outlaw" emotions are often subordinated individuals who pay a disproportionately high price for maintaining the status quo. (144)[4]

Accounting for this would involve two further points. First, the theory would need to explain the perceptual aptitude of certain emotions, that is, how certain emotions have the capacity to provide a new and potentially liberating view of the world (145). Secondly, it would have to account for the way in which the emotional responses of the oppressed can take epistemic priority over those of oppressors (146). In the absence of a justification for such a prioritization, there can be no way of accounting the ethical significance of "outlaw emotions" over against the more conventional, but quite possibly no less intense, emotional responses against which they may have to contend.

I shall take up Hegel's discussion of the place of the emotions in the ethical life in greater detail below. Already, however, it should be clear that the place of emotional engagement in his ethics and politics offers a theoretical ground for a more adequate accounting of the emotions. In the first place, for Hegel the "passions" are neither involuntary nor devoid of conceptual content. They are no less than the concrete expressions of Spirit, without which the "right" would remain abstract and indeterminate.[5] As discussed in chapter 3, the conceptual content of the moral law is not fully meaningful when it cuts against the desires of the community (its system of needs). The "right" fully exists if and only if it is integrated into the emotional life as a functioning social whole (1821: 123–125, 130, 163A, 183–187, 241–242, 253R, 260, 263–264, 268R). In contrast to the Kantian account wherein the passivity of sensuous desire is absolutely contrary to the spontaneity of reason, for Hegel rational rules (concepts) take on meaning only through their articulation in the system of needs of a community. Thus, emotional response is never "dumb" but is, on the contrary, always inhabited by reason and purpose to some extent.[6]

Secondly, Hegel's concept of the cunning of reason in his chronology provides an account of how desire can function as the goad to historical progress. In contrast to Kant's moral psychology, in which reason's call can make itself felt only in its opposition to "pathological" desire,[7] Hegel makes passion (as manifested in specific historical persons and movements) the vehicle of reason itself.[8] As discussed at length in chapter 4, the manner in which Hegel's account permits motives that are both "partial" and "interested" to function as the vehicles for advances in the ethical life can serve as a justification for the particularistic concerns of social movements. In this, it underpins the claim for the epistemic privilege of oppressed groups in moving toward a more embracing conception of universality.

Of course, it must emphasized that Hegel's defense of the motive force of desire derives from his claim that reason inhabits desire to a greater or lesser degree. To the extent that desire finds its justification only with reference to reason, however, it may itself be taken as symptomatic of a kind of rationalism. This is the charge lodged by Lawrence Blum in his "Kant and Hegel's Moral Rationalism: A Feminist Perspective" (1982). Blum specifically charges that Hegel's account fails to get beyond a rationalistic bias that it inherited from Kant and thus falls short of the demands of a feminist ethics. While Blum grants that Hegel's vision of a reason "not sundered from passion and inclination" encompasses more than Kant's view does, he still finds the former account privileging traditional concepts of reason and universality. Moreover, he links Hegel's sexist account of the "ethical life" of the state to his alleged moral rationalism. In order to address these serious charges, it is necessary to explore Blum's description of Hegel's rationalism in greater detail.

Blum describes the qualities of rationality as including "self-control, strength of will, consistency, acting from universal principles, adherence to duty, and obligation" (287). In emphasizing these, Blum argues that Hegel diminishes the significance of such qualities as "sympathy, compassion, kindness, caring for others, human concern, [and] emotional responsiveness" in the ethical life (288). Once again, although Hegel goes further than Kant in linking reason and passion, Blum still sees reason "understood universalistically" as determining Hegelian ethics: "Progress is understood in ethical or moral terms as the increasing realization of autonomy, rationality, and universality in human life" (289).

To the extent that Hegel does accord importance to virtues such as sympathy and compassion, Blum observes that this is limited to the duties of the family. As such, these can express universality only "at a lesser or incomplete level" (290). In this, Hegel follows Kant in identifying women and their roles with feeling—"modesty, gentleness, and family piety"—and in depriving those virtues of any real significance. "They do not involve the moral fortitude implied in honesty or courage; or the active concern for and engagement with the good of others involved in compassion or kindness" (293). In contrast, the virtues associated with rationality and masculinity are specifically cut off from relationships and the emotional life of the family. Putting it in more contemporary terms, Blum states that Hegel's "men have a more 'instrumental' and women a more 'expressive' orientation," where the former calls for "adherence to principle and duty, strength of will and self-control" (296).

In line with what Blum sees as valorizing the instrumental over the relational, he argues that Hegel's politics must endorse a political order characterized by "large scale bureaucracies" governed by "impartial rules" (298). Blum concludes that Hegel would likely have approved of the bureaucratic and impersonal governmental forms that have arisen since his death, and of the compartmentalization of the ethical life of which they are a part. Encouraging proceduralism in public life, they meet the demands of rationality and impartiality that writers such as Hegel and Kant advocated. Moreover, by relegating feeling to a diminished feminine private sphere, contemporary political orders contribute to the subordination of women and the emotional life with which they are identified.

Clearly, the picture of Hegel emerging from Blum's account is at odds with many important aspects of that which I have been developing in this study. Specifically, Blum's description tends to blend some of the very elements of Kant's and Hegel's ethical thought that I have argued must be kept separate. In order to get a better sense of why these elements must be kept separate, however, it is necessary to understand the key points at issue between Kant's and Hegel's approaches to moral psychology. After discussing this issue, I shall be in a better position directly to address Blum's charges.

Was Hegel a Moral Rationalist?

It is important to note that Hegel's earliest criticisms of the "moral point of view" derived from the failure of Kant and Fichte to effect a harmony between reason and nature.[9] Hegel's criticism of the morality of "ought to be" begins with the observation that when there exists a moral rule that only ought to hold and thus must "command" the moral agent, it exists apart from the needs and desires of human beings and the communities of which they are a part. Anticipating Nietzsche's later attacks on morality, Hegel remarked in the *Difference* essay (1801) that the one who imposes the moral law over against his desires "relates himself to it like a slave" (153). It is important to explore both Hegel's criticism and his attempt to arrive at a more satisfactory ethics here in greater detail.

In seeking to overcome the dualism that he and others found in Kantianism, Hegel targeted a theory of moral motivation in which the "sensuous" dimension of human agency lacked any moral worth. While Kantians have rightly objected to the caricatures of Kant's actual views sometimes invoked by Hegel (and Hegelians) in this regard, it is fair to say that a duality of reason and nature is conceptually important in Kant's conception of moral value.[10] While it is impossible to consider all of the complexities of Kant's discussion in this space, it is useful to outline those aspects of it that stand in contrast to Hegel's account. As is well known, Kant restricted the determining or legislative role in morality to reason alone:

> [R]eason alone . . . must be able to determine my will by the mere form of the practical rule without presupposing any feeling or consequently any idea of the pleasant or the unpleasant . . . as the empirical condition of its principles. (1788: 23/24)

While reason requires some sensuous material to carry out its regulative function, this material plays no positive part in determining the law.

It does not, of course, follow from the fact that feeling cannot *ground* the moral will that it has no role to play in moral *motivation*. In fact, Kant himself argued that such an implication was impossible, since the moral actions of human beings must admit of explanations in terms of nature's own motives and principles (1785: 68f/400f, 1788: 74-92/71-89). Kant provided his most detailed account of the proper relationship between morality and sensuous motives in his discussion of "respect" *(Achtung)* in the second *Critique*. Because respect is the "feeling" that Kant associates with moral action, understanding its operation on the will is critical to understanding the relation between reason and nature in his moral thought. In the latter work, he argues that inasmuch as the immoral temptation to ground action in inclination finds its source in the natural drive toward "self-love" (cf. 1785: 75/407-408), to act purely from the moral law is none other than to defeat the inclination that is the source of the temptation. This is to defeat the natural inclination toward "self-conceit," toward making self-love the determining principle of the will. This in turn provides a critical clue toward understanding the motive force of the moral law:

> [A]s striking down, i.e. humiliating self-conceit, it is an object of the greatest respect and thus the ground of a feeling that is not of a positive origin. This feeling then is one that can be known a priori. Respect for the moral law . . . is a feeling produced by an intellectual cause, and this feeling is the only one that we can know completely a priori and the necessity of which we can discern. (1788: 74/73)

Unlike pathological inclination, respect is not a prior sensuous (positive) incentive, but is rather the effect of pure practical reason upon our sensuous nature.[11] For Kant, this is critical if moral motivation is to retain its "active" or "spontaneous" character and thus remain distinct from the passive drive to succumb to inclination.

Kant goes on to observe that imperfectly rational beings (i.e., humans who are also sensuous) possess the unique capacity to experience awe at the spectacle of the moral law's humiliation of nature's conceited drive to arrogate the role of moral legislator. This awe or respect emerges from recognizing within ourselves both our inscrutable ability to rise above the world of sense and "at the same time the unsuitability of our conduct to it, thus striking down self-conceit" (1788: 90/87). Although respect is a "natural" state, it arises from an experience of the "supersensuous" capacity of the moral will to strike down that nature. The sensuous being cannot resist a certain awe before the sublimity of the moral will.[12]

The duality in Kant between the spontaneity of reason and the passivity of nature ultimately thwarts any attempt to harmonize the two. Hence, even in his discussion of the feeling of respect, Kant characterizes that emotion as one that arises (one must say ironically) as a consequence of our awe at the dominance of reason over feeling. In his influential *On the Aesthetic Education of Man* (1967), Schiller argued against the one-sidedness of such an approach, claiming that it could occasion a division in the will no less dangerous than that of licentiousness:

> [M]an can be at odds with himself in two ways: either as savage when feeling predominates over principle, or as barbarian, when principle destroys feeling. (21)

If the will is divided against itself when natural drives are allowed to overwhelm reason, it is no less disastrously torn asunder when moral principle tramples the sensuous side of the human being.

That Schiller's work had a strong influence on the young Hegel is evidenced in his hailing *On the Aesthetic Education of Man* a "masterpiece" in a letter to Schelling in 1795, as well as by his discussions of many of the same issues in his early writings.[13] In addition to the *Difference* essay, Hegel's concern for overcoming the Kantian dualism between reason and emotion runs throughout his early theological writings. In the 1795 essay "The Spirit of Christianity" (1907), Hegel criticized Kantian morality with its ethics of duty for failing to overcome the opposition of morality and inclination and producing instead a "unity of strangers" (268).[14] In his remarkable contrast between the unity of an ethics of love with the conflicted state of mere obedience to commands, Hegel strikes at the heart of Kant's moral psychology:

> Of course, "love cannot be commanded"; of course it is "pathological, an inclination"; but it detracts nothing from its greatness, it does not degrade it, that its essence is not a dominion of something alien to it. But this does not mean that it is something subordinate to duty and right; on the contrary it is rather love's triumph over these that lords it over nothing, is without any hostile power over another. "Love has conquered" does not mean the same thing as "duty has conquered," i.e., subdued its enemies; it means that love has overcome hostility. (295-296)

Although these writings and their theological preoccupations predate the completion of Hegel's system in the *Phenomenology* and the *Logic*, their ethical concern for bringing together the rational and the sensuous sides of human life foreshadows the project of the *Philosophy of Right*, and they present that concern in a prose far less dense than the later more "systematic" writings.

In the essay on *Natural Law* (1802-1803), Hegel developed a more embracing social and political critique of the dualism between reason and sensuous nature that Kantian ethics recapitulates, linking it to the abstract individualism of the bourgeoisie. Although, as always, Hegel asserts that "there is no question of denying this [moral] standpoint," he argues that its "one-sidedness" renders its perspective a partial one, ill-suited to the "absolute" demands of the moral life (434). The latter calls for the unity of ought and is, a unity that cannot be willed from a rational point of view, but can come into being only when the rule of reason (the concept) emerges in the shape of living sensuous desire.[15] Hegel repeats the charge first levelled in "The Spirit of Christianity" in *The Philosophy of Right,* that the moral point of view (now contrasted with the "ethical life" *[Sittlichkeit])* fails to move beyond the *relation (Verhältnis)* of the actual sensuous will and the moral will in the "ought" judgment (1821: 135R). As discussed in chapter 3, though the abstract commandments of the moral point of view may constitute a "starting point for the discovery of truth," merely to know what is right in the form of an ought judgment fails to make that content "come home to our minds" (Hegel 1821: 57R). For Hegel, the call of reason can find its proper reply only in the responsiveness of desire.

Where such a response is lacking, Hegel argues that duplicity rather than morality will result. At the end of chapter 6 of the *Phenomenology of Spirit,* Hegel describes the self-conscious state of an agent who, caught up in the impossibility of acting with a pure will, does not act but *judges* the action of others. Hegel's observations on the perverse psychology of one who would will purely from duty are keen. If I am compelled to "despise" selfish motives in myself, I am likely to project my self-hatred onto the other. Moreover, the judging agent is entirely hypocritical in this, setting herself above the desires that feed her disregard for the other (1807: 666). Where the unity between my actual desires and my moral ideals is "abstract," i.e., a unity that merely *ought* to exist, I am pushed toward a duplicity that damages my social relations as well.

For Hegel as for Plato, the harmony of the individual must be realized socially. The true unification of reason and desire (as opposed to their mere coordination) takes place in and through the functioning of a living community. In *Natural Law* (1802-1803), Hegel affirms that ethical development is a communal rather than a strictly individual transformation:

> As regards the ethical life, the saying of the wisest men of antiquity is alone true, that "to be ethical is to live in accordance with the ethics of one's country." And as regards education, the reply of a Pythagorean to the question: "What is the best education for my son?" is "Make him a citizen of a well-ordered state." (470, cf. 1821: 153)

Hence political problems—issues surrounding the development of the well-ordered state—take center stage in Hegel's discussion of the ethical life. This does not mean that Hegel has replaced concern for the person with that of the state, but rather that the achievement of a will in which desire is the vehicle of true universality can be accomplished only in the broader context of a system of needs.[16]

Having outlined some of the central concerns of Hegel's approach to the problems of ethical motivation, it is possible better to address Blum's contention that Hegel was a moral rationalist. Blum's charges included: (1) that Hegel's call for universality emphasized strength of will, self-control, acting from universal principles, and adherence to duty; (2) that Hegel de-emphasized or ignored virtues such as sympathy, compassion, kindness, caring, concern, and emotional responsiveness; (3) that Hegel's conception of progress called for an increase in autonomy, rationality, and individuality; (4) that Hegel anticipated and would likely have approved of the modern bureaucratic state with its compartmentalization of life and its relegation of feeling to the private sphere.

As for the first charge, it would seem that Hegel's concern for bringing reason and nature into harmony was motivated precisely by a dissatisfaction with the Kantian emphasis on strength of will, self-*control*, and adherence to duty for duty's sake. The ethical content of Hegel's early essays, his descriptions of the duplicitous consciousness that would pursue duty for duty's sake in the *Phenomenology,* and his criticisms of the deficiencies of the moral point of view in the *Philosophy of Right* together constitute a thoroughgoing critique of a morality of willed adherence to duty. On Hegel's account, such an adherence assumed and exacerbated a truly pathological condition in which the will was divided against itself. While Hegel did maintain the importance of universality, he advocated its realization through the functioning of a well-ordered community rather than by means of willed principles.[17]

Blum's charge that Hegel ignored the "caring" virtues—sympathy, compassion, kindness, concern, and emotional responsiveness—has some merit. In fact, Hegel did consign these primarily to the "family" (i.e., to the degraded sphere of women), and one finds little suggestion of them in Hegel's world historical figures, the men whose desires supposedly embodied Spirit in the world. Here too, however, it is important to see that Hegel did not deprive these virtues of all moral worth, as Kant did. As he wrote in the passage on love from "The Spirit of Christianity," caring emotions are not diminished because they are not willed as duty. Moreover, despite the diminished part they play in Hegel's political writings, the central concern of Hegel's politics—providing a means for the sensuous mediation of universality into the community—makes his account open to the inclusion of all forms of emotional response in a way that Kant's is not.

Blum's third claim, that Hegel identifies moral progress with increases in autonomy, rationality, and universality, cannot be denied. Still, Hegel's understanding of the nature of those concepts is markedly different from that of Kant. As discussed above (and in chapter 2), an increase in universality is measured not in terms of increasing adherence to abstract rules and procedures, but in terms of a community that provides for the adequate expression of the interests and desires of its members (1821: 122–125, 130). Likewise, the "autonomy" of the members of such a community is measured not in terms of a capacity to judge or act on the basis of abstract principle, but upon their contingent capacity to come to self-actualization within that society (cf. 1821: 153–157). Thus, while reason and universality remain regulative in Hegel's ethical and political thought (a point to which I shall return below), these concerns cannot be separated from the concrete self-development of the members of a political order.

Blum's final charge, that Hegel would have endorsed the compartmentalization and privatization of feelings that typify modern bureaucracies likewise represents an oversimplification of his view. As noted with respect to similar criticisms raised by Benhabib (1986) in chapter 3 above, although in the *Philosophy of Right* Hegel sometimes seems to suggest that the apparatus of the functioning state could indeed be willed by a bureaucratic regime, this goes against the fundamental principles upon which Hegel's state was founded. Its purpose, once again, is not merely to coordinate the desires of the various classes from above, but genuinely to embody their interests within a functioning whole.[18] The alienation that is the hallmark of the interaction between individuals and an impersonal bureaucracy is far removed from the ends of Hegel's state. Having said that, Blum is certainly correct that much "feeling" is privatized within the family on Hegel's account, another point to which I shall return in the next section. It should be noted, however, that in securing a place for love within the context of a political tract such as the *Philosophy of Right* (albeit a limited and sexist account), Hegel cannot be accused of having ignored its place in the state altogether.

If I am right, Hegel's ethics and politics, whatever their deficiencies otherwise, cannot simply be construed as "moral rationalism." Although Hegel does consider his to be an ethics of "reason," Hegelian reason *(Vernunft)* represents the surpassing of a dichotomy between sensuous nature and the understanding *(Verstand)* that remains operative in Kantian moral philosophy.[19] For Hegel, reason cannot simply impose an "active" rule on a "passive" desire, because reason is itself the expression of a concept the full meaning of which only takes shape through the sensuous content that it mediates. Moreover, as discussed in chapters 3 and 4, the fact that interests and desires actively inform the concept in no way detracts from its universality. On the contrary, it is precisely by means of this sensuous content—often unruly and rebellious as well—that access to genuine universality is made possible. Hegel's account thus meets two critical conditions for an adequate theory of the emotions laid down by Jaggar: that emotions must be intrinsically active and intentional and not merely under the external tutelage of a "cognitive" component, and that they possess the perceptual aptitude that permits them to be the vehicles of freedom and liberation.

Toward an Integrated Approach

Although a Hegelian account of the emotions need not fall into the sort of rationalism of which writers such as Blum have been critical, the very fact that Hegel's synthesis culminates in "reason" makes it an odd-sounding theory for meeting the needs of an approach to ethics that has sought to retrieve the moral value of concepts such as care, sympathy, and emotional response. In this final section, I hope to show that the integration of universality and abstract right in Hegel's account is not a deficiency, but is of importance in the development of a complete account of feminist moral psychology. In making this argument, it is useful to begin by contrasting Hegel's theory with that of another recently "rehabilitated" non-feminist canonical figure, David Hume.

In her resourceful and influential work on the ethics of Hume, Annette Baier (1987, 1994) has established a kind of model for the "retrieval" of non-feminist philosophers of the past. In making the case that Hume has something to offer feminist ethics, Baier observes that Hume "plays up the role of feeling in moral judgment" while de-emphasizing reason and its attendant concern for autonomy (1987: 41). Hume famously argued that reason was itself incapable of providing any ends or motives for the ethical life, and assigned this task to "the passions." In stark contrast with Kant's account, Baier notes that Hume's is "historicist" and "conventionalist," and not concerned at all with issues of universality and autonomy. For Hume, the characteristic problems of the moral life concern the development of sympathetic emotions and responses to others. Baier observes:

> Morality, on Hume's account, is the outcome of a search for ways of eliminating contradictions in the "passions" of sympathetic persons who are aware of their own and their fellows' desires and needs, including emotional needs. (41)

Though Hume does not include reason in his account of morality, he does have a place for the "correction" and "progress" of the sentiments that is independent of rationality (47).

To oversimplify a bit, we might say that while Hume's endorsement of emotion over reason reverses the downplaying of the former in traditional normative theory, Hegel's synthesis of intellect and feeling represents an attempt to get beyond the duality altogether.[20] The very fact that Hume can speak of reason as a slave of passion, and variously "play up" the side of feeling, shows that the separation of feeling and intellect remains operative in Hume's theory in a way that it does not in Hegel's. While this may enable a Humean account to attend to issues of emotional responsiveness and sympathy in a way that Hegel's cannot (a point to which I shall return below), it restricts the Humean approach in other ways that are of importance to feminist social criticism.

In the first place, as discussed the previous chapters, while politically conservative background assumptions in the understanding and application of such concepts as freedom, rights, and autonomy can shroud oppressive social relations, those concepts can also undergo a radical reconceptualization when employed in ways that challenge or undermine those assumptions. Once again, to use Hegel's expression, universalist appeals to the categories of *Moralität* can serve as the starting point for a more integrated development of the ethical life. Such a formal starting point with its appeal to freedom and rights is of particular importance to a critique of traditional values, since social conventions and the feelings to which they give rise are likely to be among the biggest stumbling blocks to social change. This limits the effectiveness of a Humean approach with its unabashedly conventionalist account of moral value (40).

Although Hegel does not think it possible for a modern theory of the right simply to abandon the categories of traditional liberal ethical and political thought, his philosophy of history emphasizes the manner in which liberating emotions give life and meaning to those categories. The great moments of ancient history were not forged with duty in mind, and the abstract categories of right remain underdetermined apart from the emotions that animate them. Because the idea of right is inseparable from "the concept of right and its actualization," justice is vulnerable to the passions and needs that move its practitioners (1821: 1).[21] While the latter cannot articulate themselves into warranted claims apart from universal concepts, as discussed in chapter 2 the concepts themselves may undergo a transformation as previously unarticulated desire takes shape through them. The passions without justice are blind and justice without the passions is empty.

By integrating abstract right and emotion, Hegel avoids the pitfalls associated with a simple endorsement of conventional emotional orientations. This is important, for if de-emphasizing traditionally "feminine" emotions such as sympathy or care expresses the social devaluation of women, simply reversing our estimation of those emotions might have deleterious effects on women as well.[22] First of all, as discussed in chapter 4, the history of feminist thought has been one of defying traditional emotional bonds as well as one of care and sympathy. Consciousness raising and the various projects to which it has given rise (women's health collectives, rape awareness campaigns, the battered women's movement, etc.) has involved bonds of political solidarity rooted in a collective commitment to rights and equality, even as it has reconceptualized those concepts.[23] The feminist reconceptualization of liberal rights has sent women into legislatures and courtrooms not merely seeking redress for harms done, but in the process doing the important political work of further "universalizing" our conventional (i.e., masculine-centered) legal categories.

Moreover, as many feminists have pointed out, a simple endorsement of care as opposed to justice, as suggested by Gilligan (1983),[24] or the "unidirectional" care of Nel Noddings (1984), has problems of its own.[25] Women's identification with care has come primarily from their having provided it to men and children, often at great expense to themselves. The primary location of care for women has been in the traditional, male-dominated household, where they have performed the economically unrecompensed labor that Sandra Lee Bartky (1990) aptly terms "feeding egos and tending wounds" (99-119).[26] The fact that such work is unpaid occasions further difficulties for women. As Susan Moller Okin (1989) has argued, because women are paid less in the workforce, and because they are the ones (in part because of their social mission to "care" for others) most often left with children, it is extremely costly for women to exit the marital relationship. This puts women in a position of asymmetrical vulnerability vis-à-vis their male partners, and may compel them to stay in a relationship at great personal cost to themselves.[27] This vulnerability is worsened, of course, in the case of abusive husbands. Moreover, as a number of writers have emphasized, women's caring (i.e., *other*-oriented caring) orientation can both make it difficult for them to leave their abuser and exacerbate the problem of blaming themselves for their victimization.[28]

In light of these considerations, Marilyn Friedman (1993) observes that "Caring remains a risky business for women" (156) and recommends an "integrated" approach that brings together elements of a caring and a justice perspective (142-143). What I hope to have shown here and in previous chapters is that Hegel's critique and redevelopment of a Kantian justice perspective may serve as a model for coming to a precise understanding of how such an integration might work. In that sense Hegel may be useful in providing at least part of "what women want in a moral theory" (cf. Baier 1994).

It must be added, however, that Hegel's stated political theory also suffers from a failure to integrate the emotional dispositions traditionally associated with women into an account of the history and development of the social and political world. Critics such as Blum (1982) are quite right in noting this. As I shall discuss in greater detail in chapter 7, while Hegel did stress the importance of the love of wife and family in the life of the *male* individual (cf. 1821: 158A), he took for granted the emotional orientation of a woman whose "vocation *(Bestimmung)* consists essentially only in the marital relationship" (164A). As noted in chapter 3, in striking contrast to his concern for the men of impoverished classes, Hegel's description of the "ethical life" consigned women to a world of patriarchal authority and enforced servitude.[29]

The exclusion of feminine emotions from Hegel's politics may correctly be thought either more or less important than similar exclusions in more traditional theories. Its importance depends upon what one is looking for in Hegel's theory. On the one hand, precisely because Hegel argues that the content of formal principles takes shape through their sensuous vehicles, his exclusion of feminine emotions from political theory is more important than it might be in a more "formal" system such as that of Kant. As stressed in chapters 2 and 3 above, the *Philosophy of Right* does not consist of a set of abstract principles that one might simply "apply more broadly," but seeks to describe the unfolding of the concept of right in the "objective reality" of a living social order. To alter the application of the principles is to change the social order and thus to alter the content of the principles. Precisely because Hegel takes history seriously, the implications of Hegel's anti-feminism for his project of providing a practical political agenda are extremely serious. On the other hand, if one looks to Hegel for a theory of the relationship between reason, intellect, and emotion, then Hegel's omission, however deleterious it may be for the practical political goals of the *Philosophy of Right,* is of less concern. In fact, to the extent that Hegel's theoretical account is true, it provides a means for understanding why Hegel's own description of the proper relation of state, civil society, and family holds so little appeal to anyone who is aware of "feminist reality."[30]

Conclusion

At first glance, it seems difficult if not incoherent to reconcile Hegel's concern for the reign of "reason" with the spirit of feminist ethics. Once it is understood, however, that Hegelian reason is meant precisely to overcome the Kantian dualism of active reason and passive nature, it need not be taken to betray a covert rationalism. If my arguments here have been convincing, then I have shown that Hegel provides a coherent account of how the concerns of equality and justice need not be at odds with fully valuing the emotions. While Hegel's specific account of the place of reason in history falls short (and more likely falls victim) to feminist critiques of moral rationalism, his theory provides a number of important desiderata of a feminist ethics: (1) it provides a positive accounting of sensuous forces in ethical action; (2) it preserves a place for the justice and rights without which the feminist critique might lose its normative force; (3) it provides a rationale for taking the point of view of historically oppressed groups more seriously than that of the oppressors.

In the following chapters, I broaden my discussion of Hegel and feminism beyond the critique of Kantian moral theory that has guided the discussion of the last three. In the next chapter, I reassess certain aspects of Simone de Beauvoir's early and extraordinarily influential use of Hegel in *The Second Sex*. In chapter 8 I use some of the conclusions from my discussion of de Beauvoir to provide a Hegelian reading of recent debates in feminist theory on equality and difference.

PART THREE

AGENCY, VICTIMIZATION, AND DIFFERENCE

CHAPTER 7

SLAVES WITHOUT FEAR
Hegel and the Feminism of Simone de Beauvoir

> *Woman herself recognizes that the world is masculine on the whole; those who fashioned it, ruled it, and still dominate it today are men. As for her, she does not consider herself responsible for it; it is understood that she is inferior and dependent; she has not learned the lessons of violence, she has never stood forth as a subject. . . .*
>
> —Simone de Beauvoir
> *The Second Sex*

No account of the relationship between feminism and Hegel would be complete without a discussion of Simone de Beauvoir and the complex interweaving of Hegelian and existentialist themes in *The Second Sex* (1980). In fact, her extraordinarily detailed description of women's position as the "absolute Other" relies upon a number of important Hegelian assumptions.[1] While these derive most notably from the parable of master and slave in the *Phenomenology of Spirit* (1807), they are not limited to this.[2] In fact, as I shall argue below, in certain important respects, de Beauvoir's account of women's situation is quite in accord with the letter of the accounts offered by Hegel in the *Phenomenology* and the *Philosophy of Right*. In striking contrast with Hegel, of course, de Beauvoir could not accept this account as doing justice to the agency of women.

It should also be observed, however, that, despite the events that were to unfold in the years following the book's publication, de Beauvoir's discussion in *The Second Sex* neither envisioned nor endorsed a collective movement of women as a corrective to the condition she described. This distinguishes the approach to what came to be labelled as "sexism" in *The Second Sex* from that of later activists and theorists of the feminist movement, many of whom were profoundly influenced by it.[3] Although de Beauvoir clearly took "human transformation" as her overall political aim, in 1949 she thought that the transformation of women's agency could come about only in the wake of a socialist revolution.[4] In this respect, as in others that I shall note below, de Beauvoir's work remained at the edge of the feminist movement that was soon to follow its publication. Still, by attempting *both* to assert that feminine agency is absolutely subordinated in the institutions and practices of culture *and* to argue as a woman for changing those institutions and practices, de Beauvoir anticipated what has become a paradigmatic conflict of contemporary feminist theory.[5]

In this chapter, I shall argue that despite her many references to Hegel's parable of master and slave in the *Phenomenology of Spirit,* de Beauvoir does not employ Hegel's conceptual apparatus as far as she might have in addressing the condition of women. In particular, I shall argue that had she fully applied the dynamic of recognition, fear, and creative labor to women's situation, her account of the possibility of a positive appreciation of women's activities and values might not have been as pessimistic as it was. I shall also address briefly some of the reasons why de Beauvoir may have failed fully to grasp the significance of Hegel's account here.

In the next section, I compare and contrast Hegel's description of woman's place in the ethical life of the family with de Beauvoir's account of feminine alterity in that same role. After that, I consider Hegel's account of Lordship and Bondage and its relevance for de Beauvoir's analysis of alterity. I conclude by arguing that Hegel's description of the relationship of master and slave has implications for women's condition that may go beyond de Beauvoir's rather limited use of it. If I am right, some of the central contentions in Hegel's account have relevance not only for an analysis of the sources of women's subordination, but also for the recovery of women's difference, a subject that I discuss in more detail in chapter 8.

Hegel's "Ethical Life"

The genius of de Beauvoir's critique lies with her ability to develop a thoroughgoing criticism of women's condition in the form of a detailed and penetrating description of the characteristics, roles, activities, and myths by which women come to self-consciousness in the institutions and practices of Western culture. In this she articulates the antithesis of Hegel's descriptions of the family in which that institution functions so as to mediate the proper ethical life of all its members. In order to come to a better understanding of the political significance of this fundamental disagreement, it is most useful to return to Hegel's descriptions of the function of the family in the *Phenomenology of Spirit* and the *Philosophy of Right.*[6] For although de Beauvoir obviously did not endorse Hegel's account of women's "vocation" in the life of the family, she nevertheless draws upon certain important features of Hegel's descriptions, and even cites them in cataloguing some of the most important and frustrating limitations on women's agency.[7] By recontextualizing Hegel's remarks in her own discussion of women's oppression, de Beauvoir disputes their status as depicting the institutions of an authentic "ethical world," and reveals them to be a shocking violation of the agency of women. In this sense, parts of the *Second Sex* may be understood to perform a kind of immanent critique of Hegel's ethical family and its account of gender.[8]

In his discussion of the life of the modern community, Hegel singles out the family as a unique ethical (*sittlich*) community, and, in so doing, distinguishes the principles governing its order from those of either nature or the state (cf. 1807: 446–463, 475; 1821: 158–181). Although the structure of relationships within the family is "immediate" and thus lacking the conscious and explicit legal structure of the state, like that larger community, Hegel rejects the Romantics' view of the relationships of the family as merely "natural."[9] For Hegel, the justification of the family does not rest primarily with the expression of the "love" or "feeling" of family members toward one another, but with the unique and irreplaceable function that the family and those feelings to which it lends expression perform in the modern social order (1807: 451).[10]

As the last stronghold of the Divine Law *(göttliche Gesetz)*, it is the ethical role of the family to exert control over death as it enters the life of the male citizen:[11]

> The family keeps away from the dead this dishonouring of him by unconscious appetites and abstract entities, and puts its own actions in their place, and weds the blood-relation to the bosom of the earth. . . . The family thereby makes him a member of the community which prevails over . . . lower forms of life, which sought to unloose themselves against him and to destroy him. (452)

Although it is only through the mediation of the particular institutions and practices of civil society and the state (labor, sports, military service, etc.) that the male receives the recognition necessary for achieving self-conscious individuality, this achievement itself involves pitting the man against the power of death. Moreover, whatever the triumphs of youth, that power is destined to overtake him in the end. The state that requires the life of the man for its ends (in war, for example) may confer posthumous honors on those who willingly undertake such a risk (455). Still, from the point of view of the state, the *particular* individual is always expendable, and the loss of *his* life inconsequential.

It is as a member of the communal life of a family that nature's power over the individual in death is challenged, and thereby that the citizen achieves a full sense of his self-worth. The dignity that the male receives in the family is of a fundamentally different order from that which the state or civil society accords him, since as a son, a father, or a husband, he is not expendable, but individually essential in that relational role. In the context of this set of relationships, his individual death assumes its rightful importance, and he finds himself recognized accordingly. Without a medium for such recognition, the significance of an individual man's death would lack embodiment in any social institution, and would remain, in a critical sense, "irrational."[12] Thus, Hegel argues that the completion of the self-conscious sense of individuality that marks the citizen, requires that his specific individuality receive its due in the family that he legitimately heads.[13]

In carrying out its ethical function of developing citizenship, the family gives rise to distinct roles for the genders: "The two sexes overcome their [merely] natural being and appear in their ethical significance" (1807: 459).[14] From the ethical household, the husband goes forth into the world of public affairs as its representative, leaving the wife to serve the needs of the (his) household. The feminine life revolves entirely around the private relationships of the family and the duties that these relationships entail. Not a part of the "transcendent" activities of civil society and the state (i.e., those activities in which the man proves himself over against other men), the woman never achieves recognition as an individual, and so "remains alien to the particularity of desire" (457). Possessed of an *intuitive* awareness of her role as guardian of the divine law of the family, the woman resigns herself to that role and leads a life uninterrupted by the drive to achieve recognition for her agency over against others in the wider community.[15] To the extent that that particular desire enters into the wife's relations with the husband, those relations lose their "ethical" character:

> In the ethical household, it is not a question of *this* particular husband, *this* particular child, but simply of husband and children generally; the relationships of the woman are based . . . on the universal. (457).[16]

Absent such particular desire, the woman remains "without the moment of knowing herself as *this* particular self in the other partner." This moment belongs to the husband, who, by contrast, "is sent out by the Spirit of the Family in the community in which he finds his self-conscious being" (457).

There can be little question with regard to the conservative and even outright reactionary strains of Hegel's account of gender. Hegel is ambiguous, however, on the extent and the nature of the distinctions that he draws between women's and men's roles. While on the one hand the "Addition" to paragraph 164 of the *Philosophy of Right* states clearly that women are "destined in essence for the marriage tie and that only," as noted above Hegel also states explicitly in the *Phenomenology* that he is offering a functional as opposed to a biological explanation of the development and sustenance of masculine and feminine gender roles (cf. 1807: 459). In fact, it makes more sense on Hegel's account to see the distinctive psychological dispositions of the sexes as the consequence of the division of activities that he endorses. Enmeshed in the private traditions of the family, the wife defends her husband from meaningless death in the world only by cutting herself off from the sphere of self-conscious activity in which she might achieve public recognition as an individual. Never engaged in competitive or "life-threatening" activity, the consciousness of the woman remains *merely* communal or "universal" — never particularized in the risk-laden challenges of the state or civil society. Hegel consistently understands that such an arrangement must leave women not merely with a diminished range of opportunities as compared to men, but with a deficiency in *desire* itself. Because women's action is restricted to the sustenance of relationships in the community, the desires and intentions that are the precipitates of this activity likewise reflect a deficiency in *self*-interest. To the extent that women do not participate in the institutions and practices of masculine society, they never attain to the "particularity" which Hegel understands as necessary for participation in the State.

The structure of Hegel's gloss on *Antigone* (discussed at length in chapter 1 above) offers further evidence that Hegel's "ideal" role of women *(Weiblichkeit)*[17] requires the proper functioning of a particular social order. In the latter account, Hegel famously introduces a scenario where the social order breaks down and results (among other things) in a disruption of gender roles. This is manifest in Antigone's failure to remain immersed in the world of the family, and her coming forth to challenge the law of Thebes. Of course, this seemingly radical transgression remained grounded in a traditional assignment of gender roles, in that its motivation was the state's violent encroachment on the religious rights of the family. In one sense, Antigone was merely acting in accordance with her feminine role as the defender of religion and the family in exposing the clash between the duty of the family to bury its dead with honor and that of the state to avenge its attackers.[18] Nevertheless, the very possibility of states of affairs that could occasion such a disruptive emergence of agency has important implications for Hegel's generally negative accounts both of women in particular and political movements more generally. Women's "essence," in Hegel's view, must be one that comes to realization only in a particular social order, and is thus socially and historically contingent. Unlike more conventional "essentialists," it is central to Hegel's chronology in the *Phenomenology* that historical changes in social conditions can in fact disturb the nature of the gender roles that he describes.

Despite this contingency, and despite the fact that women's agency plays an instrumental role in Spirit's emergence toward self-consciousness, however, the quiescent and unreflective nature of the feminine remains in the Hegelian state as it is described in Part III of the *Philosophy of Right*. For Hegel, the emergence of women's particular agency plays only a transitional role in history, doing the "necessary" work of destroying the old order, yet returning to an unmediated "universality" at the end of history. Notably, this kind of sinking back into the universal differs from the "cyclic" return to earlier stages that characterizes Hegel's system. A kind of return to origins is, in fact, central to the logic of the *Phenomenology*, since Hegel takes the return of the categories back to their origin as a proof that his enumeration of them is complete. As he observes near the end of chapter 8:

> For the self-knowing Spirit, just because it grasps its Concept, is the immediate identity with itself which, in its difference, is the *certainty of immediacy*, or *sense-consciousness*—the beginning from which we started. (1807: 806)

Unlike the earliest stages from which it began its epistemological journey, however, the shape of consciousness that emerges at the end of history has the self-conscious capacity to comprehend its movement and so to achieve a level of awareness that was lacking at the initial stage of "sense-certainty." There is no indication, however, that women partake in such a conceptual return to beginnings. On the contrary, Hegel asserts that women lack the conceptual capacity for genuine self-knowledge at all (cf. 1821: 166A). For the author of the *Phenomenology of Spirit* and the *Philosophy of Right* women remain an *irony*—instrumental in bringing about and sustaining the ethical life of the state, but failing to develop intrinsically as a result of that role (Hegel 1807: 475).[19]

In denying that the assertion of women's agency has any positive significance in itself, and in endorsing a socio-political order that effectively contains (rather than positively develops) that agency, Hegel puts women in a position with respect to the state that bears an important resemblance to that of the penurious "rabble" in Hegel's discussions on poverty. For Hegel, the political indignation of a materially impoverished class, while inevitable in the modern state, lacked any positive significance, and represented only a destructive threat to rational social order.[20] And although Hegel's rejection of collective consciousness as a progressive force in world history is well known,[21] it is interesting that his account of gender has never been taken to represent a variation on this same rejection. From a feminist point of view, however, a striking symmetry exists between the socially pernicious agency that Hegel attributes to the "rabble" and the ubiquitous menace to social order that he perceives in feminine agency. Moreover, this symmetry is manifest in the parallel solutions that he proposes for both threats. In the case of the rabble, the potentially disruptive claims of the poor can be kept in check only by the proper management of the estates by the bourgeois state. For women on the other hand, the collective development of feminine desire is managed through the effective functioning of the institutions of marriage and the patriarchal family. In each case, a functioning social institution serves to set the conditions in which some kinds of desire emerge and others are kept at bay. In both the state and the family, Hegel must assume the existence of a class of "managers" (the landed aristocracy and men, respectively) whose privileged access to the interests of the other classes places it in a position effectively to control their potentially disruptive claims.[22]

If Marxism and related popular movements can be understood to have turned Hegel's account of the estates against itself, de Beauvoir's descriptions in *The Second Sex* may be understood to have performed a similar task with regard to his account of women. Moreover, she did so more or less in spite of herself, since, despite the part that her writings played in the development of the feminist vision of the Second Wave, de Beauvoir held out no positive role for women's collective agency in them. In a manner not unlike her Left-Hegelian predecessors, however, de Beauvoir employed Hegel's parable of master and slave in focusing attention on the relation of domination and subordination implicit in women's restriction to the sphere of the patriarchal family in the modern state. Reexamining the division of activities entailed by that restriction as a reflective member of the class[23] of women, de Beauvoir was able to accept the accuracy of many of Hegel's descriptions, but was unable to accept them as ethically justified. De Beauvoir's revolutionary descriptions of women's situation deviate remarkably little from the substance of Hegel's reactionary account except that she, unlike he, explores them from the point of view of a free person who is consigned to them.

In the first place, de Beauvoir grants the accuracy of Hegel's description of a cultural order in which masculinity is marked by "transcendence" of nature while "the female remains wrapped up in the species" (23).[24] Likewise, she understands this state of women's consciousness to be a product of the activities in which her agency develops. Much of *The Second Sex* is devoted to detailed descriptions of precisely how the passivity that marks women's traditional role takes shape in the actions that women perform (or refrain from performing) in identifying with that role. For de Beauvoir, however, this passivity is no virtue, but functions to frustrate the development of women's agency. In the first place, she takes the biological constraints associated with childbirth to have initially played a critical role in chaining women to "Life" and thus closing them off from the prestige that becomes available to men with the risk of life. She contends that had women been able to engage in acts of transcendence—in the hunt, in warfare, and in the public activities of risk upon which recognition is conferred—then "woman would have accomplished *with* man the conquest of nature" (77).[25] Although de Beauvoir's discussion of women's tie to nature and "Life" largely follows Hegel's description, in criticizing the consequences of such an identification for women, she clearly rejects Hegel's endorsement of it.[26]

De Beauvoir's evaluation of women's condition further distinguishes itself from that of Hegel by redescribing what was for him merely the proper functioning of state, family, and civil society as a set of positive and debilitating *exclusions* for women. Women are actively kept from those activities where they might test their abilities against others. De Beauvoir argued that the social cultivation of a "passive nature" could be achieved only by means of considerable social restraint:

> [T]he passivity that is the essential characteristic of the "feminine" woman is a trait that develops in her from the earliest years . . . . The great advantage enjoyed by the boy is that his mode of existence in relation to others consists in a free movement toward the outside world . . . . Climbing trees, fighting with his companions, facing them in rough games, he feels his body as a means for dominating nature and as a weapon for fighting. . . . In woman, on the contrary, there is from the beginning a conflict between her autonomous existence and her objective self, her "being-the-other." (280)

For de Beauvoir, women's character is neither essential nor the outcome of a benightedly benign social order, but is learned and enforced by keeping girls and women out of certain activities, while compelling them to take up those that conform to their domestic roles.[27]

As regards the latter, de Beauvoir argues that the everyday acts that women perform have served further to reinforce their alterity. These include both the activities associated with the rearing of children and those in which the woman engages in fulfilling her household duties. Although a woman gives birth to her child, "she does not really make the baby, it makes itself within her" (496). Unlike a creative act in which an agent fashions an object according to her will, a woman's procreative function, though it may have been undertaken willingly, gives birth to a child "as a product of her generalized body, not of her individualized existence" (p. 496). Likewise, de Beauvoir attends to the concrete details of labor in the "ethical" household, and weaves them into a narrative of frustrated creativity. On the one hand, these tasks are largely "negative"—confining women to the drudgery of an "endless struggle without victory over the dirt" (451). No matter the woman's successes, her achievement is short-lived and destined to be repeated.[28] Moreover, the execution of these tasks offers little space for originality, inasmuch as they are but monotonous "technical operations" (598). Even in those societies where women do play a role outside the household, their activities are largely restricted to subsistence agriculture. While men go about the conquest of nature, woman is left with responsibility for the earth where "nothing can hasten the ripening of grain" (75).

In short, de Beauvoir did not so much dispute the content of Hegel's descriptions of gender roles, as she undermined the (masculine) point of view that Hegel assumed in reaching his positive normative evaluation with respect to them. From the point of view of a woman such as de Beauvoir, both the degrading nature of the feminine activities and their arbitrary imposition on women pose a challenge to the "objective" status that Hegel would confer on them.[29] Of course, de Beauvoir's use of Hegel did not end with her reinterpretation of the ethical life. At least equally important was her unique re-deployment of the narrative of master and slave in developing that reinterpretation, and it is to this that I now turn.

Slaves without Battle

The passage entitled "Lordship and Bondage" in chapter 4 of the *Phenomenology of Spirit* has long served as a framework for theorists seeking insight into the dynamics of power between individuals and groups. In the historical chronology of the *Phenomenology,* the passage actually recounts a very early and pivotal stage in the development of self-consciousness where Spirit moves through a series of dramatic steps from self-less immersion in the world, to a primitive shape of consciousness arising out of domination and submission, to the more enduring self-satisfaction of creative labor. Weaving his story around the basic components of desire, recognition, fear, and work, Hegel attempts rationally to reconstruct how these found embodiment in the relationship between master and slave, and how they at the same time ensured the demise of that institution.[30] Moreover, Hegel's story suggests a generalizable model for understanding both the psychological conditions underlying relations of subordination and the internal mechanisms that render them unstable. In coming to a better understanding of de Beauvoir's peculiar application of this model, it is useful to outline certain parts of its own basic structure.

As is well known, "Lordship and Bondage" concerns the development of a moment in which two consciousnesses "*recognize* themselves as *mutually recognizing* one another" (1807: 184). At this primitive stage of Hegel's chronology, mutual recognition is the occasion of mutual hostility. Lacking the cultural institutions and practices necessary for the embodiment of "self-certainty," each consciousness finds its identity thrown into disarray by the presence of the other. Lacking specific social roles by which their identities could be mediated and remain intact, they engage in a futile struggle to maintain their identities by "negating" each other's disturbing existence:

> They must engage in this struggle, for they must raise their certainty of being *for themselves* to truth . . . . And it is only through staking one's life that freedom is won; only thus is it proved for self-consciousness, its essential being is not [just] being, not the *immediate* form in which it appears, not its submergence in the expanse of life . . . . The individual who has not risked his life may well be recognized as a *person*, but he has not attained to the truth of this recognition as an independent self-consciousness. (187)

It is by virtue of its willingness to risk its life in the presence of the other that consciousness publicly confirms (i.e., proves for itself and for the other) its transcendence of "life." The combatant who surrenders displays his valuing of life over risk, and becomes the slave of the conqueror.

Hegel's narrative is most important, however, for its ironic turn of events in which the slave, who is compelled by his servitude to respect the limitations of the objective world and who must alienate his action in the objects of his labor, comes to the superior shape of self-consciousness. Precisely because he is forced to exercise his labor upon a world that is not the object of his own desire—i.e., not there to be consumed at his pleasure—the slave is able to come to an awareness of his creative powers as a laborer:

> Work . . . is desire held in check, fleetingness staved off . . . . The negative relation to the object becomes its [the object's] *form* and something *permanent*. (195)

In his capacity to shape objects through his action, the slave discloses his superiority to those objects. The material objects that have served as the medium for publicly expressing his bondage further reveal themselves as a means for his own self-expression. Moreover, the slave's capacity to express self-awareness by *shaping* rather than by merely *destroying* his object represents a genuine advance over the consciousness of the master who finds himself implicated in a "bad infinity" of conquests and surrenders in maintaining his self-certainty.

Of central importance in de Beauvoir's use of the passage, however, is Hegel's important claim that the activity of labor is not a sufficient condition for effecting the slave's self-awareness. The object into which the slave invests his labor can mediate his self-conscious agency only because the slave, like the master, has known the risk of life—the "absolute fear" of imminent death in battle. To exist in a moment of absolute fear, where consciousness experiences that very existence in jeopardy, is to find all one's ties to the world cast into insignificance and thereby to experience oneself in complete "independence." In Hegel's story, it was precisely this fear that compelled the slave to capitulate to the master, and to cling to the life that he had previously put at risk. Hegel argues that in the absence of this moment, the state of the conscious agent "is not negativity *per se,* and therefore its formative activity cannot give it a consciousness of itself as essential being" (196).

For Hegel, this last point is of no small importance. Although conquest without the "formative activity" of labor lacks the embodiment necessary to transcend the moment of victory, it is equally true that mere activity without the concrete experience of fear for one's life lacks a genuine subject to embody. In the first place, in the act of surrender to the conquering consciousness, the slave played a part in effecting his condition. Because he did in fact choose life over death, he is possessed of the knowledge that his fate is not simply given, but taken up. He is not a slave in the same manner that objects in his world "are what they are" (e.g., the way that oaks are trees) but is a slave by virtue of his own capitulation in the face of death. Of course, the slave's full awareness of this break may remain "immediate"—he is conscious only of his fear and of the servitude into which he is subsequently impressed. Nevertheless, the moment of fear and surrender represents a transformative break from his immersion in the world, the full significance of which can later emerge in the context of his service.[31] As discussed in chapters 1 and 3, for Hegel a mental phenomenon can "exist" in a potential form, awaiting its emergence into full actuality.

It is not only the act of surrender which Hegel took as necessary for the future development of the slave's awareness, however, but also the fear of death in the battle itself:

> If [consciousness] has not experienced absolute fear but only some lesser dread, the negative being has remained for it something external, its substance has not been infected by it through and through . . . determinate being still *in principle* attaches to it. (1807: 196)

This claim is more controversial in that even if it is granted that the fear and risk associated with interpersonal conflict can play an essential part of coming to full self-awareness, it is not obvious that the fear of death is solely efficacious in developing that awareness.[32] For Hegel, however, it is only by severing all its opaque, "unmediated" bonds to the world that consciousness can arrive at the starting point for genuine self-awareness. To have been moved by the fear that one's death is imminent is to come to awareness of the contingency of *all* one's connections to the world. By being emptied of all its former unmediated content, consciousness has the capacity to *re*-gain self-identity in the formative activity of work. Hegel states that while an agent who has never undergone this "self-emptying" may display technical skill and cleverness in her labor, that activity cannot serve as the means to "self-recovery" that marks authentic self-certainty.[33]

The precise content of this moment of fear and risk takes on central importance for de Beauvoir's account of women because, despite the parallel that she claims exists between Hegel's slave and woman, she also contends that unlike the bondage of the slave, women's oppression does not find its original moment in a life and death struggle. As in Hegel's story, two consciousnesses find themselves "united by a reciprocal need" which fails to liberate the subordinated group. The fact that men's needs, "sexual desire and the desire for offspring," cannot be satisfied except through the actions of women, does nothing to improve women's situation (26). On de Beauvoir's account, however, the origin of that situation is not a violent one:

> The advantage of the Master . . . comes from his affirmation of Spirit as against Life through the fact that he risks his own life; but in fact the conquered slave has known this same risk. Whereas woman is basically an existent who gives Life and does not risk *her* life. (64)

Although, like Hegel's slave, the woman finds herself bound to the world of objects—to "Life"—her bondage was not occasioned by surrender in a primordial battle with another consciousness. "She has not learned the lessons of violence, she has never stood forth as a subject" (598).[34]

In the context of Hegel's parable, the absence of an initial struggle makes women's condition actually worse than that of the slave.[35] Whereas the objects upon which the slave labors serve to mediate the relationship between him and the master, women *are* in fact objects of mediation. De Beauvoir cites Lévi-Strauss's observation on marital relations: "The reciprocal bond basic to marriage is not set up between men and women, but between men and men by means of women, who are only the principle occasion for it" (71). Because woman's subordination is not the outcome a conflictual relation *with* a man, but reflects her status as an object for the mediation of a relation *between* men, she is left with no standing to affect her condition at all.[36] De Beauvoir points out that even the debate over women's rights has historically been a quarrel among men and not between men and women (104-105).

It is precisely this dimension of de Beauvoir's account that renders it both an insightful analysis of women's subordination, and seemingly without a positive vision for altering that condition. On the one hand, by linking women's alterity to the broad range of traditionally feminine activities and identities, de Beauvoir offers an explanation for the peculiar intransigence of women's subordination even across divisions of class and culture. At the same time, however, by identifying that subordination with women's place in everything from childhood play, to adult sexuality, to the mythical and symbolic structures of society, she appears to offer women no escape from it, save by abandoning feminine roles and activities and taking up masculine ones.[37] In other words, there is no obvious place for the *transformation* of feminine agency, for the kind of self-disclosure that characterized the slave's service and gave that activity a positive meaning.

I shall return to the specific question of the "recovery" of feminine agency in chapter 8. At this point, however, it is critical to emphasize that de Beauvoir's well-known rejection of authentic feminine values does not follow simply from her descriptions of the drudgery and the demeaning nature of characteristically feminine identities and activities. Rather, it is because these identities and activities have fallen upon women *in the absence of a struggle,* without the moment of violence and fear, that they lack the self-creative possibilities of the slave's service *(Dienst)* in Hegel's account. From this it also follows that had women assumed feminine activities and roles in the face of a risk of life, then the pregnant moment of self-emptying decision would inhabit their activities and roles and hold out the promise of transformation. As Hegel's slave came to an altogether unexpected and ironical moment of self-satisfaction in his labor, we might find women coming to a similarly surprising reconceptualization of the "service" into which they were impressed.

Women's Values and Women's Victimization

Despite the theoretical significance of de Beauvoir's claim that women lack a moment of fear and risk, that assertion also appears to be seriously at odds with some of her own descriptions of women's experience in *The Second Sex.* On the basis of these, it is abundantly clear that de Beauvoir did not miss the fact that women's identities and activities have often taken shape against both real and threatened masculine violence. In her extensive discussion of cultural myths in Part III, for example, de Beauvoir draws attention to the importance of the image of violation in masculine sexuality:

> It is not only a subjective and fleeting pleasure that man seeks in the sexual act. He wishes to conquer, to take, to possess; to have woman is to conquer

her; he penetrates into her as the plowshare into the furrow; he makes her
his even as he makes the land he works. . . . (152, also 226)

Here, as well as in her later discussion on women in works of literature, de
Beauvoir repeatedly calls attention to the role that being "taken" plays for the
woman in traditional sexual encounters:

> The act of love for woman is still considered a *service* she renders to man,
> which therefore makes him seem her master . . . . [H]e can always *take* a
> woman who is an inferior, but it is degrading if a woman *gives herself* to a
> male who is socially beneath her; her consent is in either case in the nature
> of a surrender, a fall. (553) *(italics de Beauvoir's)*

De Beauvoir also makes frequent reference to the *fear* that this engenders
among women. She asserts that the fear of rape and molestation at the hands
of men looms large in the sexual thoughts of many young women (317, 322),
and even that "It is not uncommon for the young girl's first experience to be
a real rape" (383). She observes that it is often out of "the fear of violence, of
rape, that the adolescent girl gives her first love to an older woman rather than
to a man" (346). She further develops this theme in her chapter on "The
Lesbian," noting that the renunciation of the "protection" of a member of "a
superior caste that is aggressive, sneering, amused, or hostile," and "capable of
knocking you down with a blow of his fist" plays a part in some women's
choice of lesbianism (421, 423).

While such descriptions clearly foreshadowed the full emergence of the
feminist critiques of rape and domestic violence some twenty-five years later,
de Beauvoir herself did not integrate these powerful depictions of violence into
a full-blooded account of women's *victimization* before men. This had enor-
mous significance for her use of Hegel's account. For surely her contention
that Hegel's narrative of master and slave applies better to the relation between
men and women could have been further supported and enriched had she
understood the relation of women to men as importantly originating in a
struggle for sexual domination (64). Even if violent conquest does not encompass all the meanings of the sexual relationship between women and men, its
importance in conditioning those meanings can scarcely be ignored.[38] Though
de Beauvoir was obviously sensitive to the impact of this ideology on the
women she describes, however, it did not enter significantly into her political
analysis. She states instead that women have not known fear and struggle
against men. In light of the theoretical importance of this claim, it is worth
considering what might have motivated it.

An attractive explanation might be thought to lie in de Beauvoir's explicit reliance upon Sartrean existentialism, with its characteristic emphasis on "choice" as the basis for all meaning. De Beauvoir does in fact identify her perspective as that of "existentialist ethics," and consistently affirms that, despite the obstacles to which she calls attention, women cannot escape responsibility for their condition (1980: xxxiv-xxxv, 50). Despite occasional references to women's having chosen their slavery (553), or to their "bad faith" (655), however, de Beauvoir's primary focus throughout *The Second Sex* remains the absolute alterity of women, and the seemingly impossible difficulties that this implies for the woman who would seek to overcome that condition. This is consistent with the "ambiguity" that she attaches to the choices of oppressed groups in her more explicit discussion of existentialist ethics in *The Ethics of Ambiguity*.[39] Moreover, even if it is argued that women must "choose" their situation as victims, their socially imposed "situation" as the objects of sexual violence is not a choice.[40]

Of greater importance in explaining de Beauvoir's de-emphasis of violent victimization would seem to be her frequent observations on the "passive" dispositions that are cultivated in women. Because she maintains that women have been influenced from earliest childhood not to engage in struggle, de Beauvoir concludes that they lack the ability and the desire to engage males in contests of strength and skill: "Everything influences [woman] to let herself be hemmed in, dominated by existences foreign to her own" (713). Even if women have been conditioned to eschew struggle, however, it does not follow that women have not known fear and violent suppression. Few "influences" are more effective in enforcing passivity than real and threatened violence against those who would act differently. Ironically, this very point is not lost on de Beauvoir. In her account of a young woman who attempted to maintain an attitude of defiance toward males in the streets, she remarks:

> One or two unpleasant experiences . . . showed her that brute force is on the side of the males. When she had become aware of how weak she really was, she lost most of her assurance; this began her evolution toward femininity. (332)

This would appear to be a typical example of how women, from a very early age, "learn the lessons of violence" only too well.

It would appear that de Beauvoir's failure to move her account of alterity toward a critique of victimization finds its source neither in the existentialist concept of choice nor in her account of feminine dispositions, but in certain psychological assumptions that guide her analysis of women's oppression. Most importantly, de Beauvoir assumes that violence, to the extent that it plays a constitutive role in the oppression of a group, will be obvious and noncontroversial. Rejecting the psychoanalytic category of the "unconscious," de Beauvoir must assume that if one group has been violently subordinated by another, members of the victimized group will be "conscious" of that fact. Because women, quite unlike other socially subordinated groups, lack such a historical memory, de Beauvoir concludes that their subordination "was not something that *occurred*" (xxiv). If the event of subordination did not occur, then neither could the moment of risk and terror that might transform the activities through which that subordination is mediated.

As discussed in chapter 4, however, the development of the feminist movement led to a heightened consciousness of the previously suppressed issue of violence against women. As the experience of the survivors of sexual violence made increasingly clear, when that violence and the fear that it engenders become "internalized," they can cease to be transparently recognizable as a feature of experience, even as they are exerting a powerful influence on the survivor.[41] Because the grasp of a phenomenon such as victimization depends critically upon a set of descriptions that govern our perception of it, it is possible even for victims to be oblivious to a state of affairs that may appear unbelievably obvious in retrospect. Although women have always known fear before men (as de Beauvoir's own discussion amply illustrates), to apprehend that fear under a *concept* such as a fear of rape, of battery, of harassment, or of some other form of generalized violence against women retrieves it from the unnoticed background of experience. For Hegel, to *universalize* such phenomena conceptually makes possible a new self-conscious grasp of the meaning of these actions.[42] Moreover, it may be only in light of these new (and even now far from universal) meanings that a full apprehension of the various ways in which women's roles have been enforced by violence and the threat of violence can come into actuality. Despite her remarkable cataloguing of certain aspects of the terror that women face, even de Beauvoir did not fully integrate the meaning of that terror and its function into her account, permitting her to conclude, rather astoundingly, that "Woman is . . . deprived of the lessons of violence" (1980: 712). Moreover, her failure to grasp the "moment" of violence in the social construction of women's agency conceptually underpins her skepticism regarding the possibility of a politically viable retrieval of feminine difference.

In this critical respect, *The Second Sex* and its account of Otherness remains situated at the brink of the feminist analyses of women's political situation that were to appear some two decades later. While de Beauvoir's *descriptions* dramatically called attention to the intolerable effects of Western social institutions and practices upon women, her *analysis* does not—or rather does not consistently—expose this situation as an instance of the violation of the agency of one social class by another. In a certain sense like Hegel before her, de Beauvoir's descriptions never develop into a theory of "exploitation" or victimization of feminine interests by masculine ones.[43] That development would have to await the collective consciousness raising of the next twenty years, a phenomenon for which, as already noted, de Beauvoir held out little hope in *The Second Sex*. On her account, women as a group still have no genuine collective agency that could be violated.[44] Hence, it is only as "a free and autonomous being" *(une liberté autonome)* that a woman experiences her alterity as oppressive, and it is as this transcendent being (emphatically not a woman) that she can be liberated (xxxv).[45]

De Beauvoir's existentialist appeal to the unencumbered freedom of the transcendent consciousness, however, represents a departure from the description of self-realization through fear and service in which Hegel's narrative of master and slave culminates. It is precisely the destructive and vanquishing "transcendence" of the lord that is overcome in the consciousness that the bondsman achieves through his formative activity. Hegel's slave arrives at a higher stage of self-knowledge only insofar as his desire to consume is "held in check" by virtue of the service that was imposed upon him in his defeat. Perhaps foremost among the elements that have made Hegel's account of enduring political interest is its peculiar irony: the narrative of the transformation of defeat into a moment of self-creation from which the "victor" is excluded by the very conditions of his victory. If this transformation is to occur, however, it requires a consciousness of the initial defeat—the moment of absolute self-emptying before the other that permits consciousness to emerge from its initial *immersion* in the world. The recognition of victimization (fear) is the starting point for the transformation of agency in labor.

Of course, it was this initial moment of self-recognition that de Beauvoir effectively ruled out with her contention that women have never engaged in a life and death struggle with men. If, however, that contention is taken as a mystification of the violent conditions under which women's passivity has been enforced (as I have argued that it should), then Hegel's narrative of fear, dependence, and service may be applicable to feminist transformations of consciousness in a manner that goes well beyond de Beauvoir's suggestive reading of the passage. To the extent that women's characteristic activities and values are imposed as that which mediates a relationship of bondage, such activities and values can be *service* in the Hegelian sense, and may themselves be the site of genuine self-creative activity. They may serve as a means to self-recovery in the face of domination.

This interpretation of women's condition, of course, goes beyond the letter of Hegel's account in the *Phenomenology*. For Hegel, the consciousness of victimization in fear is the first stage toward self-recovery in formative activity. As feminist consciousness raising (as well as movements of empowerment among other oppressed groups) makes clear, however, the awareness of the "moment" of fear and surrender cannot be taken for granted, but may itself require a lengthy process of discovery.[46] Although this repression contrasts with the transparency that is assumed in the description of the battle of "consciousnesses" in the *Phenomenology of Spirit*, the fact that it could develop is also entirely consistent with its logical structure. If the moment of fear is the starting point of self-recovery, then the mystification of the fear and domination in which an oppressive relationship originated would be a most effective means for suppressing the agency of the oppressed group. On this account, the collective development of an awareness of victimization may be a necessary condition for the members of an oppressed group to achieve self-recovery in the characteristic medium of their oppression. Accordingly, de Beauvoir's outright rejection of "feminine values" reflected a consistent understanding of women's condition at a stage in which the nature of women's victimization remained less than fully transparent.

Conclusion: From Domination to Difference

If this argument is right, de Beauvoir's failure to perceive any possibility for positively appropriating feminine difference and her consequent espousal of a politics of "transcendence" do not derive directly from her Hegelian influences, but from those influences in tandem with her assumption that the oppression of women lacked a violent history. Once that violent history has come to light, however, a thoroughgoing re-conceptualization of women's lives and activities may become possible. One important implication of this view is that a political focus on the violence that has accompanied women's assuming the place of the Other is more than either wallowing in one's victimization or a moral attack on men. Rather, it may serve as a starting point for the recovery of women's agency, and a new appreciation of the activities, roles, values, and orientations that have been imposed on them. As in the case of Hegel's slave, consciousness of the moment of fear and risk can enable women to come to self-recognition in the very activities and roles that have also been the medium of their oppression. It is to this point and its relevance for recent feminist debates concerning victimization and "difference" that I now turn.

CHAPTER 8

JUSTICE, RECOGNITION, AND THE FEMININE

> *The repossession by women of our bodies will bring*
> *far more essential change to human society than the*
> *seizing of the means of production by workers. The fe-*
> *male body has been both the territory and machine,*
> *virgin wilderness to be exploited and assembly line*
> *turning out life. We need to imagine a world in*
> *which every woman is the presiding genius of her*
> *own body. . . .Sexuality, politics, intelligence, power,*
> *motherhood, work, community, intimacy will develop*
> *new meanings; thinking itself will be transformed.*
> —Adrienne Rich
> *Of Woman Born*

While much of the discussion of the preceding chapters has assumed the legitimacy of feminist criticisms of masculine structures of power and domination, in recent years many of the most influential of these criticisms have themselves been subject to feminist scrutiny. The condition of women as victims or survivors of male power, which was the centerpiece of the movements of consciousness raising discussed in chapter 4, has come under increasingly strident criticism from both feminist and non-feminist sources. The grounds of this critique within feminism have been varied and sometimes incompatible. One strand of criticism comes from broadly liberal critics of cultural feminism such as Alice Echols (1989) and Christina Hoff Sommers (1994).[1] These writers contend that an overemphasis on victimization is linked conceptually to an undesirable theoretical focus on women's difference as opposed to equality. Interestingly, Drucilla Cornell (1991, 1993) has brought exactly the opposite charge against some of the same writers. Developing her own theory from the French postmodernist critique of transcendent individualism and "equality," Cornell challenges the dominant feminist approaches of American feminist jurisprudence, especially that of Catharine MacKinnon, for failing fully to grasp the positive dimensions of feminine difference,[2] and for implicitly calling upon women to adopt the ideals of masculine transcendence.

In this chapter, I employ certain aspects of the Hegelian conception of subordination and self-recovery developed in previous chapters to dispute Drucilla Cornell's critique of the constructionist accounts of MacKinnon. While a Hegelian approach to political change could be employed to challenge the individualist critics as well, Cornell's work represents a deeper and more interesting challenge to some of the feminists whose work I have relied upon, in part because Cornell accepts a number of Hegelian assumptions. In what follows, I argue that calling attention to the manner in which the characteristic roles, activities, types of relationship, ethical orientation, and myths of women originated in their victimization and oppression, need not be incompatible with valuing women's difference as a feminist goal. Secondly, I show that attempts to empower women within the (masculine) legal system is not only consistent with such a goal but may be a necessary condition for its realization.

In the next section, I take up Cornell's approach to feminine difference, briefly exploring its roots in French postmodernism. After that, I turn specifically to Cornell's critique of MacKinnon. Using elements of Hegel's historical realism as well as his account of master and slave, I defend MacKinnon against Cornell's charge that her approach leaves women with an unchangeable patriarchal "reality." I continue that discussion in the following section, arguing that the important point at issue between Cornell and MacKinnon does not concern feminine difference, since each calls for a kind of "difference" as a goal, but concerns rather the means necessary for asserting it. I use certain elements of Hegel's discussion of self-actualization in defending MacKinnon's approach.

The Transformative Potential of the Feminine

In her "The Institutionalization of Meaning, Recollective Imagination and the Potential for Transformative Legal Interpretation" (1988), Cornell broke important new ground by bringing Hegel's political philosophy to bear on contemporary legal theory. Cornell argued that the relationship between the individual and the state that Hegel developed in the *Philosophy of Right* (1821) provided the starting point for a credible theory of critical legal interpretations. Although Cornell argues that the "conservative impulses in the Hegelian fusion of truth and history and of meaning and being" keep his philosophy from providing an adequate basis for legal interpretation, she sees his insights into the relationship between the individual and the community as going beyond the inadequate conceptions of contemporary legal theorists such as Ronald Dworkin (Cornell 1988: 1175–1179).

Cornell's approach to Hegel's political philosophy is importantly different from the one that I have developed here. While she criticizes what she takes to be an ineliminable conservatism in Hegel's commitment to historical realism, I have tried to exploit certain subversive elements of that theory in taking it beyond Hegel's explicit ends. Nevertheless, we are in agreement on the significance of Hegel's contention that individuality cannot subsist except in an abstract and unmediated shape apart from the practices of a state for political theory. As Cornell states:

> [I]ndividuality [cannot] be separated from the social and the communal structures that sponsor its flourishing. Mutual codetermination is not just an ideal; it is the reality of who we are as members of the state. We cannot completely sever the "being" of the individual from the "reality" of the community. (1988: 1190-1191)

In light of this concern, it is interesting that Cornell takes feminist theorists such as MacKinnon, who have sought to link women's subordination with patriarchal society's failure to embody their individuality as women, to be fundamentally opposed to her view.[3] To understand precisely why this is so, it is necessary to begin with the philosophical sources of Cornell's critique.

Consistent with her earlier criticisms of liberal legal theory, in her more recent work Cornell has argued that an adequate feminist approach to the law must aim to lend social expression to "the feminine" itself. The embodiment of the feminine in the law, however, cannot simply imitate the means and methods by which men have found recognition in those structures. Following contemporary French theorists, including Lacan and especially Derrida, Cornell argues that "the feminine can never be identified with any set of rigid cultural designators" (1993: 57). Although actual women have certainly taken on definite roles, activities, types of relationship, and ethical orientations, as well as suffered very particular forms of violence and injustice, the category "woman" eludes simple identification with any property or set of properties. Precisely because woman is the Other, that which is excluded from the simple "presence" of the knowing subject, she falls outside the range of simple linguistic representation. Accordingly, feminist jurisprudence cannot be satisfied with the demand that woman be treated in a manner that is strictly "symmetrical" with the man. It is not enough, indeed it is itself an injustice simply to place woman in the role of the masculine litigant so that the visible injustices done to her as such a subject could be addressed. An adequate feminist legal theory must aim not only at eliminating sexist harm, but at the positive embodiment of the characteristic roles, activities, types of relationship, ethical orientation, and myths of woman. While these do not encompass the full reality of women, "We cannot separate the Truth of Woman from the fictions in which she is represented and through which she portrays herself" (88).

In keeping with this project, Cornell allies herself with those positive attempts to retrieve feminine "difference" found in French writers such as

Helène Cixous, Luce Irigaray, and Monique Wittig. While Cornell eschews a simple celebration of "difference" that would fail to encompass legal remedies for the harms that real women have suffered, she likewise resists the claim that the feminine encompasses no possibilities beyond that of an oppressed other.[4] Cornell finds in French feminist postmodernism not only a challenge to the manner in which traditional conceptions of the feminine have served the interests of men, but an articulation of the disruptive possibilities that lurk in feminine roles, language, and myth. This disruptive capacity enables those roles, language, and myths to become vehicles of creative social change even while they remain largely shrouded in the regressive meanings of patriarchal culture. While a simple affirmation of the feminine as a "different voice" must run the risk of celebrating women's deficient social condition in that culture, it is equally mistaken to try to escape feminine difference altogether. In a positive reference to Irigaray's attempt to develop an authentically feminine discourse, Cornell writes:

> Feminine style is this constant experimentation to write the unspeakable, knowing all the while the inherent contradiction in the effort. But without the effort, we can only have the wordless repetition of the same, in which the feminine is denied and repudiated, and our desire is rendered inexpressible, and therefore non-existent in its specificity. (1991: 156)

Cornell specifically takes up Irigaray's description of the subversive power of *"mimesis,"* arguing that it may serve as a kind of model for the project of positive feminist jurisprudence. Such a power suggests a model for challenging the masculine social order that also can avoid falling into the "sameness" of masculine discourse:

> One must assume the feminine role deliberately. Which means already to convert a form of subordination into an affirmation, and thus to begin to thwart it. Whereas a direct feminine challenge to this condition means demanding to speak as a (masculine) "subject". . . (Cornell 1991: 147)

In *mimesis* Irigaray sees women actively rebelling against imposed social roles without abandoning the feminine altogether. However oppressive the structures of the feminine have been for actual women, these are never just "there" to be grasped by the subject of knowledge, but exist as "beyond [that] can only be glimpsed through the 'reality' of gender identity" (1991: 141). Thus, the writing of difference itself takes on a transgressive character, lending expression to latent and unexpressed feminine desire.

It is out of this orientation that Cornell goes on to criticize what she perceives as the victim-oriented approach of MacKinnon. On the one hand, she praises MacKinnon for having pursued "a relentless genealogy of our current conceptions of justice," a necessary task for coming to a grasp of "the masculine bias that undermines the claims of our legal system" (1991: 116, cf. 1993: 112). For Cornell, however, such a genealogy, when it becomes the centerpiece of feminist legal scholarship, leaves women with only a negative conception of their place in the law. Cornell alleges that this negativity has several distinct debilitating aspects, and it is to these that I shall now turn.

MacKinnon and Death of Difference

Cornell traces MacKinnon's approach, with its identification of feminine difference and male oppression, to de Beauvoir's descriptions of woman as absolute Other in *The Second Sex* (1980). As discussed in chapter 7, de Beauvoir grounded her ethical condemnation of woman's construction on the explicit charge that "otherness" constitutes a violation of the freedom of a transcendent consciousness. Because the woman is a transcendent freedom, her consignment to "immanent" roles in the division of labor, in her personal relationships, and in cultural lore represents a failure of respect. Cornell consistently concludes from this that "the desire to return woman to humanity" remains the normative underpinning of de Beauvoir's critique (Cornell 1991: 192).

Moreover, de Beauvoir consistently applies her Hegelian political theory to this situation. Inasmuch as the humanity of the subject has found expression in the roles, relationships, activities, and myths of masculinity, then it will be by means of these alone that women will achieve their freedom. As noted in the last chapter, de Beauvoir was emphatic in her denial that women possessed values of their own upon which to found a new future (de Beauvoir 1949: 65). Any so-called "feminine values" are no more than ideals expressing the prerogatives of men and reinforcing their superior position. Cornell concludes from this that de Beauvoir's politics of returning women to humanity is precisely a call on women to repeat the "sameness" of masculinity: "There is perhaps no greater example of the writer who constantly calls us 'to be' like them than de Beauvoir" (Cornell 1991: 193).[5]

If de Beauvoir's descriptions of woman as Other laid the philosophical groundwork for the rejection of feminine difference, MacKinnon's legal theory articulates such a rejection point by point. Setting her focus on MacKinnon's descriptions of the condition of women in *Feminism Unmodified* (1987) and

Toward a Feminist Theory of the State (1989), Cornell charges that these descriptions make the "central error" of diminishing "feminine reality by *identifying* the feminine *totally* with the real world as it is seen and constructed through the male gaze" (Cornell 1993: 98). As does de Beauvoir, MacKinnon fails to perceive women's characteristic roles, activities, types of relationship, ethical orientation, and myths as anything other than an expression of the interests and desires of men.

Although Cornell's precise argument against MacKinnon is not always easy to follow, it takes shape around three broad charges. First, she claims that MacKinnon's descriptions of the relations between women and men constitute "an unshakable, objective, unmodified, 'reality,'" in which the feminine was not merely historically constructed by and for masculine interests, but is so rigidly defined that it cannot change (Cornell 1991: 131). Secondly, Cornell claims that MacKinnon's constructionism holds out no possibility whatever for a positive valuation of the feminine. Because she identifies the feminine solely with the violence and victimization suffered by "actual women," MacKinnon consistently understands any celebration of difference as no more than a tacit endorsement of that same violence and victimization. For women to celebrate difference is, however unknowingly, to celebrate their chains. Thirdly, Cornell charges that MacKinnon's feminist reform agenda can do no more than call for reversing gender relations as they currently exist, i.e., insist that women rather than men take their place "on top." Such a charge appears, at least *prima facie*, to be at odds with Cornell's initial claim that MacKinnon defined gender relations in such a manner that they simply could not change at all. Before turning to an evaluation of the charges themselves, however, it is important to consider their basis.

For Cornell, MacKinnon's argument that women are "completely" constructed by the male gaze means that MacKinnon, no less than de Beauvoir, is left with a politics in which women strive "to be like them" (1991: 120). She cites MacKinnon's claim that the reality of women is itself imposed by the masculine point of view in order to emphasize the depth of MacKinnon's position here: "The way men see women defines who women can be" (1991: 124). In Cornell's view, MacKinnon's interpretation of women's condition manifests a "militant, programmatic, anti-utopianism" in which "feminism loses its critical edge because it can only reinforce the masculine viewpoint as all of reality" (1991: 128, 130). To the extent that women's interests and desires are themselves organized so as to perpetuate women's subordination, no hope exists for a positive conception of the feminine. To be a woman just *is* to be subordinated. For Cornell, simply to identify the feminine with the victimization and

violence suffered by actual women fails to recognize the transgressive possibilities of difference that render "the status of our current system of gender identity as a 'fici-fact,'" and not fully real (97). Moreover, because MacKinnon rejects
the mimetic project of using difference creatively, she must seek to place women
in the role of the masculine subject: transcendent, fully self-present, and removed from the darkness of the feminine. Women cannot recover their freedom
as women, but must follow the rules of governing the old masculine subject, the
law of the father.

In Cornell's view, this affirmation of the masculine subject has devasta-
ting practical implications. In the first place, she claims that constructionism
effectively calls upon women to "make the masculine *our* world by insisting
that we 'are' what men have made us to be" (1993: 105). Attempts made by
women to recover feminine difference in art, literature, or spirituality can
only further the subordination of women. Secondly, Cornell argues that
MacKinnon's skepticism with regard to women's capacity to alter their sexual "reality" through *mimesis* in their sexual practice implies an ethics of
sexual repression. Cornell claims that because MacKinnon holds that "sex
for women does not bring empowerment," this entails that women must
repress their own desire in hopes of eventually coming to take their place
"on top" (1993: 105). Cornell argues that MacKinnon has failed to grasp the
manner in which utopian retrievals of feminist difference, the "writing of the
real as 'fici-fact,'" is a critical component in asserting their sexuality and not
conforming to masculine "reality" (1991: 163).

Given MacKinnon's failure to provide a positive vision for women's future,
Cornell argues that such a future can only be an empty one of revenge and
conquest. If men have attained and held their power by occupying the role of
the reality-defining subject, then the empowerment of women can take place
only when men are dislodged from that privileged place and women take it
over. Cornell does not cite MacKinnon's endorsement of such a view, but she
holds that where an empowering assertion of women's difference is a contradiction in terms, the only remaining possibility is to advocate that women
change their situation by assuming the masculine role of conquerors. Cornell
notes that MacKinnon's concrete proposals for positive legal reform, from her
The Sexual Harassment of Working Women (1989) right up through her most
recent and controversial writings on pornography and the First Amendment,
seek to empower women by placing them in the role of *litigants* (1991: 151).[6]
Although Cornell does not deny that gains are possible through this means,
she takes this to be at best an incomplete approach to feminist jurisprudence
in that it leaves women with no *positive* means for legally embodying what is

uniquely their own—the "feminine." MacKinnon's feminist legal theory can only arm women in a battle against the male adversary in his courtrooms.

Social Reality and Social Construction

Cornell's claims that MacKinnon's social constructionism cannot brook a positive conception of the feminine, and must therefore advocate a politics of revenge and conquest, rests on the assumption that MacKinnon's descriptions of women's condition are simple descriptions of reality. If it is the case that MacKinnon "only leaves us with their reality," then we must assume that MacKinnon's descriptions of women's subordination are more than historically and socially situated claims about that condition, since in the latter case the future would remain underdetermined (Cornell 1991: 147). Thus, a full evaluation of Cornell's argument requires us to look more closely at the precise nature of MacKinnon's discussion.

It is clear that MacKinnon does not explicitly intend her account of women's condition to be that of a detached or otherwise transcendent observer:

> Theory [is] a social endeavor inseparable from the collective situation. Situated theory is concrete and changing rather than abstract and totalizing, working from the viewpoint of powerlessness to political understanding toward social transformation . . . . inside the world and the work, not above or outside them . . . (MacKinnon 1989: xvi)

At the same time, however, MacKinnon declares emphatically that her situated theory "is about what *is*, the meaning of what is, and the way what is, is enforced" (xii). Of course, the claim that what "is" requires enforcement already means that we are not dealing with the "is" of strict identity. Nevertheless, MacKinnon's repeated claim that she is describing reality, and her insistence that it is self-deception to believe that one can escape that reality,[7] raises an important question: to what extent can a claim about "reality" also be a criticism of that state of affairs?

As discussed at length in chapter 7, the exposure of previously hidden relations of power and subordination between groups, even if it is stated "matter of factly," may itself have an effect on the state of those relations. As Cornell herself has written, "the 'so it was' is 'seen' differently once it is 'seen' from the 'feminine' perspective" (Cornell 1991: 196). In arguing against MacKinnon's statement that under present conditions of sexism the man is active ("fucker") and woman is his passive victim ("fuckee"), Cornell asks rhetorically how

"MacKinnon, a fuckee, [can] know at all" (1991: 149). It may be that for MacKinnon, however, *that is exactly the point*. Her deconstruction of masculine reality consists of describing it from a point of view that would be impossible had masculinity truly realized its dream of unalterably constructing the limits of the "real." This is much the same point that Judith Butler (1990) makes with respect to de Beauvoir:

> Although Beauvoir is often understood to be calling for the right of women to become, in effect, existential subjects and, hence, for inclusion within the terms of an abstract universality, her position also implies a critique of the very disembodiment of the abstract masculine epistemological subject . . . . Beauvoir's analysis implicitly poses the question: Through what act of negation and disavowal does the masculine pose as a disembodied universality and the feminine get constructed as a disavowed corporeality? (11–12)

By exposing the "unshakable reality" of masculine domination from the point of view of the one who is supposed to be rendered silent in that state of affairs, constructionists such as de Beauvoir and MacKinnon remove the foundation from the edifice of domination. It is precisely to the extent that the "fuckee" can come to a grasp of sexual exploitation in its completeness and irretrievability that it is no longer complete, no longer irretrievable. In this work of undermining sexist reality, MacKinnon sees herself as part of the tradition of feminist consciousness raising discussed in chapter 4, where "unraveling and reordering what every woman 'knows' . . . forms and reforms, recovers and changes, its meaning" (1989: 96).

The manner in which MacKinnon's critique proceeds by way of describing masculine domination in its totality adds a critical dimension to the Hegelian theory of abstract moral judgments developed in chapter 3. There, I discussed Hegel's claim that the condemnation of slavery on the basis of universal human rights failed to account for the manner in which slavery, despite its wrongness, maintains a "partial validity" in a slave society.[8] MacKinnon's method, a method that she traces to feminist consciousness raising, suggests a way of developing an implicitly universalist critique of an existing set of practices that avoids the pitfalls of liberal proceduralism. Rather than asking whether or not sexual harassment or pornography constitute harms based upon our current conception of rights, MacKinnon situates these practices within the context of a broader, functioning system. Through this "relentless genealogy," it becomes clear that our very concepts of "rights," "consent," and even "equality" take on concrete meaning in light of a political system of sexual privileges for men. MacKinnon, however, does not simply abandon these concepts. A commitment to a real, but not yet fully "realized" conception of rights and equality is an indispensable condition for the moral and political outrage that her descriptions engender. Moreover, the development of a system of legal protections against the harms of such gendered offenses as sexual harassment and pornography requires that we rethink categories such as rights and consent, and not abandon them altogether.

The disruptive character of MacKinnon's narrative of gender, however, derives not only from the conceptual challenge that it poses to the ethical categories of a sexist liberal social order. The claim that the reality of women's subordination is *not* simply given but enforced by violence and fear may itself serve as a source of emotional empowerment for women. This is no incidental point. MacKinnon not only shows that the feminine has been constructed by an elaborate system that functions to support masculine interests, but draws upon women's experience to defend the distinct claim that this "construction" has developed by means of and is maintained by masculine force and violence in which "sexual abuse works as a form of terror in creating and maintaining this arrangement" (1987: 7). As noted already, no arrangement that has been and continues to be forcibly imposed can be taken as unalterably given. When a person comes to *recognize* that much of her life has been shaped by the real and threatened violence of another group, this changes her perception of that life—"calling [its] givenness into question" (1989: 95).[9]

This also distinguishes MacKinnon's constructionism from that of de Beauvoir in a way that is significant for Cornell's critique. As discussed in chapter 7, de Beauvoir explicitly denied that women's condition of alterity was the consequence of violence or sexual victimization. This permitted her to claim that woman "has not learned the lessons of violence, she has never stood forth as a subject" (1980: 598). Among the reasons that de Beauvoir held out little hope for any projects of retrieving feminine values was precisely that she saw women's characteristic activities not as imposed through a struggle, but as simply given. The possibility of the slave's activities being a means of self-recognition rested upon the absolute fear in which they were taken up. In the terms of the women's movement, the slave recognizes himself as a *survivor*. As discussed at length in the previous chapter, the self-emptying moment of fear (a moment shared by the slave and the master) was a necessary condition for the nascent self-awareness that finds mediation in the slave's work. On a Hegelian account, the awareness that one has been such a survivor is not debilitating—it is no less than a necessary condition for coming to self-awareness. To the extent that this is the case, MacKinnon's claim that women's characteristic roles, activities, types of relationship, ethical orientation, and myths find their origins in violence and victimization does not imply that the feminine is irretrievable. As noted above, by focusing attention on the sexual violence at the core of women's construction, MacKinnon performs a genuine "immanent critique" of the states of affairs that promote the construction.

It is worth noting in this regard that evidence exists for the importance of such a critique in the practice of feminist therapy. As discussed at length in chapter 4, the cultivation of a kind of righteous anger at the violence that women suffered played a key role in the feminist consciousness raising of the early Second Wave. In the subsequent development of the anti-rape and battered women's movements, accounts of how victimized women's situations have been effectively constructed so as to entrap them in a cycle of violence have been important in enabling women to escape those situations. An essential aspect of feminist therapy for battered and abused women consists of informing the survivor in a "matter of fact" way of the social origins of her victimization, linking that victimization to her social status as a woman (Smith and Siegel 1985: 18, Rosewater 1988: 142). Providing the survivor with such an account is critical if she is to overcome the tendency to assume responsibility for the violence that has been done to her (Schechter 1982: 316).[10] In this situation, informing the survivor that her "reality" was constructed in such a way that the "choices" that confronted her in the matter were all bad ones is a beginning toward overcoming self-reproach and moving toward self-recovery.

Contrary to the assumptions of the critics of "victimology," it is precisely the survivor's belief in her own capacity as a self-sufficient moral agent that leads her to the belief that she is responsible for her abuse. She takes responsibility both for the conditions that brought on the abuse (she "asked for it") and for her failure to extricate herself from it ("why did she stay?"). A constructionist account, by calling attention to the ways in which oppression structures ways of seeing, feeling, and acting for the oppressed, can begin to challenge self-reproaching beliefs. The survivor's situation of violence, her belief that she brought the male violence down on herself, her initial inability to see a way out, and the scorn of others toward her all make sense insofar as an oppressive system has come to define social reality. While such a reality is subject, in the Hegelian sense, to "contradiction" (otherwise the survivor could never see her way out), it is nevertheless *real* as was evidenced by the manner in which it effectively defined the survivor's choices and her thinking about those choices. Once she can name her oppression (and her oppressor), she begins the process of challenging that reality (Butler 1985: 35, Walker 1979: 232, 246).[11]

If a thoroughgoing constructionism such as that of MacKinnon can serve as the starting point for challenging a patriarchal conception of reality, then it cannot simply condemn women to an unmodifiably or irretrievably masculine state of affairs. In fact, to the extent that the recognition of a history of violence is a condition for an oppressed group's coming to an appreciation of its "service," MacKinnon may be understood to have implicitly begun the process toward a revaluation of feminine "difference." Before coming to such a conclusion, however, it is necessary to spell out more concretely how her theory would be consistent with such a goal. For, as the passages cited by Cornell suggest, MacKinnon's explicit remarks on such a project are far from positive.

Feminist Futures

Although MacKinnon never endorses the view that women try to assume the position of masculine conquerors, Cornell takes this to be a working assumption that underpins both MacKinnon's generally negative comments on women's difference and (perhaps as a consequence of the former view) her exclusive legal focus on obtaining for women the power of litigants. Furthermore, though I have suggested that MacKinnon's focus on the violent subordination of women might serve as the starting point for a recovery of difference, it is true that most of MacKinnon's writings tend to argue for the generally disempowering nature of that difference. This is perhaps most evident in her approving use of Ti-Grace Atkinson's observation, "I do not know any feminist worthy of the name who, if forced to choose between freedom and sex, would choose sex. She'd choose freedom every time" (MacKinnon 1989: 154). For Cornell, such a "choice" itself suggests a bifurcation in women's reality. Who, exactly, is free when she chooses freedom rather than sex? Once again, this suggests that it is a "transcendent" freedom, unrelated to a real, embodied woman.

It should be noted, however, that MacKinnon uses the quote in the context of her argument that it is hopeless to seek an equal sexuality under general conditions of inequality. Her claim thus has less to do with the possibility of freedom in the absence of sex than with the more general observation that, under conditions of sexism, sex does not bring empowerment for women. Cornell objects to this, claiming that "Sex in the best of all possible worlds should *not* bring empowerment," and moreover that "Empowerment is not and should not be the ultimate goal in any relationship" (1993: 105). Such replies, however, are not to the point in this instance. It does not follow from the claim that women are not currently empowered in sexual relations, that sex *ought* to be a source of power for women, or that it ought to be a source of power at all.[12] MacKinnon neither states explicitly nor implies that the goal of sex should be empowerment, and her general concern for equality in sexual relations appear to be incompatible with such a goal.

To show that MacKinnon's theory does not entail a feminist future of "turning the tables" on the masters, however, leaves the question as to what it might positively endorse unanswered. In fact, the bulk of MacKinnon's writings are descriptions of the present, with very little by way of either determinate implications or positive proposals for the future (a point to which I shall return shortly). Contrary to Cornell's argument, however, in those rare passages that really do have implications for the future, MacKinnon indicates that women will have to retrieve that very feminine that has been constructed in the interests of masculine hegemony. In the chapter entitled "Women, Self-Possession, and Sport" in *Feminism Unmodified* (1987), MacKinnon observes that:

> [W]e need a women's point of view that criticizes all the ways we have been created by being excluded and kept down but that also claims the validity of our own experience. This is not a transcendence operation whereby we get to act as though we don't have any particular perspective, but instead *an embrace of what we have become* with a criticism of the process of having been forced to become it. . . . (120) *(Emphasis mine)*

If MacKinnon's approach rules out an uncritical celebration of difference under conditions of domination, as noted in previous chapters, it also eschews any appeal to a universalizing transcendence (such as that which de Beauvoir took up at key points in *The Second Sex*). MacKinnon rejects the option of "turning the tables" and assuming the role of either a masculine or "transcendental" subject. This leaves the task of coming to a critically informed embrace of that "distinct meaning . . . that comes from women's oppression through our bodies" as the only plausible basis upon which to build the future.

MacKinnon goes on to flesh out this distinct meaning in terms of the future of women's athletics and sport:

> A vision of sport from this standpoint finds ritualized violence alien and dangerous as well as faintly ridiculous, every bit as much as it finds sex-scripted cheering from the sidelines demeaning and vicarious and silly. The place of women's athletics in a larger feminist analysis is that women *as women* have a survival stake in reclaiming our physical bodies. . . . (123)

Despite MacKinnon's insistence that women's difference finds its origins in masculine domination, she is equally clear that the future of women's self-re-covery must take the form of a *reclamation* of that difference. Likewise, it is women's *bodies* (and not some transcendent subject) that will be the site of that recovery.[13] Where MacKinnon differs from theorists of feminine "difference" such as Irigaray, however, is with her virtual silence about what that reclamation will look like or how it will take place. Indeed, she fears that the few things she has said may go too far and be "sentimentalized" (1987: 123).

This general refusal to develop a positive conception of the feminine, along with her singularly focused legal work on ending male violence, leads Cornell to conclude that MacKinnon has restricted the feminist political program to taking just those measures necessary to win a battle against the men. In support of this view, Cornell frequently returns to MacKinnon's rhetorical question, "Why does 'out now' contain a sufficiently positive vision of the future for Vietnam and Nicaragua but not for women?" (MacKinnon 1987: 219, cited in Cornell 1991: 128, 139, 153, 160, and 1993: 103, 122).[14] As is clear from the passages cited above, however, MacKinnon's reluctance to embrace feminine ideals is based neither on the belief that women ought to develop into violent aggressors nor on an appeal to transcendent freedom. A revalued feminine is no less MacKinnon's end than it is Cornell's or Irigaray's. What separates MacKinnon from these other authors is her worry that in a historical epoch in which sexism has social and legal "validity" (the situation today), it is perilous simply to *value* the difference that dominance has forged.

MacKinnon contends that so long as women's bodies place them in the position of sexual subordinates (i.e., so long as such practices as rape, prostitution, sexual harassment, pornography, and generalized sexual objectification of women are the *norm*), women will lack the social recognition necessary to assert their difference in a meaningful way. Before women can aspire to a genuine celebration of their otherness, the socially and legally empowered class of "men" must be compelled to recognize women as deliberative agents with the capacity to claim their bodies and their sexuality as their own. Bringing this about will involve the largely negative task of ending those practices by which women's bodies are a mark of subordination. In this, MacKinnon's concerns are in keeping with the reservations expressed by a wide range of feminist ethicists concerning an ethics of "care."[15] Furthermore, despite Cornell's insistence on distinguishing her assertion of the transgressive difference of "woman" from writers who would simplistically affirm the difference of "actual women" as they have been constructed under patriarchy, for MacKinnon both share a similar difficulty.[16] So long as actual women are in a condition of subordination, woman's difference and its creative capacity cannot become actual.

On a Hegelian reading, it might be ventured that MacKinnon is doubtful about any project that aims at positively asserting woman's difference while her capacity as a "person" (the subject of abstract right) and that of a "subject" (one capable of moral judgment and action) lack effective recognition in society at large. In the absence of these admittedly abstract but still necessary forms of recognition, legally enshrining women's characteristic roles, activities, types of relationship, ethical orientation, and myths (e.g., Irigaray's "sexuate rights"[17]) institutionalizes women's place within a set of practices that are not their own. In this, it suggests the problems of Hegel's account of women in part 3, section 1 of the *Philosophy of Right*, where he assigns the ethical life of women, a class of persons who remain effectively unrecognized as subjects of abstract right within Hegel's system (1821: 158-181). On this account, if MacKinnon seems concerned to establish women's position as the subjects of abstract right, that need not betray an adherence to a metaphysics of transcendence. Rather, just as Hegel endorsed the abstract subject of rights as a starting point for his ethics of *Sittlichkeit*, we may understand MacKinnon as working toward a similar starting point for a positive feminist jurisprudence.[18]

If this reading is right, then the real distinction between MacKinnon and the postmodernist approach suggested by Cornell lies not with a different vision for the future, but with a different assessment of what will be necessary to achieve it. For MacKinnon, *mimesis*, a retrieval of feminine difference that is not a hollow repetition of the "sameness" of masculine domination, cannot take place in the absence of the social and legal recognitions that would permit women to claim difference as their own.[19] If MacKinnon is skeptical with regard to "the feminine" as it presently exists, that need not be the symptom of an inflated regard for the masculine subject. It may be the considered observation that the blossoming of creativity that accompanies the liberation of the oppressed cannot ever be adequately anticipated while their oppression continues (cf. Hegel 1821: 57R).[20] Because a change in power relations brings about changes in the characteristic orientations and activities of both the oppressed and the oppressors, it is impossible to predict with precision what will survive and what will go under.

Conclusion

In this chapter, I have argued that a thoroughgoing social constructionism such as that of Catharine MacKinnon entails neither that women are cast in the role of permanent victims nor that they are condemned simply to engage in a battle for (masculine) transcendence. A narrative of complete and total subordination, when told from the point of view of the oppressed, must be subversive. In itself it occasions a contradiction in the totality of the system and begins its deconstruction. Moreover, just as a moment of absolute fear was a critical starting point for the emergence of consciousness and its coming to self-recognition in labor in Hegel's parable of Lordship and Bondage, so a narrative of feminine construction under conditions of sexual violence can serve as a starting point for women's self-recognition.

Likewise, constructionist accounts need not endorse a politics of revenge in which the oppressed strive merely to reverse the structure of domination without dismantling it. I have argued that despite her negative descriptions of women's condition under domination, MacKinnon does not reject a retrieval of the feminine, nor endorse the freedom of the transcendent subject. MacKinnon's endeavor to empower women "as litigants" does not entail that this is her final goal. Using Hegel's own account, I have argued that this may better be understood as the necessary starting point for an authentic recovery of "difference." If constructionists such as MacKinnon are right, even such prosaic political changes as enabling the oppressed to assume roles as litigants for their causes may be the means for animating a radically different vision for the future.

EPILOGUE

Hegel's critique of abstract universalism, at least when it is understood in all its ramifications, does not so much dispute universalism's claims as it offers a way for understanding how it must come to expression in the world. Although Hegel embraced the Enlightenment dictum that the "infinite" will of the autonomous individual was indeed the starting point for morality, he likewise insisted that it was only through cultural practice that we could come to grasp the full meaning of this concern. Outside of particular social orders and the passionate historical struggles by which they are transformed, universality and rationality remain empty ideals. This does not mean that they have no purpose to serve, but rather that their precise meaning must elude the abstract understanding.

In the preceding chapters I have explored the implications of Hegel's historical realism with the particular concerns of feminist social critics in mind. It should be observed, however, that Hegel's account has applications beyond the development of women's agency. In addition to the well-documented transformations of universality and rationality discussed in Marxian Critical Theory, it would be most interesting to apply a Hegelian reading of this kind to the continuing movement against the oppression of African Americans. Historical figures such as Frederick Douglass were particularly skillful at using the existing categories of liberty and equality to justify actions that went well beyond the prevailing conceptions of the slaveholding society.[1] As with the feminist social criticism with which I have been concerned here, African-American critique of American society has more often than not drawn upon and reconceptualized the ethical and political values of that society. As such, it too could provide an interesting site for coming to a more embracing grasp of Hegel's social theory.

If I have succeeded in my purpose here, the preceding chapters should have established that certain important parts of Hegel's philosophical approach are effective instruments for understanding the implications of social critical movements such as feminism. Once again, this is not because of any explicitly feminist or otherwise "radical" aspects of Hegel's own political theory, but due to its unique manner of combining the concerns of universality and reason with concrete historical practices, persons, and movements. It is precisely because Hegel's conception of the right takes on its concrete meaning through those practices, and through the historical agency of the persons and groups who serve to undermine and transform them, that the content of Hegelian political theory is itself ever changing. As the unfolding rather than the application of categories, Hegel's thought is open to new and unexpected revisions.

If this is right, it may explain why a political theory that is so explicitly sexist in many of its concrete proposals has nevertheless maintained the interest of a wide range of feminist theorists. Just as importantly, however, it suggests a reason that Hegelians who are not feminists have a reason to be interested in what the feminist critics have to say. Just as Hegel could not construct an effective theoretical barrier against the onslaught of historical movements for which he seemed to have had little sympathy, contemporary Hegelian thought is ever subject to rethinking with the reality of social and political change. In the end, such a vulnerability may be its greatest strength.

NOTES

Introduction

1. See, for example, Carla Lonzi's (1991) "Let's Spit on Hegel."
2. See also O'Brien 1976, Irigaray 1977, Benjamin 1983, and Ring 1991.
3. On this point, see Baier 1987: 39.
4. Hegel 1821: 322, 322R, cf. 1837b: 53. For Hegel, autonomy accrues primarily to the state, and only secondarily to individuals as members of the state.

Note: unless otherwise specified, references to the *Philosophy of Right* (1821) are to *paragraph* numbers in the Nisbet translation.

5. I employ the masculine pronoun here because, as I detail in chapters 1 and 7 to follow, Hegel provides no indication that women partake of this right, as their life remains tied to the "universal" and apart from the particular interests of the individual (Hegel 1807: 457, 463; 1821: 166, 166R, 166A).

Note: Unless otherwise specified, references to the *Phenomenology of Spirit* (1807) are to *paragraph* numbers in the Miller translation.

6. Cf. Wood 1990: 30-32.
7. This kind of work has been most famously associated with theorists associated with the Frankfurt School. See, for example, Habermas 1968, 1973, and Marcuse 1932, 1968. (See also Lukacs 1954, 1978.) I shall assume that Hegel's political thought can be at least as interestingly "re-thought" in light of feminist critique as it has been in light of class struggle. (On this point, see Balbus 1982.)

Chapter 1. Historically Emergent Agency

1. See, for example, Taylor 1979, Smith 1989, Wood 1990, and Brod 1992. Such a focus was also in evidence among those who sought variously to employ parts of Hegel's analysis in the *Phenomenology of Spirit* (e.g., Sartre 1956; de Beauvoir 1980, Kojeve 1947, Marcuse 1968, Habermas 1968).
2. This point has been argued at length by Charles Taylor (1967, 1974, 1983). Although (as will become clear below) my discussion here is deeply indebted to Taylor's

approach to Hegel, it will also call into question the degree to which Hegel's concerns parallel those of Wittgensteinian action theorists (e.g., Anscombe 1963, Kenny 1965, Melden 1961). While the latter concern themselves with attempts to describe the distinction between action and non-action, Hegel's concern is primarily with the transition from action to self-conscious action.

3. Hegel's critique of the Cartesian assumption of a capacity for immediate "self-illumination" follows that of thinkers in the *Sturm und Drang* movement, especially Johann Georg Hamann. For Hamann, the creative co-presence of God in our actions renders self-knowledge (i.e., knowledge of our agency) subject to all the difficulties accruing to knowledge of the Divine. To know ourselves, it is first necessary that we grasp all aspects of our being (Beiser 1987: 21). Although Hegel rejects Hamann's "mystical" solution to the problem of self-knowledge, his approach to the problem in terms of Spirit's rise to self-consciousness out of unthinking activity reflects a similar set of concerns.

4. Taylor likens this kind of agent-knowledge to Anscombe's (1963) account of "non-observational" knowing.

5. For a more detailed account of this objection to the causal theory, see Taylor 1970: 75–80.

6. The use of the term "self-ignorance" to describe Hegel's account of the development of agency originates with Frithjof Bergmann.

7. It should be noted that this divisive role is necessary for the development of self-consciousness, and cannot be dismissed as merely "evil." Nevertheless, Hegel's subsequent devaluation of women's role in the ethical life of the *Philosophy of Right*, as well as their insignificance in the first ethical unity immediately preceding the breakdown, makes it clear that Hegel conceives women's agency as merely instrumental, and, moreover, that it is excluded from the movement toward universal self-consciousness. Writers such as Jean Bethke Elshtain (1981) and Patricia Jagentowicz Mills (1986) have argued that this constitutes a critical limitation of Hegel's system. Susan Easton (1984), however, detects a contradiction between Hegel's claims about the merely instrumental role of women, and the activities they actually perform in his narrative. Easton argues that the role taken up by Antigone in particular, and women in general in this part of the *Phenomenology* may well have to go beyond what Hegel seems to have intended if their agency is to be effective in the manner that he suggests that it is.

8. The emergence of the "individual" is thus linked in Hegel's chronology to the breakdown of the unity of the religious and civil life of the community.

9. It is worth noting here that on Hegel's account self-conscious agency develops through the law *(Gesetz)*, and its historical evolution. The diremption of the law of the ethical state in the Spirit section of the *Phenomenology* corresponds to the diremption of consciousness ("Lordship and Bondage") in the section on Self-Consciousness, indicating that Hegel understood the latter to be the social embodiment of the former conflict. On a Hegelian account, at least some conflicts within the law are reducible neither to conflicts among individuals or between individuals and the state, nor to relations within some more basic system (e.g., economics). Rather, the law and disputes within it express the life of a community, and the forms of agency operative within it. (For a detailed discussion of the "three-fold structure" of the *Phenomenology*, see Lukacs 1954: 466–533.)

10. "Innocence . . . is merely non-action, like the mere being of a stone, not even that of a child" (Hegel 1807: 468). For Hegel, even the child has the capacity to be educated to the ethical life of the community, and, thus, to come to a transformation of agency. As I shall discuss below, Hegelian "autonomy" is defined in terms of the capacity for an ethical education of this kind.

11. Compare this to paragraphs 119-128 of the *Philosophy of Right* (1821). Here too, Hegel condemns the right of subjective intention wherein the agent lays claim only to those consequences of an action which she knew subjectively from the start, as "an empty assertion of the abstract understanding" (124). To the extent that the self-conscious subject only becomes actual, only becomes a "self" as an *agent,* "What the subject *is, is the series of its* actions. If these are a series of worthless productions, then the subjectivity of volition is likewise worthless" (124). To the extent that self-conscious subjectivity, "the dignity *(Ehre)* of being a thinking individual and a will," is a precipitate of "objective" activity (i.e., activity that takes on its particular meaning in the context of the beliefs, practices, and institutions of a community), the former is not at liberty to flee the objective characterizations of that community toward the innocence of some pure willing in the past (120R).

12. Hegel uses the term "guilt" *(Schuld)* to refer both to the sense of "moral" responsibility to which we are most accustomed, and responsibility for the condition of the one's community (what is at stake in this passage). He writes in the Introduction to the *Philosophy of History* (1837c):

[Man] can be guilty—guilty not only of evil but of good, and not only concerning this or that particular matter and all that happens around him *(Sittlichkeit),* but also the good and evil attaching to his individual freedom *(Moralität).* (44)

13. This is consistent with Hegel's view in the *Philosophy of Right* (1821), that the concrete interests of the individual within a state must be those of a class (308R, 311R). Hegel was aware (and apparently worried as well) about the political implications of this doctrine for the ills of a complex modern state. After noting the dangers of poverty for the state, for example, he observes that "within the conditions of a society hardship at once assumes the form of a wrong inflicted by this or that class" (244A).

14. Already this suggests a coherent account of broad political claims such as "All men are sexist" or "All whites are racist." I shall cover the issue of collective responsibility in detail in chapter 5.

15. Hegel uses the case of Oedipus to illustrate this point:

[T]he son does not recognize his father in the man who has wronged him and whom he slays, nor his mother in the queen whom he makes his wife. . . . [A] power which shuns the light of day ensnare the ethical self-consciousness, a power which breaks forth only after the deed is done, and seizes the doer in the act. (1807: 469)

16. Hegel's linking social meaning with universality may have a significance in German that does not carry over into the translation. In what appears to be an early argument against "private language" at the end of chapter 1 of the *Phenomenology,* Hegel argues that it is impossible to *mean (meinen)* solely by appeal to what is personal or mine *(mein);* one must appeal to what is general or universal *(allgemein)* (1807: 110).

What is *allgemein* is shared by the community (*Gemeinshaft*). On this point, I am indebted to Michael Forster. (See also 1821: 104R.)

17. To say that my action embodies the interests of a group does not entail that the group whose interest it embodies is my own. Cases of self-defeating action, where the interests of a dominant group are supported by the action of a subordinated group will be central to the discussion of feminism below. To find my actions embodying the interests of (and thereby actualizing) a group whose self-concept is defined over against that of my own group is the mark of Hegelian "subordination."

18. It will be an another important implication of this account that "victimization" and its articulation is part of the development of self-conscious agency. This is manifest not only in the discussion of the *Antigone* but in the parable of "Lord and Bondsman," where the bondsman's awareness of his subordination is a necessary condition for the transformation of his agency. As I shall argue at length in chapters 5 and 6, developing a consciousness of victimization need not be a defeatist strategy for feminism (as some have recently argued), but may be a necessary step in the development of feminine agency.

19. As I shall argue in greater detail in chapters 2 and 3, by revising the Kantian conception of intention, Hegel will attempt to adhere to an ethics of "autonomy" which nevertheless assigns moral worth to the social consequences of action.

20. The social psychological implications of "privatizing" intention, i.e., severing it from its reception in the community, underpin Hegel's critique of Goethe's "Beautiful Soul" *(schöne Seele)* at the end of Chapter VI of the *Phenomenology of Spirit* (1807: 632–671, see especially paragraph 649).

21. "What the subject *is, is the series of its actions.* If these are a series of worthless productions, then the subjectivity of volition is likewise worthless; and conversely, if the series the individual's deeds are of a substantial nature, then so also is his inner will" (Hegel 1821: 124).

22. This is understood by Hegel as the "right" of self-consciousness to be *punished* for its crime. In his view, the criminal, as a conscious subject within the community, has the *right* to retribution:

> He is denied this honor if the concept and criterion of his punishment
> are not derived from his own act; and he is also denied it if he is treated
> simply as a harmful animal which must be rendered harmless, or punished
> with a view to deterring or reforming him. (Hegel 1821: 100R)

Likewise, on the side of the community, its law is "actual" only to the extent that it is embodied in the actions of individuals. The criminal, in breaking the law, attempts to assert mastery over the law and transform it according to her will. Hegel asserts that because an injunction is a law only if it is universal, and because universality is *actual* only if all persons *act* in accord with it, by "breaking the law," the criminal is, in effect, canceling the injunction's universality, and posing crime as law. Therefore, if the law is to retain its force, it must assume the shape of negativity, of "punishment," and negate that act by which it is negated:

> [A]n injury to [the criminal] as an existent will is the cancellation *(au-*
> *fheben)* of the crime, *which would otherwise be regarded as valid,* and the
> restoration of right. (1821: 99)

By the "negation of its negation," the law undergoes a transformation from abstract universality (law as a mere "ought") to a particular punishment, to actual universality (the law expressed in the actions of individuals in the community) (1907: 280). Crime is never merely an "infraction" of the law (as if the law really existed apart from the agency of individuals), but a *perversion* of the law, a potential rival universal which must be "negated."

23. Hegel's sense of the rational freedom of human agency recalls a distinction made by Friedrich Schiller:

> The psyche *(Gemüt)* may be determinable simply because it lacks all de-termination (is indeterminate), or because it is determined in such a way as not to exclude anything, i.e. it embraces all reality. (Schiller 1967: 145)

For Hegel, to respect human freedom is to recognize its capacity to take responsibility for the full compass of its actions (i.e., the "right of the objectivity of action").

24. This applies to both Kantian autonomy, as expressed in the formula, "Never to choose in such a way except that in the same volition the maxims of your action are also present as a universal law" (Kant 1786: 440), and more modern injunctions to act only on certain kinds of rationally endorsed desires.

25. In understanding autonomy as a "consequent" capacity, Hegel follows the conception of human nature developed by Schiller in his letters on *Aesthetic Education* (1967). There he writes of the human being that:

> [W]hat makes him man is precisely . . . that he does not stop short at what Nature herself made of him, but has the power of *retracing by means of Reason* the steps she took on his behalf, of *transforming* the work of blind compulsion into a work of free choice, and of elevating physical necessity into moral necessity (italics mine). (p. 11)

Reason is the capacity to transform what was mere compulsion and drive to free action. What was initially the outcome of other forces must *become* self-conscious choice, and thus take on moral significance.

26. In Hegel's "absolute idealism" both subject and object are constituted by the activity of Spirit. As applied to ethical action, this will mean that both intention and consequence are "constituted" in a single act, and that one cannot take precedence over the other in the evaluation of the act. I shall have more to say about the implications of this for evaluations in normative ethics in chapter 3.

27. Hegel's "right of the objectivity of action" may be seen as the precursor to Sartre's concept of "choice" (or at least his more interesting use of that concept). The "right" to claim that the consequences of my actions, however unforeseen, are my own, implies a kind of responsibility for the rational agent that encompasses the whole of life. Hegel, however, offers an explanation for this responsibility in the collective nature of agency that is largely lacking in Sartre.

28. It has been argued that Hegel's use of "necessary," in at least some cases, comes to little more than "not arbitrary" (see for example, Bergmann 1964, Kaufmann 1965). In a like vein, it might be argued that his use of "universal" sometimes seems closer to "not particular." As already noted, his sense of *allgemein* importantly includes the concept of a community of meaning, though it does not seem (e.g., in his discussion of the clash between the divine and the human laws in chapter 6) that the judgments of such a community need be from, or even aspire to "universality" in the rigorous sense.

29. This has important implications for feminist critique. On the one hand, it opens the possibility for critiques of individual agency on the basis of functional accounts on the social level (see chapter 6 for a discussion of how this may justify a seemingly problematic aspect of feminist normative criticisms). On the other hand, however, it underscores the importance of developing feminist community as a basis for the kind of transformative criticism to which feminism seems to be committed (see chapter 4).

30. The agent cannot "deny" responsibility in the sense that he cannot *authentically* deny it. This is not to say that he cannot "deny" it in the Freudian sense of denial. On a Hegelian account, it would seem that collective denial or rejection is a primitive form of epistemic access to certain kinds of action. I shall take up this theme in my discussion of masculine denial and moral responsibility in chapter 6. (For a rather different account of the link between Hegelian negation and Freudian rejection, see Julia Kristeva, *Revolution in Poetic Language* [1981: 109–164]. For a general discussion of the link between Hegel's and Freud's thought, see Jean Hyppolite [1957], "Hegel's Phenomenology and Psychoanalysis.")

31. "[W]hat the bondsman does is really the action of the lord. The latter's essential nature is to exist only for himself . . . . while the action of the bondsman is impure and inessential" (Hegel 1807: 191). The freedom and autonomy of the individual can *actually* exist only to the extent that they find embodiment in the *action* of the individual. Where an agent's action is defined as other than her own, such freedom is impossible. (For a more detailed discussion of Hegel's "Lordship and Bondage" passage, see chapter 7.)

32. This, of course, is also the plight of Hegel's unpunished criminal, who also finds himself "unrecognized," as an agent, and is not given his due as a rational agent on that account (see note 24 above, and Hegel 1821: 100R).

33. Indeed, the argument might be made that more recent examples of slave systems (in the antebellum southern United States, for example) have not been so confining. To the extent that slaves have been afforded a certain, however tenuous and restricted, sphere of activity for themselves, they have not fallen into the category of absolute denial of self-conscious agency that Hegel describes in the *Phenomenology of Spirit*. Of course, to the extent that the deprivation of "agency" is not absolute, it will be possible for agents to identify with their roles, even if they are relatively bad ones. This kind of identification is of no small importance in coming to a full grasp of the complexity of oppressed agency.

34. Cf. Hegel 1821: 118R.

35. In moving away from this aspect of Taylor's interpretation, I am also setting aside (for my purposes) the issue of whether intentions can stand in a causal relation to action. Still, it is worth noting that Hegel's conception of self-awareness as an achievement does not, by itself, imply that mental phenomena cannot stand in some kind of causal role with respect to action. Even if epistemic access to my intentions and purposes is not immediate, and requires that I engage in certain kinds of activity, it is not clear why this entails that my intentions cannot be ontologically distinct from my action. All that would follow from this is that action would be a necessary condition for my coming to *know* its intention.

Discerning Hegel's own position here is difficult for two reasons. As noted above, Hegel was primarily concerned with the transformation of agency that occurs within the context of society (the emergence of *self*-conscious action), rather than with the distinction between action and non-action taken in the abstract. Secondly, the sense in which action is primitive for Hegel derives from its role in constituting both a set of "external" consequences and an "internal" motive or purpose. As such it is reducible to neither. Although it would be incorrect to say that an intention stands in a causal relation to *action,* however, agency is itself expressive of a contingent relation between intention and consequence. Just as the "triadic" relationship between Spirit, subject, and object defies any easy reduction to realism or idealism in metaphysics, so the relationship between action, intention, and consequences will defy simple reduction in ethics and the philosophy of action.

Chapter 2. Hegel's Critique of "Emptiness"

1. As in previous chapters, unless otherwise specified, I shall use the expression "moral point of view" in Hegel's sense, i.e., to designate the perspective aimed at in applying a formal criterion of right such as the categorical imperative. For my purposes, "impartial" and "moral" may be understood as interchangeable.

2. Seyla Benhabib (1986a) suggests that Hegel's analysis of Kant's moral philosophy can be understood to focus on three major themes: the "procedural" critique of universalizability; the "institutional deficiency" critique; and the critique of Kantian moral psychology (72). My criticisms in this chapter will focus on the procedural critique, although (following Solomon's reinterpretation of Hegel's "emptiness" critique), I shall link this to the institutional deficiency critique. I shall return to some of the issues of moral psychology in chapter 3.

3. For a similar assessment of Hegel's reading of Kant in the context of a more negative assessment of Hegel's own approach to ethics, see Heimo Hoffmeister (1974), "Moral Autonomy in Kant and Hegel," in O'Malley, Algozin, and Weiss, eds.

4. In Hegel's *Phenomenology*, the test of a system, be it a cultural, artistic, religious, or philosophical one, lies with the historical shape of consciousness to which it gives rise. It is through the internal contradictions of each shape of consciousness that a new shape is developed. Just as importantly, however, that new shape also preserves what is consistent in the shape it supplants. In this sense, Hegel's "critiques" always purport to show that past philosophers, insofar as their doctrines escape contradiction, in fact must support his view. With regard to Kantian ethics, Hegelian "phenomenology" tracks its development as a form of self-consciousness, its triumphs as well as its failures.

5. For a discussion of the relationship between Hegel's moral epistemology and constructivism, see Benson 1991.

6. Although this argument is first and most fully articulated in *Natural Law*, its significance extends beyond the aims of Hegel's *Jugendschriften*. This is evident in its reemergence in *The Philosophy of Right* (1821: 135, 135R), the *Phenomenology of Spirit* (1807: 429-434), and the *Lectures on the History of Philosophy* (1837a: III, 460-461).

7. The latter "psychological" line of argument is detailed in section C of Chapter VI of the *Phenomenology of Spirit* (1807), "The Spirit that is Certain of Itself: Morality" (pp. 596-671).

8. In the *Philosophy of Right* (1821), after briefly restating the argument first raised in *Natural Law* (1802–1803) against the use of the categorical imperative to forbid keeping a loan (see below), Hegel continues:

> But if a duty is to be willed merely as a duty and not because of its content, it is a *formal identity* which necessarily excludes every content and determination. The further antinomies and shapes assumed by this perennial *obligation* among which the merely moral point of view of *relationship* simply drifts to and fro without being able to resolve them and get beyond obligation I have developed in my *Phenomenology of Spirit*. (135R)

Clearly, Hegel intends to link the psychological description of the shape of "moral" consciousness to his earlier argument that the categorical imperative is empty.

9. Though Hegel's interests in raising such an objection was not to argue against the institution of private property *per se* (for Hegel's own defense of the holding of property in the context of his account of the development of self-consciousness, see 1821: 41–70, also 1830: §486), he was concerned to show the contingency of that or any other part of the social order.

10. Hegel in fact conflates two distinct charges under the heading of "empty formalism": (1) that "duty . . . willed merely as a duty and not because of a content . . . is a *formal identity*," and excludes "every content and specification"; (2) that "[i]f it is already established and presupposed" that some action or practice is justified, then any line of conduct can be endorsed by Kant's procedure (1821: 135R, cf. 135A, 1802–1803: 438). While (1) may be taken to support the claim that Kant's test is consistent with any line of conduct whatever, (2) tends to support the weaker claim that it is consistent with those actions and practices that are "already established on other grounds." In this chapter, I am concerned with the implications of the weaker claim at (2). (On this distinction, see W. H. Walsh 1969: 24.)

11. See, for example, Marcus Singer 1963: 251–253, Christine Korsgaard 1985: 27–32, 38–39, and Allen Wood 1990: 156–158.

12. "If the specification can be taken up into the form of the pure Concept, if it is not cancelled thereby, then it is justified and has itself become absolute . . . as law and right or duty" (1802–1803: 75).

13. As Onora O'Neill (1975) argues, when Kant enjoins the moral agent to "Act only on that maxim through which you can at the same time will that it should become a universal law," he is really requiring that *two* things be subjected to inspection: "Maxims which are not contrary to duty must be conceivable as a universal law *through* the maxim and *at the same time as* the maxim is held . . . " (69). Kant's first formulation of the categorical imperative in the second section of the *Groundwork* requires that the agent test the coherence of *simultaneously* willing both her maxim *(M)* and its universalization *(UM)* (70). If she cannot consistently hold both the intention expressed in *M* and that expressed in *UM*, then it is not morally possible to act on *M*. Although this appears to be a version of Kant's contradiction in will test, O'Neill argues against earlier writers (Kemp 1958, Dietrichson 1964) that it is implied in the contradiction in conception test as well.

14. This assumes, of course, that all so acting will serve to *eliminate* poverty and not occasion Hegel's other scenario where all are in poverty. Determining which state of affairs would actually be occasioned in a given case remains an important consideration for the Kantian.

15. In fact, (2) also rules out using a charitable practice to achieve one's ends where the universalization of a maxim would will a situation in which that practice does not exist. Korsgaard fails to take account of this because she understands the "succoring the poor" as an isolated action, and not as participation in a practice that would be self-eliminating (1985: 39).

16. It might be thought that in keeping the deposit *A* must be contradicting her purpose, since it involves her in a case of false-promising which would violate the relations of trust and loyalty necessary in any social order (cf. Kant 1785: 403). As Timothy O'Hagan (1987) argues, the duty to pay back deposits may embody a "higher order" duty to keep promises (140–141, see also Wood 1990: 158). If Kant is right, however, that an injunction against lying promises must hold in *any* order, then to the extent that *A* is willing a different social order she is also willing the embodiment of the higher order principle. Unless it is assumed that a system of deposits and loans is the only manner in which that higher order duty can be expressed or that *A* is simply being selfish, both of which are in dispute here, it is impossible to rule out the universalization of her maxim to destroy *P*.

17. For a discussion of the need for normative assumptions in applying the test of the categorical imperative that is sympathetic to Kant's project, see Barbara Herman 1985.

18. Cf. Singer 1961: 292.

19. Singer (1961: 292–295) takes up this objection as raised by Arthur Kenyon Rogers (1922: 67). Stephen Darwall (1986b), in "Kantian Practical Reason Defended," replies to what appears to be a very similar claim against Kant raised by David Gauthier (1986) in his "The Unity of Reason: A Subversive Reinterpretation of Kant" (perhaps lending credence to Singer's observation that "This type of criticism, which stems from Hegel, can probably never be totally eradicated, since there will probably always be someone new to rediscover it" [292]).

20. Kant 1788: 67–71, cf. 1785: 454. Nevertheless, there is a certain asymmetry between theoretical and pure practical reason for Kant. Because the morally good is "supersensuous," it can have no sensuous counterpart, as do the concepts of the understanding. Kant argues, however, that by universalizing the maxim of my action, I can judge my act according to moral principles: "If the maxim of action is not so constituted as to stand the test of being made the form of a natural law in general, it is morally impossible" (1788: 69–70).

21. It will also be necessary to appeal to empirical data in carrying out the test. The conclusion, for example, that no one would leave deposits in a society where everyone stole them rests upon certain psychological and perhaps sociological facts. These, however, do not in any way *ground* the moral judgment. See Wood 1990: 156–158.

22. Hegel discusses this in terms of the multiplicity of "virtues" in different cultures and in different historical epochs of the same culture (1907: 294–295).

23. I am indebted to Elizabeth Anderson for this example.

24. Hegel's own account in the *Philosophy of Right* (1821) describes "Morality" as historically emerging out of "Abstract Right" due to the contradictions of a revenge system. He concludes that the individualistic character of the execution of such a system contradicts its universal ends:

> [R]evenge, as the positive action of a *particular* will, becomes *a new infringe-ment;* because of this contradiction, it becomes part of an infinite progression and is inherited indefinitely from generation to generation. (102)

Although not fully "rational," the revenge system nevertheless has validity at a certain stage of history, and, moreover, the "bad infinity" it occasions is the historical condition for the emergence of a more rational order. The failure of revenge to embody self-sat-isfaction is a historical and systemic failure, not transparent in the formally isolated actions of individuals at the early stages of its development. Hence, the "concept of *Morality* [as opposed to revenge] is not just a requirement; it has emerged in the course off this movement itself" (103). (Whether or not it would have to "emerge" in so obvious and logical a manner as Hegel suggests is another question. The actual social norms governing revenge in "simple societies" are in fact quite complex, and can often avoid falling into the self-contradiction that Hegel suggests [see, e.g., Jon Elster 1990, "Norms of Revenge," *Ethics* 100: 862-885].)

25. It does however introduce an element of cultural and historical relativism into the Kantian picture. For differing Kantian perspectives on this issue, see O'Neill 1989: 206-218, and Herman 1985.

26. Of course, the legitimation conditions governing this conflict will vary ac-cording to the social and historical conditions of a given social order. In chapters 3 and 8, I shall explore the modern conflicts which Hegel sees as occasioned by a moral commitment to rights. For Hegel, it is just this tendency of the moral point of view to engender ethical progress through conflict that is its own greatest "virtue."

27. Though this has been the focus of most Hegelian objections. Walsh 1969, for example, cites the possible purposes of convinced totalitarians as counting against Kant's argument (24-25). Singer 1961 deplores such appeals to "abnormal" agents who "do not care what happens at all" (294). As I point out below, however, the greatest problem for the Kantian concerns not agents who do not *care,* but those whose cares are structured differently.

28. This would, of course, be the Marxist interpretation of the system of private property assumed in the example. As noted above, however, this is not Hegel's view, nor should his critique in *Natural Law* be understood to represent a difference of opinion with Kant regarding the actual "rightness" of a system where the bourgeoisie pay back their loans. Hegel's point, rather, is that the "right" just *is* a function of the actual practices and institutions of a social system.

29. For Hegel, as for Kant, to act in a manner that does not respect the freedom of others is to be unfree oneself. Hegel's concern with socially opaque *collective* rela-tions of oppression is evident in his criticism of the ancient Greeks in *Reason in History* (1837c):

> [T]he Greeks . . . and the Romans likewise, only knew that some are free—not man as such. This not even Plato and Aristotle knew. For this reason the Greeks not only had slavery, upon which was based their whole life and the maintenance of their splendid liberty, but their freedom itself was partly an accidental, transient, and limited flowering, and partly a thralldom of human nature. (23-24)

30. In chapter 6, I shall examine some of the most significant and controversial of the "revelations" of early feminist consciousness-raising along these lines. Most

importantly, consciousness-raising groups provided an alternative "objective" space, where certain background assumptions no longer held. This made it possible to morally ground certain kinds of generalizations (e.g., "Women have a *right* to abortion"), which could not be so grounded given the assumptions of the prevailing ("patriarchal") political order. As I shall discuss in detail there, the "moral point of view" has a critical function here, but only in the context of assumptions provided by a particular form of community.

31. Such a state of affairs may, somewhat anachronistically, be read into the gloss on *Antigone* (1807: 464-476). Before Antigone's action against the law, the violence of Creon's decree remained "unmediated" and not accessible to reflective awareness. Only when that decree was reexamined in the light of the considerations that Antigone's rebellion embodied was it possible reflectively to grasp the nature of the violation. Although the account of *Antigone* is "pre-moral" in the chronology of the *Phenomenology,* tragic acts that serve to transform rather than to honor the categories of the ethical life are of continuing importance in Hegel's account. I address how such epic change might occur after the appearance of the moral point of view in chapter 3.

32. "Even if . . . by its utmost effort [the will] accomplishes nothing, and only good will is left . . . it would shine like a jewel for its own sake as something which has its full value in itself" (Kant 1785: 394).

33. "It must be maintained that since morality is something absolute, this is not the standpoint of morality and there is no morality in it" (1802-1803: 434). It is this same perceived demand for absolute purity, i.e., that morality make no appeal to sensuous content, that forms the backdrop for Hegel's attack on Kant's moral psychology in the *Phenomenology of Spirit* (1807).

34. This shift in emphasis will prove important in providing a groundwork for feminist ascriptions of agent-responsibility, where the intentions of the offending agent, *qua* individual, are not primarily at stake. As the discussion in chapters 7 and 8 will make clear, sexism can persist in the absence of any "egoistic" motivations on the part of individuals.

35. Kant himself called attention to the opacity of the "inner principles" that guide our acts. For him, however, it is the impossibility of eliminating psychological egoism that underlies our inability to credit ourselves with moral worthiness (1785: 407).

36. In chapter 3, I take up how this applies specifically to "moral reality."

37. As with other aspects of Hegel's account, this point is, of course, closely akin to Schiller's critique of Kant's moral psychology. For further discussion of the relation between Schiller and Hegel, see Kaufmann 1965: 45-58, and Shklar 1976: 113-115.

38. I shall suggest a concrete example of this in my discussion of consciousness raising in chapter 4.

39. "As long as background beliefs can be articulated and subjected to criticism from the scientific community, they can be defended, modified, or abandoned in response to such criticism . . . . [O]bjectivity, then, is a characteristic of a community's practice of science rather than of an individual's, and the practice of science is understood in a much broader sense than most discussions of the logic of scientific method suggest . . . . [S]cientific method . . . involves the subjection of hypotheses and the background assumptions in light of which they seem to be supported by data to varieties of conceptual criticism, which is a social rather than an individual activity" (74).

Though Hegel would undoubtedly have agreed with the passage in spirit, he would likely have drawn the contrast between universality (the social) and particularity (the individual in abstraction from society), with the "individual" as that which mediates the two (see the next section).

40. Longino thus concludes that the fact that feminist critiques of science have generally been limited to biology and the social sciences (see, e.g., Doell and Longino 1988) need not show that the "hard sciences" are more objective. Their apparent invulnerability to political critique may instead indicate a debilitating lack of critical discourse with respect to their guiding assumptions.

41. As Hegel remarks in *Reason in History* (1837c):

Spirit's development, its progression and ascent to an ever higher concept of itself . . . is connected with the degradation, destruction, annihilation of the preceding mode of actuality which the concept of Spirit had evolved. This is the result, on the one hand, of the inner development of the Idea and, on the other, of the activity of individuals, who are its agents and bring about its actualization. It is at this point that appear those momentous collisions between existing, acknowledged duties, laws, and rights and those possibilities which are adverse to this system, violate it, and even destroy its foundations and existence. (38–39)

Hegel believes that these conflicts also mark the "Moral" stage of Spirit, though through dramatic "conflicts of duty" rather than outright violations (cf. 1821: 112R, 139R). For Hegel, the appearance of the moral point of view, which reaches its apex in the Kantian concern for the autonomous will, decisively alters the ethical world (cf. 21R, 135R). I shall take up Hegel's understanding of the moral point of view as a "starting point" in chapter 3.

42. It is, of course, a key feature of Hegel's historical account of rationality, that actions may be *more or less* rational, depending upon what stage of "self-satisfaction" they represent. Systems of revenge, for example, do represent a certain kind of rational development, but not advanced to the degree of a social system based upon legal rights (Hegel 1821: 104).

43. Onora O'Neill, in "Reason and Autonomy in *Grundlegung* III" (O'Neill 1989), argues that Kant's emphasis upon universalization may be linked to his concern that rational agents adopt a "strategy" for developing an autonomous will, free from all alien influence:

One corollary of refusal to bow under an alien yoke is that what count as the principles of reason cannot hinge on variable and contingent matters, all of which, however, intimately human, are alien causes. Would-be reasoners must then at least adopt the strategy of not acting on principles that accept such alien authorities. They must act only on maxims on which others whose contingent circumstances and character differ can also act. (58)

By adopting something like the Formula of the Universal Law as a test of our will, we may be developing a useful psychological disposition toward the performance of right action.

On a Hegelian account, however, such a strategy may prove ill-suited to its task. To the extent that achieving self-conscious agency is, at least in part, a matter of receiving a certain kind of recognition from another, one's contingent position in a relationship of power may affect what an agent can and cannot will, consistent with respect for oneself and others. If a master insults a slave, that action serves merely to reaffirm the slave's subordinate status. For the slave to direct the same insult toward the master, however, might be an assertion of agency, and of the right to be respected. Though the slave could not will that she receive the same treatment, to the extent that such behavior (perhaps in concert with other slaves) serves to embody the agency of the slave (and, thus, her worthiness of respect), such action would be justified. (Of course, on Hegel's account, it might also be a display of respect on the part of the slave, since her submission fails to recognize the self-consciousness of the master.) This gives an interesting twist to Hegel's remark that the agency of the individual who would advance history "is not so sober as to adjust [its] ambition to circumstances; nor is [it] very considerate" (Hegel 1837c: 43).

44. Nevertheless, it is not clear that *all* applications of the Formula of the Universal Law need rely upon socially particular background assumptions in so damaging a manner as does the "loan" example upon which Hegel focuses his attention. For a response to Hegel that seeks systematically to "organize" Kant's various examples, see Timothy O'Hagan's "On Hegel's Critique of Kant's Moral and Political Philosophy," in Priest, ed. 1987: 140–142.

45. It also does not show that a formal procedure could not do more to take account of historically opaque background assumptions than Kant's Formula of the Universal Law did. Contemporary Kantians such as Rawls have sought to interpret Kantianism in such a manner as to permit principles and judgments mutually to inform one another toward a "reflective equilibrium," when developing a formal criterion (1971: 20–21). This flexibility makes Rawls's procedure more sensitive to transformations in social and political awareness than the test of the categorical imperative. Sibyl Schwartzenbach (1987), for example, develops an interesting "Rawlsian" argument that Rawls's claim that the two principles of justice could be consistent with either welfare state capitalism or market socialism relies on background assumptions that exclude women's reproductive labor from consideration. (Similar "radical readings" can extend to metaethics as well. See, for example, Lynne Arnault's (1989) critique of Hare, "The Radical Future of a Classic Moral Theory.")

46. This commitment to rationalism has motivated writers such as Lawrence Blum (1982) to treat both Kant's and Hegel's approaches as both antithetical to feminist aims. I take up these charges in detail in chapter 6.

47. "Those who speak philosophically about right, morality, and ethics and at the same time seek to exclude thought, appealing instead to feeling, heart, emotion, and inspiration, bear witness to the profound contempt into which thought and science have fallen" (Hegel 1821: 21R). Of course, Hegel is equally critical of the ethical "rationalism" that would take abstract universality as something more than a starting point for ethics. I discuss the implications of Hegel's commitment to reason for feminism in chapter 6.

48. Of course, it is perhaps Hegel's most enduring contribution to have underscored the very limited usefulness of a purely abstract standard, and the difficulties that follow from failing to take note of the limits.

49. Of course, in Hegel's epistemology such errors *might* in fact challenge the standard, if they showed that the standard could not, effectively, be met. As Hegel remarks in the *Phenomenology of Spirit* (1807):

> [T]he criterion for testing is altered when that for which it was to have been the criterion fails to pass the test; and the testing is not only a testing of what we know, but also a testing of the criterion of what knowing is. (85)

Hegel's target in the passage is the "standard" (*Maßstab*) implicit in Kant's epistemology, and the latter's conclusion that knowledge of the things-in-themselves is impossible. As Taylor (1975) notes, Hegel adopts a pragmatist approach here: "Knowledge there is, and it is . . . the realization of a standard. If the standard we conceive is unrealizable, we have to conceive again" (136). As regards ethical standards, however, it may be the case that Kant has struck on the correct *criterion* (universality), but has gotten the procedure for meeting it wrong. As my discussion below will suggest, in a complex and highly qualified sense, Hegel may be saying something very much like this.

50. Some of Hegel's own remarks in *The Philosophy of History* (1837b, 1837c) might be read to reinforce such a view:

> The application of the [Christian] principle [that all men are free] to secular conditions, the thorough molding and interpenetration of the secular world by it, is precisely the long process of history. (1837c: 24)

51. In the *Encyclopedia* (1830a), Hegel details this dialectical division:

> (1) The first is *Universality*—meaning that it is in free equality with itself as in its specific character. (2) The second is *Particularity*—that is, the specific character, in which the universal continues serenely equal to itself. (3) The third is *Individuality*—meaning the reflection-into-self of the specific characters of universality and particularity; which negative self-unity has complete and original determinateness, without any loss to its self-identity or universality. (§ 163)

In the remarks to §163 and in the *Philosophy of Right* (1821), Hegel ties this to the universality at which his ethical theory aims (1821: 5–7).

52. Hegel alludes here to his distinction between the analytic and ahistorical grasp of reality afforded by the "Understanding" *(Verstand)* and the dialectical and historical grasp of "Reason" *(Vernunft)*. Although Hegel (in contrast to the Romantics) accepts the need for the "divisive" role of the Understanding, it is his ubiquitous complaint against Kantianism that it remains moored at that level and never attains the "conceptual" grasp that Reason provides (see Hegel 1807: 32; 1831: 45–48).

53. The power of Spirit *(Geist)* to bring about what is, for the Understanding, an "inconceivable transformation," calls up themes from Christian theology. Augustine describes the power of the Holy Spirit *(Heiliger Geist)* to justify human beings in terms of a similarly inconceivable transformation which lies outside their direct willing by "grace" (Augustine, *Sermons* 109, 5; 342, 5, in J.P. Migne, ed. 1841-1842: XXXVIII, 675; XXXIX, 1504). The conceptual structure of the fundamental problem of Patristic theology—how essentially sinful humanity could be worthy of being taken up into the Godhead—bears an interesting similarity to the Kantian problem of how a sensuously affected being could perform an action of moral worth. Patristic theologians conceived the grace of the Holy Spirit manifest in the Church as a source of inner transformation through which human beings could participate in the Divine life. Hegelian Spirit, manifest in the living institutions and practices of a community, has a like capacity to transform the agent's willing. Hegel called the concept of the Trinity "the principle of all speculative philosophy." (See Hegel 1837a, III, 10–23.)

54. "[F]or us men it is wholly impossible to explain how and why the *universality of a maxim as a law*—and therefore morality—should interest us" (Kant 1785: 460).

As Findlay (1958) remarks: "[T]he function of Reason is to integrate such notions into new unities, where they will be shown to require each other and to be the necessary conditions of each other." (66). See also Hegel 1837c: 15–16.

55. As I shall discuss in chapter 4, on a Hegelian reading, a critical part of feminist political critique centers on the inability of a self-conscious agent to embrace "feminine agency" as it has been defined in the institutions and practices of modern Western societies. In chapter 7, I argue that this underpins Simone de Beauvoir's seminal discussion of woman as "Other."

56. She *will* find her grasp transformed, and not merely feel obliged or rationally compelled to transform it, only if (1) she is a *self-conscious* agent, i.e., not in some state of denial, and (2), the judgment is consistent with respect for her as a free and responsible individual. The irresistibility of the social judgment, however, is not merely, or even primarily, a matter of the agent's "conscientiousness," but of the extent to which it is embodied in the life (law, religion, etc.) of the community. This underscores the need for institutional change as a precondition of moral transformation.

57. It is the positive role of the "moral point of view" to engender social conflict, thereby mediating the ills of a given set of conventions (Hegel 1821: 112R, 139R). It is thus a "beginning" toward universality, but no more than a starting point toward it (57R, 135R).

58. Moreover, Hegel has a developmental argument for the existence of such a "power." Because (1) self-consciousness is constituted by its action, and (2) it can come to a conceptual grasp of that action only by taking up *as its own* the intersubjective meaning of that action in its community, the fact that we can internalize (and feel responsibility on the basis of) the social meanings of our acts at all is evidence for a capacity to "absorb" universality within us. See chapter 1 for a more detailed discussion of this capacity.

59. Such a view appears to be endorsed in the Additions to Paragraph 7:

"I" as such is primarily in the first place pure activity, the universal which is with itself *(bei sich)*; but this universal determines itself and to that extent . . . ceases to be the universal. Then the third moment [Individuality] is that "I" is with itself in its limitation, in this other, as it determines itself, it nevertheless still remains with itself and does not cease to hold fast to the universal. This moment, then, is the conscious concept of freedom, whereas the two previous moments have been found to be thoroughly abstract and one-sided. (1821: 7A)

The passage goes on to assert that we have access to this universal freedom in "friendship and love," where "we willingly limit ourselves with reference to another even while knowing ourselves in this limitation of ourselves." By conceiving a kind of determinate relationship such as love as the dialectical completion of, and thus higher than "abstract" universality, Hegel's account anticipates feminist criticisms of universalism (e.g., Carol Gilligan's [1982] criticism of Lawrence Kohlberg's "stages" of moral development). For further discission, see chapter 6.

60. Once again, Hegel's concerns appear to recapitulate those of Patristic theology. The Arian heretics denied that a particular human being (Christ) was "consub-

stantial" with universal Being (God the Father), and made the kingdom of God ever beyond the earthly community of the Church. Similarly, Hegel believes that Kant's denial that we have access to the genuine (Ideal) union of particular desire and universality makes morality an endless "ought-to-be," always beyond the grasp of human community. (There is, of course, a critical distinction between the Arian and the Kantian claims, since the former simply denies that the union of particular and universal is possible, while Kant famously asserts that we cannot know *how* it is possible.) Compare Hegel's assessment of Arianism in the *Lectures on the History of Philosophy* (1837a, III, 20-22) with that of the "Postulates of Practical Reason" (461-464). For a discussion of Hegel's criticism of Kant and Fichte in the light of his specifically theological and religious writings, see Rose 1981: 92-120, esp. 107.

61. See Avineri 1972: 155f, and Taylor 1975: 443-446, 1979: 108-112.

62. It is characteristic of Hegel's system to assail the "rationality" of particular forms of understanding by consigning them to a relatively "primitive" rank in his chronology. His discussion of Newtonian physics in chapter 3 of the *Phenomenology of Spirit* (1807), i.e., at the pre-self-conscious level of "Force and the Understanding," may be a striking example of this. (I am indebted to Michael Forster for this observation.)

63. "The later universal . . . is potentially but not yet actually present in the preceding one . . . . Spirit, in taking this new historical step, is . . . in a state of unconsciousness, which the great men arouse to consciousness" (1837c: 38, 40).

64. These observations are based upon the conception of agency and ethical transformation discussed in previous chapters, and thus prescind from other aspects of his philosophy of history (for a similar reading, see Taylor 1979: 95-100). It is among the most controversial aspects of that philosophy whether or not Hegel consistently understood his own judgments to issue from a chronological "End of History." For a discussion of this issue favoring an "absolutist" view, see Plant 1983: 233-243.

65. All of these concepts take on a certain technical meaning in Hegel's philosophy of history and its account of the ethical transformations of Spirit. I shall take them up specifically in chapter 3.

Chapter 3. Hegel's Phenomenology and Impartial Justification

1. As discussed in chapter 1, Hegel also uses the term *"Sittlichkeit"* to describe the primitive ethical unity of ancient Athens. As will be discussed below, Hegel does not think that this kind of unreflective communitarianism is possible or desirable in the modern state. His use of the term *"Sittlichkeit,"* however, serves a dual purpose. Firstly, it distinguishes his approach in ethics from that of more conventional moral philosophers (in particular, Kant and Fichte). Secondly, it conveys the sense in which the modern *Sittlichkeit* represents the completion of the dialectical process beginning with the breakdown of the ancient unity. It is central to Hegel's demonstration of the completeness of his system that the categories with which he begins reemerge (after having been mediated through the contradictions of history) at the end: "[T]he [philosophical] science exhibits itself as a *circle* returning upon itself, the end being wound back into the beginning, the simple ground, by the mediation . . ." (Hegel 1831: 842; see also 1807: 806-

807, 1830a: §§14-15). The modern *Sittlichkeit* must both recapitulate the unity of its primitive forerunner and accommodate the hard-won "rights" of self-consciousness upon which modern societies are based.

2. See, e.g., Taylor 1975: 449-461. Seyla Benhabib (1986a) has called attention to the managerial control of the state implicit in the point of view that Hegel takes up Part III of the *Philosophy of Right* (1821), with its "System of needs" (97-101). I shall address this point briefly below. As noted in the Introduction, however, my approach to Hegel, while closely tied to the doctrines articulated in his writings, is in no way tied to the kinds of political conclusions that he sought to draw from them. As Walter Kaufmann has pointed out, "What Hegel actually did in his works was quite different from what he thought . . . needed to be done" (note to Friedrich Nietzsche, *The Gay Science* (1966): §369).

3. See Hegel 1821: 244, 244A. Plant (1983) notes that Hegel is "strikingly modern" in his understanding of how social attitudes and material conditions both play a part in the development of a collective sense of social injustice (214-215). If the reader of the *Philosophy of Right* is an administrator, this will have precisely the "managerial" overtones of which writers such as Habermas and Benhabib have been critical. If, on the other hand, the reader is a member of the "penurious rabble" (or some similarly situated class), then its implications may be entirely different.

4. See Railton 1986: 172. For a parallel account of the paradoxical aspects of Hegel and epistemological realism, see Westphal 1989: 1-3.

5. In the phenomenological account of the *Philosophy of Right* (1821), the moral point of view emerges specifically in the context of the development of property relations. The contradictions of the more primitive relations of the social contract (revenge), establish the conditions for a universal conception of moral "wrong." Hence, Hegel can say that "*[M]orality* is not just a requirement; it has emerged in the course of this movement itself" (103).

6. Hegel traces this development historically in the *Phenomenology of Spirit* (1807). Emerging from its destructive and anarchic development in the wake of the French Revolution ("Absolute Freedom and Terror"), Spirit finds its willing stripped of all positive social determination, and thrown back upon its own pure willing:

> [T]he universal will itself . . . it now knows itself to be insofar as it is a pure knowing or a pure will. Consequently, it knows that will to be itself, and knows itself to be essential being; but not essential being as an *immediate existence*, not will as revolutionary government or anarchy striving to establish anarchy, nor itself as the centre of this faction or the opposite faction; on the contrary, the *universal will* is its *pure knowing and willing* and *it* is the universal will *qua* this pure knowing and willing. (594)

As the dialectic of master and slave in Greek and Roman antiquity marked the beginning of self-consciousness as we know it, it is only with the Enlightenment (and its culmination in the "Reign of Terror" following the French Revolution) that the identification of right with the will of the self-conscious individual "conceptually" emerges.

7. This is consistent with the dialectical account discussed in chapter 2, section 4 above, where the synthesis of the universal and the particular is the "Individual" (cf. 1821: 5-7, 1830: §163).

8. Hegel is particularly concerned with how the central concerns of modern morality differ from those that he perceives in earlier ethical systems:

> In recent times especially, it has become customary to enquire about the motives of actions, although the question used simply to be: "Is this man honest *(rechtschaffen)?* Does he do his duty?" Now we seek to look into people's hearts, and thereby presuppose a gulf between the objective realm of actions and the inner, subjective realm of motives. (Hegel 1821: 121A; see also 1830: §147R)

9. See also 1802–1803: 434–435.

10. Though Hegel here recognizes the need for a moral "refuge" from socio-political "alienation," as I shall discuss below, deliverances from the moral point of view may also serve as the goad to change by stirring a conflict between the person and the law.

11. For a similar account of the "completion" of *Moralität* in the institutions and practices of *Sittlichkeit,* see Taylor 1979: 82–95.

12. Hegel explicitly employs the term "empiricism" in his early contrast between classical social contract theorists and Kantian *"a priorism"* in the *Natural Law* essay. There, he assails the former's uncritical (and, he thinks, inconsistent) reliance upon peculiar inclinations and capacities in a state of nature. This contrast is strongly suggested in the dichotomy discussed in paragraph 57 (e.g., in the parenthetical allusion to a Lockean justification for slavery), although in the *Philosophy of Right,* Hegel is primarily concerned to contrast Kantianism with the appeal to feeling that characterized Romanticism:

> Those who speak philosophically about right, morality, and ethics and at the same time seek to exclude thought, appealing instead to feeling, heart, emotion, and inspiration, bear witness to the profound contempt into which thought and science have fallen. (Hegel 1821: 21R)

13. Hegel's "phenomenological historical" account of the rise and demise of slavery occurs in the transition from "Lordship and Bondage" to the "Unhappy Consciousness" of Christianity in the *Phenomenology of Spirit* (1807). This initial historical flowering and demise did not involve any function for the "moral point of view" as discussed here. On Hegel's account, its historical passing occurred with the demise of ancient Greece and Rome, many centuries before "morality" in its characteristically modern forms had entered onto the stage of world history. More importantly, as will be discussed below, the historical development of slavery represented a rational, though primitive, embodiment of Spirit, the "immorality" of which was inaccessible until the time of its passing. The background assumptions necessary for coming to a formal grasp of slavery's inconsistency with the universal law were not yet in place.

14. The distinction between mere existence and actual existence is poignantly illustrated in the additions to paragraph 21:

> Truth in philosophy means that the concept corresponds to reality. A body, for example, is reality, and the soul is the concept. But soul and body ought to match one another; a dead body, therefore, still has an existence *(Existenz),* but no longer a true one, for it is a conceptless existence *(Dasein):* that is why the dead body decomposes. The will in its truth is such that what it wills, i.e. its content, is identical with the will itself, so

that freedom is willed by freedom. (Hegel 1821: 21A, see also 10, 270A, and 1830: §7)

15. Hegel employs a similar line of argument in criticizing a hereditary caste system (1821: 206R). Because they fail to accord recognition to the transcendent self-conscious agency of the human being, such systems are necessarily unstable.

16. Hegel explicitly acknowledges that his discussion assumes the earlier discussion in the *Phenomenology* in a footnote to the passage.

17. By characterizing the moral grasp of a concept as "subjective," Hegel means to draw a contrast between that kind of knowledge and the intersubjective or "objective" grasp that comes when a concept is embodied in the practices and institutions of culture. "Subjective" thus becomes a way of expressing *not*, or at least *not-yet* objective. This loose kind of usage, of course, mirrors that sometimes employed with respect to terms such as "necessary" and "universal."

18. Hegel's conception of "morality" is thus rather idiosyncratic. Ordinarily, in asserting that "Slavery ought not to exist," we do not think it necessary to be referring to any actually existing practice. For Hegel, however, for a prohibition to be strictly "moral" as opposed to "legal" or "ethical" it must express a *conflict* between an actual state of affairs and the moral law. Thus, to state that slavery is wrong in a society where the practice of slavery does not exist, either because no practice of slavery exists or because it is legally prohibited, is not to utter a *moral* proposition. The replacement of "morality" with a society guided by an "immanent theory of duties" is central to Hegel's project in the *Philosophy of Right* (cf. 1821: 135R, 138A; see also 1807: 637).

(Should one assert, in the context of a non-slave society, that slavery is wrong *somewhere else* [either historically or geographically], where a slave system does exist, then that is a moral proposition in Hegel's sense, and thus subject to complications. This last category will prove important for my consideration of feminist critique in chapter 5. On a Hegelian account, cross-cultural "applications" of feminist criticisms will thus differ essentially from the "consciousness raising" in which awareness arises initially. Such applications have also occasioned some of the most critical difficulties for feminist theory.)

19. For a detailed discussion of the importance of Kantian morality as a source of dialectical conflict for Hegel, see Lukacs 1954: 146–166.

20. As I shall detail in chapter 6, a parallel case may be made with regard to the freedom and self-expression of men under patriarchy.

21. As noted in chapter 3, for Hegel, achieving individual identity requires that the agent come to self-consciousness as a member of a social class or estate.

> When we say that a human being must be *somebody (etwas)*, we mean that
> he must belong to a particular estate. . . . A human being with no estate
> is merely a private person and does not possess actual universality. (Hegel
> 1821: 207A)

Where a prevailing conception of fairness or equality has been understood as consistent with the subordination of a class of which I am a member, that conception may itself have to be re-thought if it is adequately to reflect my interests.

In the next two sections below, I shall take up the issue of "re-conceptualizing" ethical categories in greater detail. There I shall argue that when a conception of freedom (and the attendant set of practices that has concretely embodied it) has failed systematically to honor the self-conscious agency of a class, that conception may have to be overhauled or "re-conceptualized" by the emergent class before it can adequately reflect its interests. I shall further specify this with respect to the interests of women as an oppressed class in chapter 4.

22. For Hegel, of course, such conflict is important, insofar as it plays a critical role in spurring the development of new social forms. In this, Hegel is far from Romantic calls for the simple unity of the will. He nevertheless faults "morality" for its satisfaction with the split between the particular and the universal, and for not attempting to overcome it:

> It is *not* that the point of view of division . . . ought never to appear at all—on the contrary, it is this which constitutes the distinction between the unreasoning animal and the human being. But the will must not stop short at this point and cling on to particularity instead of the universal as the essential; the point of view of division should be overcome as null and void. (Hegel 1821: 139R)

23. Cf. Hegel 1837c: 23–24. I could, of course, have the latter interest even if I were a slave, or a potential slave. Depending upon the social allocation of essential goods, a subordinated individual may have a (self-defeating) "interest" in her own subordination. This will have important implications for my discussion of sexist subordination in Parts II and III below.

24. For a discussion of Hegel's criticism of repression in Kantian morality, see Peter Laska (1974), "Kant and Hegel on Practical Reason," esp. 134–138.

25. In this sense, the agent is not self-sufficient in freeing herself from the grip of oppressive forms of agency. Such freedom could exist only if her action could express the practices of a society in which oppression did not exist. Though a Kantian conception of autonomy need not exclude reliance upon external influences in moral reflection (at least if that reliance is itself grounded in moral reflection), it likewise assumes the capacity of the morally autonomous agent to act rationally apart from "alien influences." This is an important basis for the "inalienability" of autonomy. For Hegel, it is only when the agent's interests and desires reflect her place within a rational social order (i.e., an order in which the freedom of all persons is embodied concretely) that rational agency is possible. This means that autonomy is impossible *apart from* the influence of a society in which the agent's interests as a self-conscious being are recognized and supported. (Cf. Taylor 1975: 378. For a discussion of the distinction between autonomy and self-sufficiency, see Arthur Kuflik [1984], "The Inalienability of Autonomy," and Stephen Darwall [1988], "Self-Deception, Autonomy, and Moral Constitution.")

26. As Taylor (1979) points out, Hegel politicizes a Kantian ethical theory that "remained at the edges of politics" (82). This is a move that goes beyond the obvious implications of Romantically inspired critiques that called for the cultivation of a capacity in the individual without any explicit reference to the political preconditions of that project.

27. This use of the term "Idea" *(Idee)* is, of course, not that most familiar to contemporary English-speaking philosophers. For Hegel, the Idea is the concept at the end of its process of development. For the more familiar use of idea as a "representation," Hegel reserves the term *Vorstellung.* As Taylor (1975) observes, this distinction is critical in understanding Hegel's idealism: "'Idealism' here does not refer us to the

'ideas' of Cartesians and empiricists, i.e., ideas as the content of the mind; but on the contrary to the Ideas of Plato" (109-110). Nevertheless, it may be questioned how well Platonic Ideas, which exist most fully outside the sensible world, serve to explain Hegelian concepts that *must* be embodied to be fully real. For this point, I am indebted to Frithjof Bergmann.

28. Because the economic system plays such a critical role in shaping social reality in Hegel's account, it is essential to the embodiment of the right that this system be subject to the law (cf. Avineri 1972: 141-152). This point, which recurs through the third part of the *Philosophy of Right*, occasions a typical word-play on the double-meaning of *"Recht"* as both "right" and "law."

29. Slavery is "primitive" in a double sense. First, as an institution, it represents a historically early stage of consciousness's drive to self-satisfaction. Because ontogeny recapitulates phylogeny for Hegel, however, it is also a "primitive" of each individual human consciousness that must be developmentally overcome, or "negated." In chapters 4 and 7, I shall interpret Simone de Beauvoir's feminism as an attempt to understand oppression in general, and women's oppression in particular, as the historical embodiment of this doubly "primitive" stage.

30. This focus upon the public "fitness for subordination" has important implications for such issues as the feminist argument against pornography, as I shall argue in chapter 6.

31. I shall argue in chapters 4 and 8 that this analysis may be useful in clarifying what is at stake in some feminist critiques (e.g., Catharine MacKinnon's (1979) contention that relationships of domination are simply assumed in discussions of "sex difference" [8-10]).

32. Cf. chapter 2, section 3.

33. "To consider something rationally means not to bring reason to bear on the object from outside in order to work upon it, for the object is itself rational for itself; it is the spirit in its freedom . . . . [T]he sole business of science is to make conscious this work which is accomplished by reason of the thing *(Sache)* itself". (Hegel 1821: 31R).

34. This important point has not always been grasped with regard to phenomenological description. For an interesting discussion, see Rose 1981: 79-91.

35. As Lukacs (1954) has noted:

Hegel reached the point where he could see through the formalistic and impotent definitions of constitutional law and grasp the underlying issues of political power. But this vision was blurred by his inability to perceive the creative force inherent in a revolutionary movement of the people. (291, see also Taylor 1975: 73)

Nevertheless, as I shall suggest below, the potential of groups within modern societies to serve as the agents of ethical transformation is strongly suggested by Hegel's conception of collective action, even if Hegel himself did not advocate the exploitation of such potential in his mature political writings.

36. Benhabib goes on to conclude that Hegelian "administrators" could be satisfied where "the pangs of moral conscience" remain unresolved, and social institutions merely "neutralize the distinction between the 'is' and the 'ought'" (89). It is important to emphasize, however, that Hegel never abandoned his concern (taken from earlier writers such as Goethe and Schiller) that a society's institutions and practices genuinely

embody wholeness of character. Whatever one's assessment of Hegel's notion of a "universal class," to construe the latter as distant, bureaucratic overseers of "universality" might entail, contrary to Hegel's repeated assertions, that the universal could be imposed or applied. If the universal is to overcome the contradiction between particular interests and the right, then its administrators must act so as to "actualize and maintain the universal contained within the particularity of civil society" (Hegel 1821: 249). (For an earlier, but similar assessment to that of Benhabib, see Habermas 1968: 20–24. For a critique, see Rose 1981: 24–47.)

37. Hegel's dread of the "rabble" *(Pöbel)* may have roots in both the Jacobin reign of terror and the rebellions against the Bonapartist regime in Bavaria while he was rector of the gymnasium at Nuremberg. Hegel attempted to distinguish his approval of the struggles of the "people" *(Volk)* from his condemnation of the rabble, for whom, in his view, all respect for civil society was lacking. (This is especially evident in his "Letters," e.g., 1984: 195.) He linked the formation of a rabble to the illegitimate imposition of a formal criterion of right on a society. As I point out below, however, it is unclear exactly how, given a Hegelian understanding of the emergence of collective agency, the administrator of a state could be in a position to judge the legitimacy of various collective appeals (cf. 1807: 582f, 1821: 5R, 29R, 258R).

38. Moreover, Hegel seems to be very aware of the difficulty of "drawing lines" with regard to legally actionable harms, and is critical of attempts to limit these (cf. 1821: 134, 134A, 319, 319R). Nevertheless, Hegel focuses these remarks on the relation between the state and *individuals,* avoiding the potentially much more difficult issue of how to deal with dissident groups and their claims.

39. Indeed, it may be that Hegel's dire warnings as to the dangers of class warfare arise precisely from his appreciation of the nature of collective agency. As I shall suggest below, this is especially apparent in his discussion of poverty and of the penurious "rabble" that the capitalist order brings about (cf. Hegel 1821: 242–246).

40. The term "proceduralism" is taken from David M. Anderson's (1990) discussion and criticism of Rawls's "pure procedural justice."

41. As Taylor (1975) points out:

If a concept were just incoherent, it could be set aside in favor of a more adequate one. Or, if while indispensable, it was just inadequate as against incoherent, there would be no conflict in *complementing* it with a fuller one . . . . For Hegel, this [contradiction] poses no problem . . . . for reality is incoherent, that is prey to contradiction. What the inadequate categories correspond to is inadequate, partial reality, which both necessarily exists (hence the categories are indispensable), and yet being contradictory necessarily goes under (hence the categories are incoherent) . . . . [O]ur finally adequate category, which Hegel calls the Idea, . . . will exhibit . . . the necessary connection of the whole ascending chain of categories . . . . (229–230)

42. For the sake of consistency with the translation of the *Philosophy of Right,* I have changed Hartman's translation of *sittliches Gänze* from "moral whole" to "ethical whole." As I shall detail below, though a previous set of ethical conventions may be *aufgehoben,* morality has a function within that process such that it is never, strictly speaking, "surpassed."

43. In this sense, Hegel's own critique of Kant's loan example may be understood to express the disintegration of the "bourgeois" pattern of life against which the background assumptions of Kantian morality take their shape. For further development of this point see Rose 1981: 79–91.

44. "It can be said that the right which lay in wait is not present in its own proper shape to the *consciousness* of the doer, but is present only *implicitly* in the inner guilt of the resolve and the action" (Hegel 1807: 470).

45. Aside from certain suggestive passages in the section "Lord and Bondsman," Hegel's discussion in the *Phenomenology* focuses on the emergence of agency in singular events that have already occurred in history. Hence, there is no discussion of how such agency might collectively develop. (As noted at length above, Hegel placed little hope in such developments having a positive outcome.) Nevertheless, as I shall suggest below, there is no reason to believe that a collective movement could not facilitate this kind of emergent agency. In chapters 4 through 6, I shall expand on this Hegelian theme, focusing upon the relation between the alienation of collective agency and the activities of feminist consciousness raising.

46. Hegel is clear that the impact of this agency endures:

> Womankind—the everlasting irony [in the life] of the community— changes by intrigue the universal end of the government into a private end, transforms its universal activity into a work of some particular individual, and perverts the universal property of the state into a possession and ornament of the family. (1807: 475)

Hegel's sexist antagonism toward women's active capacities here seems curiously at odds with the "passive and subjective" role to which he consigns them in the *Philosophy of Right* (1821: 166). (For further discussion of women's "ethical role" in Hegel's thought, see chapter 7.)

47. It should also be noted that the "divine law" exacts respect through its capacity for retribution. The legitimacy of Antigone's cause finds its proof with the bloody price that Creon must pay for his rejection of her appeal—the death of his son Haemon.

48. As I shall argue in the next section, my interpretation here assumes that Hegel's use of the term "empty" in practical philosophy (like Kant's in theoretical philosophy) should not be taken to mean simply "useless" or "pointless," but rather as in need of embodiment or mediation.

49. "In England, even the poorest man believes he has his rights; this differs from what the poor are content with in other countries. Poverty in itself does not reduce people to a rabble; a rabble is created only by the disposition associated with poverty, by an inward rebellion against the rich, against society, the government, etc." (Hegel 1821: 244A).

Raymond Plant (1983) has noted that Hegel's view here is "strikingly modern" in recognizing poverty as a socially relative problem (214). Equally noteworthy, however, is the manner in which he links this relativity to the abstract notion of "rights." For Hegel, that which the agent claims as a matter of rights is contingent upon the emergence of certain collective dispositions. Poverty becomes a matter of justice only if an impoverished class grasps its lot as a violation of its agency, and advances that understanding through a set of claims against another class.

The passage is also noteworthy in that it displays Hegel's typical distrust of "proletarian agency" in advancing the universal. This is an interesting contrast to his assessments of the no less unruly agency of "individuals" such as Alexander the Great, Julius Caesar, or Napoleon (cf. 1837c: 39–49; 1984: 114).

50. Hegel was, of course, greatly concerned about just this issue. In the *Philosophy of Right* (1821: 239f), he is particularly critical of those who would fail to comprehend the political nature of poverty, and would leave its alleviation to good will and charity. "[W]ithin the conditions of society hardship at once assumes the form of a wrong inflicted on this or that class" (244A). (For further discussion of Hegel's views here, see Avineri 1972: 96–98, 146–151, and Plant 1983: 213–215.)

Typically, Hegel was concerned that the state provide for the subsistence of all its classes, thus preventing the development of rebellious class-consciousness. Nevertheless (as his account of *Antigone* made clear), such rebelliousness may itself be the necessary condition for knowledge of harm. Once again, the political "resolution" of the *Philosophy of Right* stumbles between the management of class conflict and the genuine mediation of the interests of the various estates.

51. If the norms of a society (1) affirm that the autonomy of the individual is inalienable (i.e., is a capacity a rational agent cannot *really* surrender), and (2) fail to recognize that particular institutions and practices are necessary for persons (i.e., members of social classes or estates) to *achieve* autonomy, then the failure of individuals to extricate, or to attempt to extricate themselves from conditions that violate their agency will itself appear culpable. Because norms in contemporary liberal societies have tended to express the conjunction of (1) and (2), not only "pity" for subordinated classes, but equally a kind of "victim-blaming" has been common. I take up this phenomenon in greater detail in chapter 4.

52. This will, of course, be even more difficult to the extent that members of an oppressed class are excluded from the institutions and practices of a society in virtue of their membership in *other* subordinated classes. This is manifest in the links between racism and poverty, and sexism and poverty (the "feminization" of poverty), in contemporary liberal society.

53. It is important to note that the conditions for recognizing that "poverty is a violation of rights" among members of the impoverished class, is related to the conditions for successfully asserting that proposition in the society in question. To the extent that the background assumptions for making rights-based claims in that society are governed by norms that exclude the agency of members of an oppressed class from recognition, even members of the oppressed class may fail to recognize their capacity to make rights-based claims. In chapter 4, I describe consciousness raising as a collective attempt to overcome this dilemma by creating a niche within society where alternative assumptions hold.

54. "The accomplished deed completely alters its point of view; the very performance of it declares that what is *ethical (sittlich)* must be *actual (wirklich)*; for the *actualization (Wirklichkeit)* of the purpose is the purpose of the action . . . . The ethical consciousness must, on account of this actuality and on account of its deed, acknowledge its opposite as its actuality, must acknowledge its guilt" (1807: 470).

55. I shall take up this transition in greater detail in the following section.

56. To fully make out *Hegel's* dialectical account, it might also be necessary to show that rights constitute an indispensable category for coming to a grasp of the right.

That we are dealing with ethical *reality* itself, and not just a historical perspective on it, requires a stronger claim.

57. For an interesting discussion of how the historical indeterminacy of "democracy" as regards not only its domain (a familiar topic for Marxian analysis) but who participates in it and what constitutes participation, see Bowles and Gintis 1987: 27-63.

58. It may thus explain the conceptual coherence behind feminists' deeply felt suspicion of the liberal values that seem to underpin some of their criticisms of liberal society, e.g., "Abstract equality undermines substantive equality, but it reinforces it at the same time" (MacKinnon 1987: 14).

59. Such an extreme case could be avoided, of course, to the extent that alternative embodiments of rights were available in a given social order. If, for example, the conception of rights in a neighboring society legitimated claims against the state for social welfare, then claims for the same in the first society might not appear so contrary to principle. This more closely describes the current situation with regard to rights against impoverishment.

In chapter 4, I shall take up a more "extreme" case, however, concerning feminist re-conceptualization of the notion of "consent." By detailing a feminist perspective on the nature of consent (i.e., the nature of consent under conditions of political subordination), feminist scholars such as Catharine MacKinnon suggest a rethinking of that concept so encompassing that it may appear to challenge the existing conception of consent altogether.

60. Of course, Hegel argued that past history has been marked by the advance of the universal by the impassioned and self-serving agency of the world historical individuals: "their own particular purposes contain the substantial will of the World Spirit." (1837c: 40) Hegel is also clear, however, that the "individual" may in fact be a collective form of agency (1837c: 15).

61. This need not entail that knowledge, or "genuine knowledge," of the relevant injustice is restricted to members of the disadvantaged class. What is epistemologically required for members of that class and everyone else as well is that public practices and institutions have the capacity to render a meaningful and politically effective articulation of the oppressive conditions. As noted below, however, the development of an alternative "subset" of institutions and practices from which members of the dominant class are excluded may be among the causal conditions required for bringing about such an articulation.

62. Under certain conditions, this may justify so-called "terrorist" aggression. When a social class has been effectively excluded altogether from the institutions and practices by which they could assert their claims against a social order, the only means for such assertion may be violent ones. The conditions under which the African National Congress refused to renounce violent action against the white ruling class in South Africa might be an example of this. Likewise, feminist support for those women who have violently retaliated against spouses who have beaten them and otherwise violently kept them in subjection may be understood to have occurred under relevantly similar conditions of exclusion. I am indebted to Elizabeth Anderson for this example.

63. It may also require that members of the oppressed class refrain from publicizing their action as aimed toward "impartiality" or the refinement of a cultural con-

ception of it, inasmuch as that too could be apprehended as an attitude of capitulation before the extant social order.

64. Indeed, it would count against a Hegelian conception of ethics if appeals to the rights and freedom of individuals were impossible altogether, insofar as these have been a part of all modern movements of liberation. As noted in the Introduction, it is among the virtues of the Hegelian account that it integrates an appeal to abstract categories of the right with the emergence of impassioned challenges to the existing embodiments of those categories.

65. "Thoughts without content are empty, intuitions without concepts are blind" (1787: A51 / B75). Of course, for Hegel the *concept* is not empty, since he uses that term to describe the dialectical unity of form and content by which the universal advances. The re-conceptualization of a moral category involves not only a new description of that category, but a new shape of self-consciousness which concretely embodies that category. As noted below, this captures Hegel's double-sense of *begreifen*, where it retains both its intellectual and sensuous meanings of "to comprehend" and "to grasp," respectively (cf. Kaufmann 1965: 159–160).

66. This may offer a concrete example of how the formal categories of morality serve their role of generating "contradictions" in the social order (cf. Hegel 1821: 30R, 112R, 139R). It is in the nature of purely formal categories (i.e., categories disembodied from all content) to "contradict themselves, and pass over into their opposites" (1830: §214). Examples such as these would suggest, however, that terms such as "opposite" and "contradiction" are meant in a rather looser sense than we might ordinarily expect.

67. It is worth noting that this reading of Hegel's approach to Kantian morality bears certain rather striking similarities to Hegel's reading of Kantian epistemology. Robert Pippin (1989) takes the latter to attempt to make sense of the conjunction of three claims:

> First, there is the claim about nonempirical constraints on what could be a possible experience, pure concepts . . . . Second, there is Hegel's denial that these are only conceptual forms, that they must be connected with intuitions to be objective; or his claim that such concepts *themselves* determine "actuality" *(Wirklichkeit)* as it is *in itself*. Third, there is the fact that Hegel accepts much of Kant's criticism of the "dogmatic" tradition, and in particular rejects a reliance on the classical notion of intellectual intuition. (9)

68. At least in certain respects, this would appear to be a more "Hegelian" approach to the problem of a deficient social order than the escape into the "inner life" suggested in the Additions to the *Philosophy of Right* (1821: 138A).

69. Kant, because he conceives desire as no more than the sensuous "inclination" of an individual agent, does take the existence of desire for granted.

70. As Harding later notes in the same text, standpoint advocates Jane Flax (1983), Nancy Hartsock (1984), and Dorothy Smith (1981) all rely on Hegel's parable of master and slave in endorsing an approach to knowledge rooted in women's particular experiences (Harding 1986: 158).

71. As Jane Flax writes: "Feminist philosophy thus represents the return of the repressed, of the exposure of the particular social roots of all apparently abstract and

universal knowledge. This work could prepare the ground for a more adequate social theory in which philosophy and empirical knowledge are reunited and mutually enriched" (Flax 1983: 249, cited at Harding 1986: 151).

Chapter 4. Consciousness Raising and Political Critique

1. I shall consider de Beauvoir's own quasi-Hegelian project in detail in chapter 7 below.

2. As Allen Wood (1990) has justly pointed out:

Though he ridicules the banal moralizing of the schoolmaster, there is something rather trite about Hegel's own admiration for the men nineteenth century schoolboys read about in their history books, and something very schoolmasterish about the way Hegel turns the history lesson into a "time to praise famous men." Some of us might have preferred an alternative history curriculum in which what Marx called "the high sounding drama of states and princes" is supplemented by an account of how history is really shaped incrementally by the deeds of countless people whom the schoolmaster never heard of and would in any case not have time to name. (230)

3. Kathie Sarachild, the author of the 1968 paper that is generally thought to employ the term for the first time to describe the specific self-education activities of feminist organizers (see Tanner 1970: 154-157), tells of a *New York Times* article referring to "a meeting called by Henry Kissinger to talk to the executives of the major television networks about the content of their programs as a 'curious consciousness-raising session with a Secretary of State'" (Sarachild, ed., 1978: 147).

4. See, e.g., Spelman 1988, and Frye 1983.

5. See Leon 1978: 152-153. As Sarachild (1978b) points out, the development of consciousness raising represented the convergence of several distinct phenomena:

The beginning of the solution, the synthesis, came in the United States with the combination of Beauvoir's analysis [in *The Second Sex*], black liberation, particularly, Black Power thinking and experience—the theory coming out of the Chinese Revolution. (28)

For a recent discussion of the effects of the Chinese model of revolutionary thought on feminism, see Sally Taylor Lieberman (1991), "Visions and Lessons: 'China' in Feminist Theory Making." For an extremely informative if somewhat idiosyncratic account of the feminist break from other Left movements in the late nineteen sixties and early nineteen seventies, see Echols 1989: 103-137.

6. See, e.g., Robin Morgan (1970), "Goodbye to All That." The close connection between the Second Wave and the activities of the radical Left in the nineteen sixties is not always recognized. In fact, the term "women's liberation" probably originated with SNCC (Leon 1978: 152). Though the moderate ("liberal") National Organization for Women was formed in 1966, it was not until the following year that women activists from the radical Left began the push toward an independent women's movement. Such a view had been anathema to earlier activists for whom any movement toward "libera-

tion" that was separate from the establishment of socialism was bound to be "counter-revolutionary" (Echols 1989: 54). (For a discussion of the evolution of Simone de Beauvoir's views on this issue, see chapter 7.)

7. As Barbara Leon (1978) pointed out, the aim of developing a "woman-centered" movement was controversial from the start. Shulamith Firestone, for example, saw it primarily in terms of building a unified movement to confront patriarchal power:

> We must not come as passive suppliants begging for favors, for power "cooperates" only with power . . . . Until we have united into a force to be reckoned with, we will be patronized and ridiculed into total political ineffectiveness. (Leaflet for the Jeannette Rankin Brigade (1968), cited in Leon, 153)

Pamela Allen, on the other hand, endorsed the "developmental" line of thought taken up more recently by writers such as MacKinnon:

> We found that there are very strong inferiority problems amongst women and that it was very productive and positive to have women meet together and find out that it is not an individual problem . . . chauvinism is a man's problem. We have enough to work out to begin to develop a sense of true identity . . . . to define who and what we are in our own terms. (Interview, Pamela Allen and Julius Lester, WBAI (1968), cited in Leon: 153)

Of course, the two aims need not be incompatible. I shall be concerned with the implications of the second (Allen) interpretation of consciousness raising as it affects normative evaluation.

8. This "speaking bitterness" was essential to the development of revolutionary consciousness in rural China (Lieberman 1991: 91). In his influential *Fanshen: A Documentary of Revolution in a Chinese Village*, William Hinton gives the following description of a meeting of a cadre of young revolutionaries:

> The meeting lasted three days and three major issues were discussed: (1) Who depends upon whom for a living? (2) Why are the poor poor and the rich rich? (3) Should rent be paid to the landlords? . . . . When the meeting broke up on the third day the three main questions had been settled in the minds of most: (1) The landlords depended on the labor of the peasants for their very life. (2) The rich were rich because they "peeled and pared" the poor. (3) Rent should not be paid to the landlords. (Hinton 1966, cited in Sarachild, ed., 1978: 149)

9. Rowbotham 1973: 27, cited in MacKinnon 1989: 84.

10. As Sarachild (1978a) remarked:

> Our meetings were called [by hostile leftists] coffee klatches, hen parties or bitch sessions. We responded by saying, "Yes, bitch, sisters, bitch," and by calling the coffee klatches a historic form of women's resistance to oppression. (146)

The issues brought up by women in the context of consciousness raising in fact differed little in their factual content from those of which women had long complained to one another in the "coffee klatches." As I shall discuss below, however, consciousness raising sought to eliminate the intrusion of elements that kept the "complaints" from becoming political critique.

11. See, for example, Anne Forer 1978: 151.

12. As Susi Kaplow (1971) wrote:

Through consciousness-raising each woman can (at least ideally) find sufficient confirmation of her perceptions to be assured of her own sanity—and can find growing strength to do so without such confirmation when necessary. (41)

13. I am assuming here, as I have elsewhere, that a "point of view" or "perspective" may properly be attributed to a group where the agency implied in that perspective is that of a collective. (For further discussion of this point, see chapter 1.)

14. As a participant of one of the early consciousness-raising sessions broadcast over WBAI in New York commented:

It seems to me that the reason we have such difficulty responding adequately either to being attacked or being put down or being used in some way, being disregarded, whistled at or whatever, is that on the one hand there is objectively a great deal of real danger . . . . but on the other hand we have internalized our fear of invoking male anger, and that we carry around within us—this powerlessness. (Rainone 1970: 71)

15. I shall take up the issue of fear before men in relation to Hegel's narrative of master and slave in my discussion in chapter 7.

16. For a discussion of the impediments to women's free expression in the presence of men, see MacKinnon 1989: 86.

17. It is interesting to note that there was no opposition to all-women's groups that were expressly apolitical. The Southern Christian Educational Fund (SCEF) fired Carol Hanisch (later to become active in New York Radical Women) when she attempted to organize exclusively female women's liberation groups. Although SCEF had no opposition to all-women groups on non-feminist issues, it insisted that women's issues be addressed by "mixed groups" (Leon 1978: 153-154). So long as the perspective of the oppressed group does not constitute a challenge to the oppressors, it may be permitted and even welcomed.

This led activists such as Barbara Leon and Kathie Sarachild to repudiate the uses of consciousness raising for purposes *other than* addressing masculine domination. Fearing the lapse into conservatism that had characterized the suffragist movement in the United States, they were critical of the "reactionary separatism" they saw suggested in works such as Elizabeth Gould Davis's *The First Sex* (1973) and Jill Johnston's *Lesbian Nation: The Feminist Solution* (1974), as well as in the women's peace movement. For an interesting discussion of the debate within the New York Radical Feminists, see Echols 1989: 72-92.

18. N.B. In Morgan's text, the "Principles" are erroneously attributed to the New York Radical Feminists (see Sarachild, ed., 1978: 149n).

19. The denial often associated with victimization may also shed light on why early consciousness raising tended to focus on what now appear to be the tamer and less violent features of women's subordination, seemingly overlooking more serious issues. Indeed, the early movement's emphasis on issues such as appearance, men who wouldn't listen, and child care was the occasion of much ridicule in the male radical Left. The first major articles addressing rape came in 1971 (Griffin, "Rape: The All-American Crime," Mehrhof and Kearon, "Rape: An Act of Terror"). Awareness of the pervasive problem of battered women came even later, and led to the conversion of some women's "homes"

originally established for consciousness raising into shelters in the mid-to late 1970s (See Schechter 1983: 29–34). While this peculiar chronology has sometimes been explained by the predominance of well-off university "radicals"—women who were relatively removed from the worst instances of masculine violence—in the early movement (see, e.g., McAfee and Wood 1969: 420–422), it may also reflect the psychological difficulties associated with unmasking violent victimization. The denial occasioned by incidents of violence suggests that, contrary to common belief, a situation of real and threatened physical violence may be far more difficult for the victim to admit to herself than less traumatic situations. Under these conditions, it is not surprising that the earliest foci of feminist critique would be the less-distressing aspects of masculine domination, nor that these would be the starting point for the collective "discovery" of far worse kinds of victimization as the movement matured.

20. I mean "harassment" here to consist in being placed in the unwanted position of having to choose between some form of sexual compliance and a real or implied threat. This can range from the case of being placed in the position of having to provide sexual favors for employment benefits (or avoiding employment harms) to that of being placed in the position of having to submit to unwanted stares and catcalls to walk down the street (see MacKinnon 1979: 37). To experience states of affairs such as these as threats, the person being harassed must experience themselves as somehow subordinate to the person making them. Hence, I am not referring to harassment as a mere annoyance.

21. This question could, however, be taken in another "deconstructive" sense, where asking what was meant is a question about the meaning of the act in women's experience, whatever the conscious intentions of the harasser may have been. As I shall discuss in detail in chapter 6, a critical part of the "grievance" procedure of feminist consciousness raising involves altering the accepted social meanings of a set of actions. On a Hegelian account, a change in the social meaning of an act entails a transformation in the agency of the actor as well.

22. Once again, as noted above, I mean harassment in the strong sense of an actual or implied threat (cf. MacKinnon 1979: 37).

23. As discussed below, advocates of "methodological impartiality" elide this point either by ignoring the possibility of persons standing within oppressive relations or by implicitly taking up the point of view of the oppressor or potential oppressor.

24. The Hegelian aspects of this problem are remarkably well stated in the passage by Minnie Bruce Pratt (1984) cited at the beginning of chapter 3 above:

It is very hard for me to know *how* to talk about this struggle [against racism and anti-Semitism] because the culture I was born and raised in has taught me certain ways of being that reduce the process of change to ought-to, that reduce the issue of how to live to ought-to. I was taught to be a *judge* of moral responsibility and of punishment . . . was taught to be a *preacher*, to point out wrongs and tell others what to do . . . . I am struggling now to speak, but not out of any role of ought-to; I ask that you try not to place me in that role. I am trying to speak from my heart, out of need, as a woman who loves other women passionately, and who wants us to be able to be together as friends in this unjust world. (14–15)

25. This implicit universalism is in evidence in the words of Catharine MacKinnon (1989) cited at the beginning of chapter 2:

The problem . . . is that the generalized, universal, or agreed-upon never did solve the disagreements, resolve the differences, cohere the specifics, and generalize the particularities. (xv)

This state of affairs emerges as a "problem" precisely because it is taken for granted that generality, universality, or agreement is desirable.

26. See also chapter 3, section III above.

27. Hence, my discussion of reconceptualization draws upon two important themes that run through Hegel's thought, expressivism and historical emergence. As Taylor (1975) notes:

[T]he notion of human life as expression sees [*self*-realization] not only as the realization of purposes but also as the clarification of these purposes. It is not only the fulfillment of life but also the clarification of meaning . . . . As such a clarification my life-form is not just the fulfillment of purpose but the embodiment of meaning, the expression of an idea . . . . Human life is both fact and meaningful expression . . . it expresses the idea which it realizes. (17)

28. Onora O'Neill (1989), for example, has written:

A [deep and historically] important understanding of the idea of treating others as persons sees their consent to actions that affect them as morally significant. On this view it is morally objectionable to treat others in ways to which they do not consent. (106)

See also Thomas E. Hill, Jr. (1980), "Humanity as an End in Itself."

29. For an interesting discussion of past approaches to consent theory and their relation to feminist critique, see Carole Pateman (1980), "Women and Consent."

30. See MacKinnon 1989: 88–89. For an early discussion, see Bengis 1973.

31. For further discussions of women and consent with relevance to my discussion here, see Brownmiller 1975, Clark and Lewis 1977, Foa 1977, MacKinnon 1987: 7, 11, 100; 1989: 174–183, 238, Medea and Thompson 1974, O'Neill 1989: 105–125, Pateman 1980, Peterson 1977, Russell 1977; 1982: 375–381, Shafer and Frye 1977, Tax 1973.

The issues surrounding feminism and sexuality have themselves, of course, been the topic of a sustained debate, i.e., the "Sex Wars." In my discussion, I shall attempt to outline concerns that are generally accepted without addressing the controversial interpretive question of what they may mean for women's sexuality *per se*. For representative essays on the "sexual liberal" side, see Snitow, Stansell, and Thompson, eds., *Powers of Desire: The Politics of Sexuality* (1983), Vance, ed. (1984), *Pleasure and Danger: Toward a Politics of* Sexuality, and Caught Looking, Inc., *Caught Looking: Feminism, Pornography and Censorship* (1987). On the other side, see Lederer, ed., *Take Back the Night: Women on Pornography* (1979), Keohane, Rosaldo, and Gelpi, eds., *Feminist Theory: A Critique of Ideology* (1982), and Leidholdt and Raymond, eds., *The Sexual Liberals and the Attack on Feminism* (1990).

32. For more recent accounts, see Robin Morgan 1989: 23–24, and Larry May and Robert Strikwerda 1994.

33. For an interesting discussion of terrorism that is informed by women's experience of the threat of rape, see Bat-Ami Bar On (1991), "Why Terrorism Is Morally Problematic."

34. The articulation of a ubiquitous *fear* of rape in consciousness raising came largely in advance of the empirical findings according to which that fear was shown to be justified. (See, e.g., Diana E. H. Russell (1980), "Pornography and Violence: What does the Research Say?")

35. To the extent that a woman's refusal to consent is not understood as such, her acquiescence is likewise compromised. As Carole Pateman (1980) remarked:

> [I]f "no," when uttered by a woman, is to be reinterpreted as "yes," then all the comfortable assumptions about her "consent" are also thrown into disarray. Why should a woman's "yes" be more privileged, be any the less open to invalidation, than her "no"? (162)

This was the precursor to MacKinnon's oft quoted query, "If 'no' can be taken as 'yes,' how free can yes be?" (1987: 95).

36. "Rape is never defined in marriage in the U.S.A. This simply means that a husband always has the right to take his wife by force regardless of her inclinations. It is next to impossible to press rape charges against a boy friend, a male acquaintance, or a male with whom one has had a single date" (Mehrhof and Kearon 1971: 232). Although most states have now taken action to make marital rape and "date rape" legally actionable, and have likewise taken steps to mitigate the demands placed on the plaintiff in rape prosecutions, the continued infrequency of reported rape, as well as notorious difficulties in obtaining rape convictions from *juries* in cases where the rapist knew the survivor, show that the legal embodiment of a women's perspective remains far from a reality.

37. Mehrhof and Kearon 1971: 232. See also Foa 1977: 356, MacKinnon 1989: 172-183.

38. "[P]art of the culture of sexual inequality that makes women not report rape is that the definition of rape is not based on our sense of violation." (MacKinnon 1987: 82)

39. "The proper scope of one's power of consent depends upon one's *domain*, and the notion of domain is inextricably linked with that of personhood, for it is as a person that one has a domain" (Shafer and Frye 1977: 336).

40. Moreover, the problems associated with the social definition of a woman's body extend to a wide range of feminist concerns not explicitly linked to sexual availability. Feminist discussions of the relationship of women to the medical profession (e.g., Ehrenreich and English 1978), of women's experience of eating and obesity (e.g., Chernin 1985), of their exclusion from sports (e.g., MacKinnon 1987: 117-124), and, of course, of abortion and reproductive decision making all reflect conditions in which women's bodies are socially defined as falling variously outside the scope of women's agency.

41. MacKinnon (1989) states this most unambiguously: "To be rapable, a position that is social not biological, defines what a woman is" (178, see also Shafer and Frye 1977: 334). Even if it is argued that the feminine is not strictly *identical* with the rapable, however, to the extent that this forms a central part of women's experience, it will have important implications for any discussion of sexual consent. (For further discussion of MacKinnon's argument, see chapter 8.)

42. For further discussion of this symmetry, see chapter 7.

43. "From women's point of view, rape is not prohibited; it is regulated" (MacKinnon 1989: 179).

44. See O'Neill 1989: 105-125. While O'Neill addresses inequality-based structures of disrespect in capitalist relations of production, however, her discussion of consent in heterosexual relations fails even to broach the possibility that it too might be based on a relation of unequal power. By assuming that "the rapist's victim is coerced rather than consenting," O'Neill glosses the most difficult issues concerning the distinction between coercion and consent in sexual relations, and thus fails to address the most interesting cases (106). She argues instead that sexual relations are "wholly different" from capitalist relations, in that disrespect in sexual relations derives from the condition of "intimacy" and its perilous intermixing of expressions of true and merely superficial commitment. (For a discussion of the question of intention in cases of group dominance and subordination, see chapter 5.)

45. I am assuming here that some of the most objectionable features of traditional rape statutes are not in force, e.g., requiring eyewitnesses to verify that a rape has actually taken place (Mehrhof and Kearon 1971: 232).

46. MacKinnon (1979) sees this problem in criminal prosecutions of both rape and sexual harassment:

> "[A] victim who resists is more likely to be killed, but unless she fights back, it is not rape, because she cannot prove coercion. With sexual harassment, rejection proves that the advance is unwanted, but also is likely to call forth retaliation, thus forcing the victim to bring intensified injury upon herself in order to demonstrate that she is injured at all" (44).

47. "The deeper problem is that women are socialized to passive receptivity; may have or perceive no alternative to acquiescence; may prefer to the escalated risk of injury and the humiliation of a lost fight; submit to survive" (MacKinnon 1989: 177).

48. As Shafer and Frye (1977) pointed out, "Rape is the exposure of the public lie that women are respected persons" (343). MacKinnon uses this point in criticizing Judith Jarvis Thomson's (1971) argument for the symmetry between a neutral "person's" obligation to be a celebrated violinist's unconsenting life-support system and a woman's obligation to be a fetus's unconsenting mother: "The parallel [in Thomson's argument] seems misframed. No woman who needs an abortion . . . is valued, no potential a woman's life might hold is cherished, like a gender-neutral famous violinist's unencumbered possibilities. The problems of gender are thus underlined here rather than solved or even addressed" (1987: 98-99, cf. 1989: 189).

49. "Rape . . . is an effective political device. It is not an arbitrary act of violence by one individual on another; it is a political act of *oppression* (never rebellion) exercised by members of a powerful class on members of the powerless class" (Mehrhof and Kearon 1971: 233).

The parenthetical reference to rebellion represents a rejection of the use of rape by men as a political act against their masculine oppressors. As Eldridge Cleaver (1968) famously remarked concerning his behavior as a rapist in *Soul on Ice:*

> Rape was an insurrectionary act. It delighted me that I was defying and trampling upon the white man's law, upon his system of values, and that I was defiling his women—and this point I believe was the most satisfying

to me because I was very resentful over the historical fact of how the white man has used the black woman. I felt I was getting revenge. (26)

50. As MacKinnon (1987) notes in a particularly "Hegelian" passage, "Abstract equality undermines substantive inequality, but it reinforces it at the same time" (14).

51. I take up some of the complex issues surrounding "willful ignorance" and sexism in chapter 6 below.

52. I mean "actual" here in the Hegelian sense of *wirklich*, i.e., effectively embodied in institutions and practices of a social order. To actually exist as a person requires that one's agency be one's own, and that this condition find expression in one's culture.

53. This phenomenon of coming to a sense of self-respect despite exclusion is of course common to all disempowered groups. As Paolo Freire (1983) has written, "We cannot enter the struggle as objects in order to later become subjects." To the extent that a genuine sense of agency can be claimed under conditions of oppression, however, that sense must exceed the conventional definitions. For a discussion of this with regard to black and feminist conceptions of self, see bell hooks (1989), "On Self-Recovery" (28–34).

54. As Melinda Vadas (1990) has remarked with regard to MacKinnon's discussion of rape law:

In whose interest is it to believe that what women who have been raped experience is *nothing like* what women who consensually engage in intercourse experience? That is, in whose interest is it to draw the dividing line (at consent) between rape and intercourse? (140)

55. This has important implications for responding to certain charges sometimes made regarding the feminist discussion of consent. It is a common observation among some men that, given the attention recently given to sexual harassment and assault, the only way to respect women is to avoid contact with them altogether. After all, if "consent" is never free under conditions of oppression, then the only way for a member of a powerful group to avoid oppression is to remove himself from all contact with the oppressed. This is manifest in the usually derisive male contention that feminism has left no opening for mutually respectful sexual relations at all (see, e.g., Levin 1987: 205). Rather than giving credence to the *possibility* that feminists might be articulating a reconceptualization of respect and sexuality that is not geared to the problematic conditions of "consent," anti-feminists have concluded that they have reduced all heterosexual sex to rape. (This reasoning displays just how little current conceptions of "consent" have to do with women's experience.)

56. There, I argue, contrary to theorists such as Drucilla Cornell (1991: 119–164) that the capacity of women and members of other oppressed groups to transform their self-conceptions does not rely upon some aspect of their agency *not* being subordinated.

57. As Luce Irigaray (1985) has written regarding the task of feminists:

[W]omen must of course continue to struggle for equal wages and social rights, against discrimination in education and employment, and so forth. But that is not enough: women merely "equal" to men would be "like them," therefore not women . . . . That explains certain difficulties encountered by liberation movements. If women allow themselves to be caught in the trap of power . . . if they allow themselves to be contaminated by the "paranoid" operations of masculine politics, they have nothing more to say or do *as women* . . . . [Women's liberation] must never disguise the fact that it is in order to bring their difference to light that women are demanding their rights. (166)

Thus, the struggle around certain liberal conceptions of justice transcends the mere "application" of them *to* women, and seeks to rethink them through women's experience. This will be a necessary condition, moreover, for coming to an understanding of what is peculiarly "masculine" in political discourse as well (see p. 128).

58. "The spirit's objective *right of particularity*, which is contained within the Idea, does not cancel out *(nicht aufhebt)* the inequality of human beings in civil society—an inequality posited by nature, which is the element of inequality—but in fact produces it out of the spirit itself and raises it to an inequality of skills, resources, and even of intellectual and moral education . . . . In consequence, the whole complex *(Zusammenhang)* evolves into *particular systems* of needs, with their corresponding means, varieties of work, modes of satisfaction, and theoretical and practical education—into systems to which individuals are separately assigned, i.e. into differently *estates [Stände]*" (Hegel 1821: 200R-201).

Of course, not just *any* system will produce a working "system of needs." In Hegel's view, the estate divisions in the system outlined in the *Philosophy of Right* are (most implausibly) intended to mediate the self-satisfaction of the members of the various estates as other systems (e.g., a slave system) could not. As discussed in the last chapter, however, Hegel's political theory has little of use to say to those of a modern social order who find themselves members of an oppressed class. Their complaint, like that of the slave, is not some unmotivated demand for "abstract equality," but a plea for the social means to realize their agency as self-conscious persons.

59. "Hegel's theory of history does not preclude the possibility that there might be such a thing as self-transparent world-historical agency. If there is, then it might be possible for you to know of your own action that it possesses a supramoral justification. You might be able knowingly to exercise the world historical right to do wrong" (Wood 1990: 234).

Wood has in mind the kinds of claims made by Marx and Engels as to the kinds of action necessary to bring about communism. The sort of agency that I have described in the context of feminist consciousness raising suggests that there may be a third alternative between self-opacity and absolute self-transparency, where, without benefit of a transparent historical justification (as in Marxist class theory), agents may act out of a particular interest.

Chapter 5. Ignorance, Oppression, and Blame

1. I shall use the masculine pronoun when referring to the "sexist agent." It is an implication of the Hegelian conception of agency developed in chapter 1 above that although women can engage in at least some sexist activities (e.g., use sexist language, contribute to sexist research, etc.), the collective agency embodied by individuals engaged in these activities is masculine.

2. The critiques' being "less than obvious" alone is insufficient, of course, to exculpate sexist agents from *culpable* ignorance. I shall address this point below.

3. Of course, on a consequentialist reading, this is the *only* justification that ascriptions of blame can have. This reading succeeds in evading the charge of disingenuousness, however, only by eliminating exclusively agent-centered concerns from the normative picture altogether. To the extent that feminist method is defined in terms of the transformation of agency of women and men (as I argue at length in chapter 3 above), such an elimination is not acceptable.

4. For a discussion of sexist practices that not only *cause* the oppression of women but *embody* it through the practice, see Susanne Kappeler (1986), *The Pornography of Representation,* and Melinda Vadas (1987), "A First Look at the Pornography/Civil Rights Ordinance: Could Pornography Be the Subordination of Women?"

5. This challenges Raymond S. Pfeiffer's earlier (1985) consideration of this issue, in which he argues that feminist reproach is indefensible on moral grounds and is concerned rather with achieving "tactical, political, (and) rhetorical" ends (227). Pfeiffer bases his argument on the claim that in order for judgments about individuals to have moral status, they must be *logically* derivable from judgments about the collectivity. It is his contention that feminists cannot show that their judgments are so derived (Pfeiffer 1985: 226, cf. Held 1972: 109). Pfeiffer's argument, however, assumes a principle of methodological individualism that is implicitly at issue in most of the feminist charges that he discusses.

6. I have in mind here the kind of scientific research into women's "deficiencies" that Ruth Bleier (1986) criticizes in her "Lab Coat: Robe of Innocence or Klansman's Sheet."

7. I am using the somewhat awkward term "exculpate" rather than "excuse" here, since to excuse is ambiguous between (1) actually *releasing* an agent from a *prima facie* obligation to perform or refrain from performing an action, and (2) merely providing a reason not to *blame* her for wrongdoing. Although certain kinds of ignorance "excuse" in the sense of (2) (that is, they exculpate the agent from blame), I do not claim that this ignorance can excuse in the stronger sense suggested by (1).

8. This, of course, assumes that *individual* motives are separable, at least for the purposes of ethical analysis, from functional accounts on the social level. As discussed in chapter 1, Hegel counts the capacity to embrace the intersubjective meaning of one's action as the mark of rational agency and autonomy. As I shall argue below, this rules out any strict distinction between individual motives and social descriptions of action.

9. It would seem that by removing all doubt as to the motives of the physicians, Calhoun puts a counterintuitive twist on her own example. It is hard for us to believe that the physicians were *really* ignorant of the relevant facts of the matter. The practice of routinely sterilizing members of certain social groups is exactly the sort of socially and politically significant act where individual motives and collective interests mesh in an ethically interesting way, making it analogous to the cases of sexist action discussed below.

10. As Aristotle states in book 3 of the *Nichomachean Ethics,* all wickedness involves the ignorance of the offender as to "what he ought to do and what he ought to refrain from." Where the ignorance is merely of "particulars, i.e. of the circumstances

of the action and the objects with which it is concerned," however, she may escape reproach: "For it is on these that both pity and pardon depend, since the person who is ignorant of any of these acts involuntarily" (1110 b 25–35). As I shall argue in the next section, the distinction between ignorance of principle and ignorance of fact plays an important role here, since collective consciousness raising not only calls attention to previously suppressed facts but reconceptualizes the ethical principles of an existing social order.

11. Calhoun uses the example of children to make the opposite point, that it is possible to excuse while also correcting. She points out that it is possible for parents to chastise a child by saying "I know you didn't know any better and I'm not blaming you." Before a child could grasp the meaning of such a modified reproach, however, she would have to know the meaning of blame. The fact that Calhoun would exculpate small children from blame in their moral education, however, makes it all the more curious that she would subject some "morally competent" adults to simple *blame* for their acts.

12. Calhoun's assumption here that scientific "neutrality" requires that research-ers refrain from exploring the normative implications of their work has itself come under feminist scrutiny. Under conditions of domination and subordination, a principle enjoining scientists from reflecting on the normative implications of their work may abet those conditions. See, for example, Longino 1990, especially chapters 5 and 8.

13. My reading of Frye's position on ignorance here prescinds from her broader consideration of the phenomenon of oppression, which is, in certain important respects, similar to that outlined in chapter 1. As she points out earlier in *The Politics of Reality* (1983), "[T]he locus of sexism is primarily in the system or framework, not in the particular act" (19). Frye, however, maintains the conventional distinction between the moral agent *qua* "person" on the one hand, and as constructed by social determinants on the other (27-28, 44f, 57, 72n). It is this distinction that, on Hegel's account, will prove problematic.

14. With her focus on "lying," Frye preserves the "liberal" (or, perhaps more accurately, "Cartesian") assumption that intentions are transparent. It is interesting to contrast this with Catharine MacKinnon's (1979) critique of what she identifies as a liberal "differences" approach to inequality in favor of a focus on "inequalities:"

> What the second [inequality] approach grasps, and the first does not, is that it is not only lies and blindness that have kept women down. It is as much the social creation of differences, and the transformation of differ-ences into social advantages and disadvantages upon which inequality can be *rationally* predicated. Discrimination is often irrational. But under the inequality approach, that is not all, nor even primarily, what is unjust about it. What is unjust about sex discrimination is that it supports a system of second-class status for half of humanity. (105)

15. Or at least this is what Bleier says. It may well appear credulous to believe that scientists engaging in such research would be quite so oblivious to the potential uses of their studies.

16. It should be noted that the same could perhaps even more plausibly be said for Frye's example from Ellison. To the extent that the "lies" and the ignorance to which they gave rise were not transparent as such to white men in a racist culture, it is unlikely

that any of these agents could self-sufficiently disabuse themselves of their ignorance. However morally thoughtful any of them might have been with regard to "Negroes," because their reflection was itself informed by "lies," the oppressive nature of their behavior might well escape the test of moral scrutiny. If Frye is right that the "inattention" here (and in her other examples as well) can persist "without any specific effort," then it hard to understand how it could be active or "willful" in any morally relevant sense (1983: 121).

17. For a discussion of the implications of this kind of collective benefit, see May and Strikwerda 1994.

18. This point takes on special relevance with regard to "hate speech" and "free speech," in that expressive practices that are directed against a particular group may function to silence that group's expression of the harm done by that practice. As MacKinnon (1987) writes with regard to pornography:

> [T]o the extent pornography succeeds in constructing social reality, it becomes invisible as harm. If we live in a world that pornography creates through the power of men in a male-dominated situation, the issue is not what the harm of pornography is, but how that harm is to become visible. (174)

19. As Frye (1983) argues, ignorance on the part of dominant groups may play a vital part in "creating the conditions which ensure its continuance" (118-121).

20. Of course, to the extent that criticisms of oppressive agency are analogous to ascriptions of legal responsibility, they may also entail a challenge to the strict distinction between legal and moral duty. As is well known, Hegel was adamant in his rejection of the Kantian distinction between *Tugendlehre* and *Rechtslehre,* and sought to articulate a unified political order in which the legal system of the state effectively embodied the ethical relations of a people (Karl Rosenkranz 1844, cited in H.B. Acton, "Introduction" to Hegel 1802-1803. On the importance of the distinction for Kant, see O'Neill 1975: 44-56). As I shall suggest below, feminist criticisms of masculine sexist agency may imply a similar rejection, in that they suggest that agent-centered criticisms fall outside the sphere of strictly "moral" critique. (Notably, the glaring exception to Hegel's "legalization" of social relations was that of the family.)

21. I assume throughout this discussion that *P* is a *universal* principle, i.e., one applying impartially with respect to persons (the sense discussed in chapter 2 above). This is in accord with the Hegelian point that once the "moral point of view" has been historically instantiated, the ethical life cannot but make reference to it.

22. This is not to say that *A* may not experience regret at what has transpired. The fact that I feel regret that I played a role in bringing about evil consequences does not, by itself, justify reproach.

23. This example is adapted from Vadas 1987: 496. The object of her example is to show that the case of pornography, where a "payoff" for ignorance is present, is relevantly different from more "innocent" cases where no such reward structure exists. When the broader structures of cultural reinforcement are taken into account, however, innocent cases are not easy to find, and seem nearly always to entail that the agent be grossly ignorant of the practices of the group in question.

24. Of course, this need not relieve her of responsibility for the unintended consequences of her behavior. At least on a conventional account of morality, whether or not she bears such responsibility is a separate issue.

25. *A*'s understanding of *P* expresses the background assumptions of her society, as discussed in chapter 3 above. As I argue there, such assumptions, while necessary in coming to a grasp of the content of any moral principle, likewise occasion the possibility of closing oneself off from other ways of apprehending it.

26. I am accepting, for the sake of argument, Calhoun's contention that a "public consensus" on the wrongness of marital rape now exists, and thus referring to the time when the critique of existing marital practice was first raised. The precise nature of the "consensus" to which Calhoun refers, however, is highly debatable. While marital rape is condemned in certain contexts of discourse, its "private" nature means that it is most often invisible, the likelihood of legal action against it extremely small, and the likelihood of successful prosecution before a jury at least as small. (See Finkelhor and Bersti [1985], *License to Rape: Sexual Abuse of Wives.*) The ease with which people in a modern liberal social order can assimilate the "moral wrongness" of certain kinds of sexist and racist practices, while at the same time effectively closing off legal remedies to the survivors of those practices is among the most vexing problems for political activists. (For a discussion of this phenomenon focusing on liberal divorce reform, see Fineman [1991], *The Illusion of Equality.*)

27. As discussed in chapter 3 above, it is the possibility of ignorance of *this* kind of background assumption that renders mere adherence to the moral point of view notoriously unreliable as a guide for action. Hegel called attention to the way in which the otherwise advanced social order of ancient Greece (one that produced the sophisticated accounts of moral agency of Plato and Aristotle) nevertheless failed to "notice" the ethical significance of its excluded class of slaves (1837c: 23-24).

28. Similarly, a woman is widely considered responsible for the well-being of her children, even her unborn children. If a beaten wife kills or seriously injures her abusive husband, she is treated as a murderer or felonious assailant. Her agency is respected to the extent that it serves the interests of men.

29. This is manifest in Hegel's classic example of Creon's refusal to accept that Antigone's act represents anything more than self-will and rebellion. Though tragic, this apprehension of the act is inevitable for the guardian of the old order.

30. Moreover, denial is even more likely to the extent that "acting on principle" is accepted as the measure of self-respect. If full-blooded blame is synonymous with ethical reproach, and the possibility of historical reconceptualizations of principle is not acknowledged, then members of powerful classes will be unlikely to accept the full force of critiques from the side of the oppressed. Their denial, backed by social power, may easily translate into backlash.

31. "For the accomplished deed is the removal of the antithesis between the knowing self and the actuality confronting it. The doer cannot deny the crime or his guilt: the significance of the deed is that what was unmoved has been set in motion, and that what was locked up in mere possibility has been brought out into the open, hence to link together the unconscious and the conscious, non-being with being" (Hegel 1807: 469).

32. Hegel's account of meaning entails that an agent's intention cannot be separated from an action. Taylor (1983) calls attention to this point but, because he does not link it to Hegel's doctrine of "self-ignorance," fails to draw out the most radical implications of Hegel's account. See my discussion in chapter 1 above.

33. Hegel in fact rejects not only Kantian deontology but consequentialism as well, as failing to get beyond the "abstract understanding." He notes in the *Philosophy of Right* (1821):

The maxim *(Grundsatz)* which enjoins us to disregard the consequences of our actions, and the other which enjoins us to judge actions by their consequences and make the latter the yardstick of what is right and good, are in equal measure [products of the] abstract understanding. Insofar as the consequences are the proper and *immanent* shape of the action, they manifest only its nature and nothing other than the action itself; for this reason, the action cannot repudiate or disregard them. But conversely the consequences also include external interventions and contingent additions which have nothing to do with the nature of the action itself. (118R)

34. *Some* agents of oppression, of course, may simply and straightforwardly reject such principles, or perhaps consciously attempt to justify excluding members of a subordinated group from the class of agents to which the principles apply. I am assuming, however, that this is not the group toward which the kinds of criticism I have discussed here is aimed. Moreover, the interesting issues for moral philosophy do not arise with regard to oppressors who would consciously espouse oppression in this manner, inasmuch as their culpability is not really in question.

35. As noted in chapter 1, this consideration lies behind Hegel's retributive theory of punishment in which the rational agent has a *right* to be punished for criminal acts (cf. 1821: 100R).

36. As Hegel writes: "The *heroic* self-consciousness (as in the ancient tragedies like that of Oedipus) has not yet progressed from its unalloyed simplicity to reflect upon the distinction between *deed* and *action*, between the external event and the purpose and knowledge of the circumstances . . . but accepts responsibility for the deed in its entirety" (1821: 118R).

37. It is, of course, characteristic of Hegel's "phenomenological" account of history that the individual must recapitulate the various stages of Spirit's own emergence:

The single individual must also pass through the formative stages of universal Spirit so far as their content is concerned, but as shapes which Spirit has already left behind, as stages on a way that has been made level with toil. (1807: 28)

In light of this, it might be ventured that only the child can experience genuinely *tragic* agency, where she is compelled to accept the intersubjective meaning of her act despite having had *no* reason—not even on the basis of a commitment to abstract principle—to take account of that meaning. This would be in the spirit of Hegel's remark that:

[W]e find that what in former ages engaged the attention of men of mature mind, has been reduced to the level of facts, exercises and even games for children; and, in the child's progress through school, we shall recognize the history of the cultural development of the world traced, as it were, in a silhouette. (28)

38. For some typical responses of men to feminist criticism, see Koedt (1970), "Some Male Responses," and Duelli Klein (1983), "The 'Men Problem' in Women's Studies: The Expert, the Ignoramus, and the Poor Dear."

Chapter 6. Feminist Ethics and Critiques of Rationality

1. The feminist discussion of the role of emotions in ethics is too extensive to list here. Much recent discussion has come in the wake of Carol Gilligan's groundbreaking *In a Different Voice* (1982). Other authors of relevance to the discussion in this chapter include Baier 1987, Blum 1980, 1982, Calhoun 1988, Diamond 1983, Friedman 1993, Held 1993, Jaggar 1989, Manning 1992, Meyers 1989, Noddings 1984, Raymond 1986, and Tronto 1987.

2. For similar arguments associating some version of a "care" ethic to women and their characteristic orientations, see Noddings 1984, and Manning 1992.

3. A number of critics have, of course, voiced similar concerns on other than feminist grounds. See, e.g., Stocker 1976, Williams 1976: 214, Wolf 1982.

4. For further discussion of the political importance of anger, see Marilyn Frye's "A Note on Anger" (1983): 84-94.

5. "[E]thical life not just the subjective form and the self-determination of the will: it also has its own concept, namely freedom, as its content. The sphere of right and that of morality cannot exist independently *(für sich)* . . . . For the right lacks the moment of subjectivity, which in turn belongs solely to morality, so that neither of the two moments has any independent actuality" (Hegel 1821: 141A).

6. Though, as discussed in chapters 1 and 5, the purposes inhabiting sensuous desire may be opaque to the individual agent. Hegel does not hold that agents are always fully aware of the purposes that they are serving, nor the rules that spur them in their desire.

7. This is not to endorse the crude and erroneous view that Kant thought that we could only do our duty by opposing our desires, but rather that it is only when duty is in opposition to our desires that we can experience its sublime force (see section 3 below).

8. "Reason is as cunning as it is powerful. Cunning may be said to lie in the intermediative action which, while it permits the objects to follow their own bent and act upon one another until they waste away, and does not itself directly interfere in the process, is nevertheless only working out its own aims . . . . God lets men do as they please with their particular passions and interests; but the result is the accomplishment of—not their plans but his . . . "(1830: 209A).

9. For further discussion of this aspect of Hegel's critique of Kant, see Bergmann 1964: 194-199.

10. For further discussion of the complex issues involved in coming to a precise grasp of Kant's moral psychology, see Henson 1979, Baron 1981, Herman 1981, 1983, Darwall 1986b, Benson 1987, Jenson 1989, Packer 1989, and Simmons 1989.

11. "Thus respect for the law is not the incentive to morality; it is morality itself, regarded subjectively as an incentive, inasmuch as pure practical reason, by rejecting all the rival claims of self-love, gives authority and absolute sovereignty to the law" (1788: 7879/76).

12. Kant makes the link between respect for the law and the sublime at 1785: 440, cf. 1788: 76-77, 87, 1790: 254-255, 264. For further discussion, see Crowther 1989 and Guyer 1993.

13. "Letter to Schelling," April 1795, in Kaufmann 1965: 303. Hegel's interest in eliminating or somehow "mediating" the dualism between reason and sensibility in Kantian thought began with his M.A. Thesis (see Plant 1983: 20n). For further dis-

cussion of the relationship between Hegel and Schiller, see Kaufmann 1965: 46-58, and Shklar 1976: 113-115.

14. Kant's separation of legal obligation from moral worth (e.g., Kant 1788: 71) is the object of an extended critique in Hegel's essay, *Natural Law* (1802-1803).

15. Once again, as noted in chapter 2 above, Hegel's rejection of the formal "ought" that must be imposed on nature in favor of the concept that comes to realization by becoming one with the nature that it transforms, bears a strong resemblance to the Christian theology of the Trinity. In the latter, creation is redeemed only if the divine Christ is fully human, only if God and creation are in unity.

16. Hegel did not think that politics could *replace* a concern for the individual, however inseparable the interests of the individual were from those of society:

> The interest in and the need for such a real individual totality and living independence neither can nor will ever leave us, however reasonable and fruitful we acknowledge the character and the conditions of civil and political life to be in their developed form. In this sense we may admire the youthful and poetic spirit of Goethe and Schiller in their efforts to recover the lost independence of their characters within the given conditions of the modern world. (Hegel, *Lectures on Aesthetics* (1835-38): v. I, 366, cited in Lukacs 1954: 205-206)

17. See my discussion in chapter 2 above.

18. Hegel 1821: 249. See Benhabib 1986: 98, and Habermas 1968: 20-24. For a criticism of the "bureaucratic" reading of Hegel, see Rose 1981: 24-47.

19. This classic piece of "Hegelian" dialectic actually derives from Schiller: Nature (sense and intuition) always unites, Intellect *(Verstand)* always divides; but Reason *(Vernunft)* always unites once more (1967: 127n).

20. Although Hume's master slave metaphor expresses a dualistic understanding of the relation between emotion and reason, as Baier points out, Hume has invested "sentiment" with a capacity not only for improvement and cultivation, but also one of "reflection" upon itself, which most philosophers would associate with the cognitive side of human agency (1987: 47, 53). Thus, Hume's approach is in fact more synthetic than his famous metaphor tends to let on.

21. As Habermas (1973) puts the point, "The actualization of abstract right has been carried out by history itself, so to speak, behind the back of theory" (124).

22. I return to this issue in a distinct context in chapter 8 below, where I take up the debate between feminist theorists who emphasize "equality" and those who seek to value "difference."

23. As Marilyn Friedman (1993) argues, a simple endorsement of dyadic care relationships may tend to de-emphasize "the sense of solidarity or commonality that most women share with at least some other women" (154).

24. It is not quite true to say that Gilligan (1983) endorses care *over* justice, since her intention was not to dismiss Kohlberg's notion of a mature justice orientation but to argue that an equally postconventional but fundamentally different ethical orientation exists. Likewise, Gilligan places importance on self-care, and argues that caring need not be associated with traditional feminine values (e.g., it can be expressed in a woman's decision to have an abortion [64-105]). For a discussion of the complexity of Gilligan's account, see Friedman 1993: 142-143.

25. The term "unidirectional" as applied to Noddings is from Hoagland 1991.

26. For a classic discussion of this issue, see Judy Syfers "Why I Want a Wife" (1973). See also Marilyn Frye's insightful comments on the "arrogant" versus the "loving" eye (1983: 66-82).

27. "Ending a marriage usually causes pain and dislocation for both adults as well as for any children involved. However . . . in all the ways that are affected by economic deprivation, women and children are likely to suffer considerably more than men from marital dissolution. It is highly probable that most wives, well aware of this fact, take it into consideration in deciding how firm a stand to take on, or even to raise, important issues that are likely to be conflictual. We cannot adequately understand the distribution of power in the family without taking this factor into account . . ."(Okin 1989: 168).

28. See Diamond 1983, Rhode 1989, Schechter 1982, Walker 1979. For more on the issue of self-blame in battering relationships, see chapter 8 below.

29. Moreover, Hegel cannot be said to have been *unaware* of the possibility of alternative arrangements. As Wood (1991) has pointed out, he simply rejected the views of Romantic writers such as Karl Ludwig von Haller and Adam Muller in their calls for equality (246).

30. This awareness is not shared by all, as is evidenced by neo-Hegelian tracts such as Christopher Lasch's (1977) *Haven in a Heartless World: The Family Besieged.*

Chapter 7. Slaves without Fear

1. The Hegelian influences on de Beauvoir's work have not always been fully appreciated by critics who focus upon her "existentialist" themes. The latter have in fact been the object of a number of feminist criticisms (see, for example, Ellen Willis (1986), "Rebel Girl," 38, and Alison Jaggar (1983), *Feminist Politics and Human Nature,* 10.) To see de Beauvoir's work only as an "application" of Sartrean existentialism, however, fails to consider the more diverse ethical underpinnings (influenced by Hegel's and Marx's social philosophies) of works such as *The Second Sex* and *The Ethics of Ambiguity.* For recent reassessments of different aspects of de Beauvoir's ethics, see Eleanor Kuykendall, "Simone de Beauvoir and Two Kinds of Ambivalence in Action," and Jo-Ann Pilardi, "Female Eroticism in the Works of Simone de Beauvoir," in Allen and Young, 1989: 18-34.

2. De Beauvoir's (often implicit) reliance on certain aspects of Hegel's model in *The Second Sex* is extensive. See, for example, xxiv, xxvi, 64-65, 70-71, 79, 140, 187, 402-403, 481, 598, 612-615, 652. Her uses of Hegel here often appear to reflect Sartre's endorsement of (his reading of) Hegel's account of "Being-for-others" over those of Husserl and Heidegger in *Being and Nothingness* (1956: 318-330).

3. See, for example Kathie Sarachild 1978: 27-29 and Alice Echols 1989: 337.

4. De Beauvoir writes in the "Conclusion" to *The Second Sex:*

We must not believe, certainly, that a change in woman's economic condition alone is enough to transform her, though this factor has been and remains the basic factor in her evolution; but until it has brought about the moral, social, cultural, and other consequences that it promises and requires, the new woman cannot appear. (725)

She later revised this belief, not only because of the continuing failure of existing socialist societies effectively to incorporate women's equality, but because of the secondary drudge roles to which women comrades were most often relegated in left activism (de Beauvoir 1984: 32–33). As is clear in her later interviews with Alice Schwartzer (1984), de Beauvoir identified herself with the feminist struggles that took to the streets in the late 1960s and early 1970s, a phenomenon that de Beauvoir's writing played no small part in bringing about, even if she failed to foresee it.

5. "[J]ust how shall we pose the [woman] question? And to begin with, who are we to propound it at all? Man is at once judge and party to the case; but so is woman. What we need is an angel—neither man nor woman—but where shall we find one? Still, the angel would be poorly qualified to speak, for an angel is ignorant of the basic facts involved in the problem . . . . It looks to me as if there are, after all, certain women who are best qualified to elucidate the situation of woman" (de Beauvoir 1980: xxxiii).

It is worth noting that de Beauvoir specifies that "certain women" are best qualified. The question remains, however, in a social order where women are, by definition, non-agents, how such women could be specified except by their success at emulating masculine agency.

6. Of course, the description of the ancient order at the beginning of chapter 6 of the *Phenomenology* represents a very different historical stage of Spirit from that of the third part of the *Philosophy of Right*. Nevertheless, it is striking that the characteristic marks of the gender identity of men and women in the ancient world are repeated without substantial alteration in Hegel's description of the modern political order. This is one indication of women's apparent exclusion from the development of Spirit in history, except in an instrumental role, a point to which I return below.

7. See, for example, 1980: 23, 162, 435.

8. Of course, more conventional criticisms of Hegel's account of the role of women in the family are also possible. See, for example, Alison Assiter (1988), "Autonomy and Pornography."

9. Because the ties of the family represent a "transcendence" of the kind of recognition accorded by the state, Hegel insists that the relationship of marriage cannot be that of a contract: "For the precise nature of marriage is to begin from the point of view of contract—i.e. that of individual personality as a self-sufficient unit—*in order to supersede it (ihn aufzuheben)* (1821: 163R)."

On Hegel's account, however, it is entirely unclear how women whose "vocation *(Bestimmung)* consists essentially only in the marital relationship" could "transcend" anything through such a relationship (164A). This is no minor inconsistency on Hegel's part, since the feminine familial role of protecting the *göttliche Gesetz* (e.g., the role that Antigone took on so effectively) requires a degree of social recognition that her place in the household order forbids.

10. This underpins Hegel's defense of the public marriage ceremony against Romantic objections (1821: 164, 164R, cf. 162R). To reduce the marital bond to one of love between two persons would be to recognize only a "natural" and not an "ethical" significance in that relationship.

11. Unless otherwise specified, I take the subject assumed in Hegel's passages on the family and the state, as well that of the narrative of master and slave, to be male.

For a discussion of the merely instrumental role that women play in Hegel's account of the family, see Jean Bethke Elshtain (1981), *Public Man, Private Woman,* 170-183.

12. Nevertheless, to the extent that the family and its practices succeed in protecting the individual man from the chthonic power of nature, they fail to confer the status that comes with the risk of destruction in the state. Because the family fails to demand the risk of the man's life, bestowing its honors gratuitously, the man is recognized merely for what he *is,* and not as an agent that transcends his immediate situation. Kojeve (1947) comments, "By loving man in his *inaction,* one considers him *as if* he were dead" (61). An institution that would preserve the man from death cannot honor him as fully alive.

(It is dubious that such an observation applies to the *woman's* role in the family, at least insofar as that role involves the deadly risks associated with childbirth and/or domestic violence. This once again underscores the androcentric perspective from which Hegel makes his observations.)

13. Though Hegel recognizes a conflict between the "rival communities" of state and family (one that explodes in the events described in *Antigone*), he does not take this tension to entail destructiveness. Indeed, it is the responsibility of the modern state to take measures to preserve the conflict creatively. See 1821: 184A.

14. See also 1821: 165-166.

15. As regards the nature of feminine self-awareness which develops through her role as guardian of the divine law, Hegel writes:

> She does not attain to *consciousness* of it, or to the objective existence of it, because the law of the family is an implicit, inner essence that is not exposed to the daylight of consciousness, but remains an inner feeling . . . The woman is associated with these household gods [Penates] and beholds in them both her universal substance and her particular individuality, yet in such a way that this relation of her individuality to them is at the same time not the natural one of desire. (1807: 457)

16. It is because an element of "particularity" inevitably does enter into the wife's relationship with her husband that Hegel's ideal ethical relationship is that between sister and brother: "The brother . . . is for the sister a passive similar being in general; the recognition of herself in him is pure and unmixed with any natural desire" (1807: 457). This underpins the *Antigone* sequence which immediately follows in the text, where Creon's disruption of the relation between sister and brother awakens feminine agency against the state.

17. See 1821: 166R.

18. See Hegel's comments in 1821: 166R.

19. For a criticism of this aspect of Hegel's account, see Joanna Hodge (1987), "Women and the Hegelian State."

20. "[T]he rabble do not have sufficient honor to gain their livelihood through their own work, yet claim that they have a right to receive their livelihood. No one can assert a right against nature, but within the conditions of society, hardship at once assumes the form of a wrong inflicted on this or that class" (Hegel 1821: 244A).

21. See, for example, Lukacs 1954: 358, and Habermas 1973: 139.

22. It is interesting to note that the managers of the State are identified as the "universal estate," whereas in the family it is the woman who is identified with the

universal (1821: 303). Because Hegel holds that feminine identity with universality remains unconscious ("immediate"), however, women cannot be the "masters" of their own interests or desires.

23. In her description of women's situation, Simone de Beauvoir in fact understood herself to be describing what was less a class relationship than one most closely resembling a caste (1980: xxvi). As she later remarked:

> A caste [is] a group one is born into and cannot move out of. In principle, though, one can transfer from one class to another. If you are a woman, you can never become a man. Thus, women are genuinely a caste. And the way women are treated in economic, social and political terms makes them into an inferior caste. (1984: 37–38)

For the sake of consistency, I shall continue to use the term "class" in referring to women as a group. Moreover, as I shall argue below, at least some of de Beauvoir's negativity with respect to women's collective capacities may reflect questionable assumptions.

24. In certain quotations from *The Second Sex*, I shall amend Parshley's translation to reflect the standard philosophical translation of key terms (e.g., I shall translate "*les données*" as "the given" rather than "data"). I shall indicate places where I have chosen to diverge substantially from the English text.

25. This aspect of de Beauvoir's Hegelianism received considerable support in first surge of feminist anthropology of the early 1970s. Influential papers including Nancy Chodorow's (1971) "Being and Doing: A Cross-Cultural Examination of the Roles of Males and Females" and (1974) "Family Structure and Feminine Personality," Sherry Ortner's (1974) "Is Female to Male as Nature is to Culture," and Michelle Rosaldo's (1974) "Woman, Culture, and Society: A Theoretical Overview." In various ways, all of these authors sought link universal male dominance with feminine gender roles which tied women to nature and the domestic sphere, and masculine gender roles which involve men in the public transcendent activities of culture. These claims came under scrutiny as other feminist anthropologists argued that the apparent "universality" of cultural value being ascribed to masculine transcendent activities over the natural and life-giving roles of women may have been more a reflection of Western ethnologists' values than those of the cultures they were studying. (See, for example, Rogers 1975, Sacks 1976, Schlegel, ed., 1977, MacCormack 1980, and Sanday 1981)

26. She contended, for example, that: "The worst curse that was laid upon woman was that she should be excluded from . . . warlike forays. For it is not in giving life but in risking life that man is raised above the animal; that is why superiority has been accorded in humanity not to the sex that brings forth but to that which kills" (de Beauvoir 1980: 64).

27. Seeing "passivity" as a function of exclusion has become an important theme of later feminist thought as well. Consider, for example, Catharine MacKinnon's discussion of the cultivation of feminine passivity by exclusion from sport:

> Women have learned a lot all these years on the sidelines, watching. Not only have we been excluded from resources, excluded from participation, we have learned actual disability, enforced weakness, lack of spirit/body connection in being and in motion. (1987: 120)

For a discussion of both how women have been forcibly excluded from sports, as well as how the distinction between men's and women's athletic achievements is diminishing at a remarkable rate, see Mariah Burton Nelson's *Are We Winning Yet? How Women Are Changing Sports and Sports Are Changing Women* (1991).

28. "Washing, ironing, sweeping, ferreting out rolls of lint from under wardrobes — all this halting of decay is also the denial of life; for time creates and destroys, and only its negative aspect concerns the housekeeper" (425).

29. "They [men] propose to stabilize her as object and to doom her to immanence since her transcendence is to be overshadowed and perpetually transcended by another consciousness which is essential and sovereign. The drama of woman lies in this conflict between the fundamental aspirations of every subject which always poses itself as essential, and the exigencies of a situation in which she is the inessential" (xxxv).

30. Or, perhaps, how they *must* have found expression in that institution, and *must*, subsequently, have brought about its demise. Nothing, however, in the arguments to follow depends upon taking the events either of this particular passage or of the *Phenomenology* more generally as entailing one another logically.

31. Hegel's characteristic concern for how an event can be "transformative" and, at the same time, awaiting its "fulfillment" also reflects the influence of Christian theology. How the incarnation in Jesus could be the single saving event of history and at the same time lack any real social or natural significance (not culminate in mass conversions, cosmic catastrophes, etc.) led to the development of various eschatologies, accounts of how the full reality of the salvific event would not be fully actual until the end time, or perhaps the end *of* time. The project of eschatology, of course, has more than a coincidental similarity with Hegel's concerns. Hegel was entirely dissatisfied with *Heilsgeschichte* and its assertion that fulfillment can come to the world in the person of Jesus:

> [F]or if the beyond seems to have been brought closer to the individual consciousness through the form of an actuality that is individual, it henceforth on the other hand confronts him as an opaque sensuous *unit* with all the obstinacy of what is *actual*. The hope of becoming one with it must remain a hope. . . . (1807: 212)

Hegel's doctrine of the mediation of what is first immediate draws on the Christian notion of a transformation that awaits fulfillment, while rejecting the latter's narrative of salvation through a single individual in history.

32. Indeed, Hegel's strong claim that fear for one's life is alone sufficient for the development of genuine formative activity has sometimes been linked to a "militarist" ideology that has been the object of feminist criticism. See Jo-Ann Pilardi (1983), "On the War Path and Beyond: Hegel, Freud and Feminist Theory," and also Elshtain (1986), "Self/Other, Citizen/State: G. W. F. Hegel and Jane Addams."

33. Hegel's concerns also suggest a kind of secularized soterilogy centering on the Christian notion of "kenosis" or self-emptying. According to the latter account, the suffering Messiah is a necessary condition for the salvation of the world. Salvation cannot be realized either in the individual or in *Heilsgeschichte*, except through an act of self-emptying (cf. Isaiah 53: 12, Mark 14: 24, 1 Corinthians 15, 2 Corinthians 5). The influence of this theme is apparent in the *Phenomenology*'s tripartite account of the development of knowledge: immediate certainty, followed by a destructive breakdown of

that certainty, culminating in mediated knowledge. Hegel acknowledges this most explicitly in his account of "Absolute knowing" in chapter 8, where he identifies self-knowledge with self-emptying and sacrifice: "to know one's limit is to know how to sacrifice oneself" (807). (For theological accounts of kenosis, see Baumgartner 1963: 19-39, and Schillebeeckx 1974: 291-294. For recent discussion of Hegel's threefold account of the self, see Stephen Houlgate (1991), "Power, Egoism, and the 'Open' Self in Hegel and Nietzsche.")

34. See also 670-671.

35. "To regard woman as simply a slave is a mistake; there were women among the slaves to be sure, but there have always been free women . . . . They accepted men's sovereignty and he did not feel menaced by a revolt that could make of him in turn the object. Woman thus seems to be the inessential who never goes back to being the essential, to be the absolute Other, without reciprocity" (de Beauvoir, 1980: 141).

36. Other authors have developed the link between women's oppression and their role as an object of exchange between men in detail. See, for example, the classic studies of Gayle Rubin (1975), "The Traffic in Women: Notes on the Political Economy of Sex," and Kathleen Barry (1979), *Female Sexual Slavery*. Nicole Chevillard and Sebastien Leconte (1986) make the case that all women are potential objects of exchange within a slave system in "Slavery and Women." In her "Pornographic Harms" (1988), Jacqueline MacGregor Davies (who also cites Lévi-Strauss) makes an interesting case against pornography involving the claim that it perpetuates a symbolic exchange of women.

37. This is implied in her repeated rejection of "feminine values" in *The Second Sex* (65, 360, 491, 597, 611), as well as in the rather brief set of recommendations found in the "Conclusion" (716-732). De Beauvoir is far more explicit in her uneasiness with women's taking up any traditional roles in subsequent interviews (e.g., 1984: 68-79). I take up de Beauvoir's seemingly total rejection of the values of the "feminine" in greater detail in chapter 8.

38. For a discussion, see Andrea Dworkin (1987), *Intercourse*.

39. 1948: 98f. For a discussion of the place of "ambiguity" in de Beauvoir's writing, see Eleanor Kuykendall (1989), "Simone de Beauvoir and Two Kinds of Ambivalence in Action."

40. Sartre's complex and sometimes confusing notion of "choice" should not be identified with an individual agent's capacity self-sufficiently to *overcome* her situation. For Sartre, the concept of choice is closely related to that of responsibility—the agent experiences her situation as chosen inasmuch as she has the ability to assume responsibility for it. The situation, however, remains a "given," perhaps entirely out of the control of the agent who chooses it. The set of conditions that de Beauvoir describes as confronting the consciousness of the woman in *The Second Sex* is not inconsistent with Sartre's discussion of freedom "in situation" in part 4, chapter 1, of *Being and Nothingness* (1956, see esp. 619-629).

41. As a member of an early (1970) feminist consciousness-raising group remarked with regard to this phenomenon:

> [O]n the one hand there is obviously a great deal of real danger, and to a certain extent if we're sensible we're going to back away. I mean that's a sensible reaction to real danger. But on the other hand we have internalized our fear of invoking male anger, and that we carry around within

us—this powerlessness. We've allowed it to shape us on the inside so that internally we're debilitated and there are also external conditions that are really threatening. The combination of the two, really, I think, is too much. (Rainone 1973: 71)

When violence has sufficiently shaped an agent "on the inside," it may impair her own capacity to recognize it as a violation. For further discussion of this phenomenon among the survivors of domestic violence, see Schechter 1982 and Walker 1979.

42. The critical importance of the development of new terms for describing women's experience has been noted by many writers. As Susan Griffin (1986) writes, "The act of naming our suffering as oppression transformed us" (28). This goes for specific forms of oppression as well. Liz Kelly (1988) writes that "a major contribution of feminist social action around sexual violence has been to provide and create new words with which to describe and name our experience. For example, the terms *battered woman* and *sexual harassment* did not exist twenty years ago" (115). Catharine MacKinnon (1989) writes that "sexual harassment was a non-issue, even a non-experience" before feminist critique (112).

43. I am employing the term "victimization," rather than "exploitation," when referring to the socially systematic domination of women by men. Whereas exploitation tends to be identified explicitly with the extraction of some commodity from members of the exploited class, I shall use victimization to mean the forcible imposition of *service* upon one (collective) agent by another. Service, as detailed in Hegel's account of master and slave, consists in the subordinated agent's alienating her consciousness in a set of activities that are socially recognized as embodying the interests of another.

44. For de Beauvoir, women are at best "comrades in captivity," lacking the material and emotional resources to bring about their own liberation (545–546). This is consistent with the aforementioned belief that she held in the 1940s that a socialist revolution was at least the necessary condition for any meaningful change in the condition of women.

45. This would seem to vindicate the charge levelled by Drucilla Cornell (1991) that "There is perhaps no greater example of the writer who constantly calls us to 'to be' like [men] than de Beauvoir. It is we who have to try harder" (193). While this is clearly true of de Beauvoir's "recommendations," however, it should be added that these are a very small part of *The Second Sex*. It was the detailed descriptions of women's experience of sexist subordination, descriptions that in many cases gestured toward a political analysis that transcended the categories available to de Beauvoir, that made the work so influential among Western women.

46. For an account of the "forgotten" fear that characterized the transition to capitalist relations and management, see Braverman 1974: 64f.

Chapter 8. Justice, Recognition, and the Feminine

1. A parallel criticism can be found in popular writings such as Katie Roiphe's *The Morning After: Sex, Fear, and Feminism on Campus* (1993) and Naomi Wolf's *Fire with Fire: The New Female Power and How It Will Change the 21st Century* (1993). In the latter, Wolf advocates the empowerment of women as individuals in mainstream

political and economic structures, an approach she terms "power feminism." The strident individualism of writers such as Wolf and Roiphe interestingly parallels (and shares some of the same deficiencies as) that developed earlier by black conservative critics of anti-racist strategies such as Shelby Steele (1990).

2. I shall use the terms "femininity," "the feminine," and "feminine difference" interchangeably to refer to women's characteristic roles, activities, types of relationship, ethical orientation, and myths, and those interests and desires that arise from and support them.

3. See, e.g., the discussion of consent in chapter 4 above.

4. Cornell is clear that she does not intend to deny the definite sufferings of actual women either:

> Even as we want to recognize that the play of feminine sexual difference is not captured by the stereotypes of any gender hierarchy, we also do not want to deny the tragedy of women's suffering. The explosive power of feminist jurisprudence can . . . also be cut off by undermining the actual experience of suffering that exists now, in the name of a possibility that "exists"—but as a dream not as an actuality. (1993: 73)

Unlike the liberal critics of MacKinnon (e.g., Dworkin 1993), Cornell does not dispute the need for specific legal remedies for the violence done to women *qua* women in such areas as rape, harassment, or pornography (see, e.g., 1993: 124-125). Her fundamental disagreement lies with the aims of those remedies.

5. As discussed in chapter 7, de Beauvoir was clear and steadfast in her rejection of "feminine values" in the descriptions of women's condition in *The Second Sex* as well in the rather brief set of recommendations found in the "Conclusion". De Beauvoir is even more explicit in her uneasiness with women's taking up any traditional roles in subsequent interviews. (See Alice Schwartzer (1984), *After the Second Sex: Conversations with Simone de Beauvoir*, 68-79.)

6. Though Mackinnon never claims this as her sole aim, her civil rights approach to feminist jurisprudence assumes the value of litigation:

> Most major advances in sex equality under civil rights law—from affirmative action to redress for sexual harassment—have come from litigation, not legislation, though Congress subsequently affirmed a commitment to sex discrimination law many times. . . . (Dworkin and MacKinnon 1988: 13)

7. For example: "So long as sexual reality remains unequal and sexual, attempts to value sexuality as women's, possessive as if women possess it, will remain part of limiting women to it, to what women are now defined as being" (MacKinnon 1989: 153).

8. "Partial validity" is a possibility for Hegel inasmuch as reality itself may be only "partial" to the extent that the categories through which it finds mediation are themselves inadequate and subject to contradiction. See Taylor 1975: 229-230.

9. Once again, this was a fundamental part of the early feminist consciousness raising discussed in chapter 4:

> After sharing, we *know* that we suffer at the hands of a male supremacist society and that this male supremacy enters into every sphere of our existence . . . . We know that our most secret, our most private problems are grounded in the way that women are treated, in the way women are allowed to live. (Pamela Allen 1970 :27, cited in MacKinnon 1989: 95)

10. For further discussion of the problem of self-blame, see chapter 4, section 3. See also Schechter 1982: 18f, Walker 1979: 8, 1985: 206.

11. Once the violence and risk of her predicament as a woman has come to self-awareness, the survivor can come to a new and more positive comprehension of her own actions in that situation. The survivor can begin to "celebrate her survival" as she comes to perceive her actions in the violent situation from which she has emerged as embodying often remarkably resourceful solutions to an impossible state of affairs (Smith and Siegel 1985: 18, Rosewater 1988: 42, Hunter 1993: 101).

12. See, for example, MacKinnon 1987: 97–98.

13. In this too, MacKinnon goes beyond de Beauvoir who, as even Butler (1990) notes, "maintains the mind/body dualism, even as she proposes a synthesis of those terms" (p. 12).

14. Perhaps more recent developments in those countries since the appearance of *Feminism Unmodified* in 1987 call the rather minimal political vision associated with "Out now" into question even for movements of national liberation.

15. See my discussion in chapter 6.

16. "We can state the difference . . . between Gilligan and Irigaray, at least to the degree that Gilligan roots her reevaluation of the feminine in a study of the way women supposedly *are*" (Cornell 1991: 150).

17. In *Je, Tu, Nous* (1990) Irigaray includes such things as a right to female virginity and a right to motherhood as essential to guaranteeing the civil rights of women. See 84–92.

18. As Cornell herself has perceptively observed with regard to Hegel, "The very ideal of modern personality *begins* and only *begins* with the legal recognition of each one of us as a person who cannot be completely identified by her social roles" (1988: 1185).

19. As Irigaray (1990) herself has written, "an autonomous identity for girls is . . . essential for the free consent of girls to sexual relationships and for the institution of marriage if women are not to be alienated by male power." (87)

20. Sandra Harding (1986), for example, cites Edgar Zisel's (1942) argument that modern science was made possible only by the elimination of systems of slavery and feudalism wherein manual labor and educated intelligence were mutually incompatible (218). Such a development could scarcely have been anticipated based upon the manual labor of slaves or serfs, but could only emerge with the new social configuration that accompanied the fall of the old system.

Epilogue

1. As Fishkin and Peterson (1990) note, "Douglass praised John Brown's actions as thoroughly consistent with the principles of the Declaration of Independence: "He believes the declaration of Independence to be true, and the Bible to be a guide to human conduct, and acting upon the doctrines of both, he threw himself against the serried ranks of American oppression." (194).

For the example of Douglass I am indebted to Elizabeth Anderson.

REFERENCES

Abel, E. and E. K. Abel, eds. (1980). *The Signs Reader: Women and Gender Scholarship*. Chicago: University of Chicago Press.

Allen, Jeffner and Iris Marion Young, eds. (1989). *The Thinking Muse: Feminism and Modern French Philosophy*. Bloomington: Indiana University Press.

Allen, Pamela (1970). *Free Space*. New York: Times Change Press. (Reprinted in Koedt, Levine, and Rapone, eds., pp. 217-219.)

Allison, Henry (1983). *Kant's Transcendental Idealism: An Interpretation and Defense*. New Haven: Yale University Press.

Anderson, David M. (1990). "Reconstructing the Justice Dispute in America." Ph.D. dissertation, University of Michigan.

Anscombe, G. E. M. (1963). *Intention*. Ithaca: Cornell University Press.

Antony, Louise M. and Charlotte Witt, eds. (1993). *A Mind of One's Own: Feminist Essays on Reason and Objectivity*. San Francisco: Westview.

Aristotle (1941). *The Basic Works of Aristotle*. Ed. R. McKeon. New York: Random House.

Arnault, Lynne S. (1989). "The Radical Future of a Classic Moral Theory." In Jaggar and Bordo, eds., pp. 188-206.

Assiter, Alison (1988). "Autonomy and Pornography." In Griffiths and Whitford, eds., pp. 58-71.

Avineri, Shlomo (1972). *Hegel's Theory of the Modern State*. New York: Cambridge University Press.

Baier, Annettte C. (1987). "Hume: The Woman's Moral Theorist?" In Kittay and Meyers, eds., pp. 37-55.

——— (1994). "What do Women Want in a Moral Theory?" In *Moral Prejudices*. Cambridge, Mass.: Harvard University Press.

Balbus, Isaac D. (1982). *Marxism and Domination: Neo-Hegelian, Feminist, Psychoanalytic Theory of Sexual, Political, and Technological Liberation*. Princeton: Princeton University Press.

Bar On, Bat-Ami (1991). "Why Terrorism Is Morally Problematic." In Card, ed., pp. 107-125.

Baron, Marcia (1981). "The Alleged Moral Repugnance of Acting from Duty." *The Journal of Philosophy* 71: 359-382.

Barry, Kathleen (1979). *Female Sexual Slavery*. Englewood Cliffs, N.J.: Prentice-Hall.

Bartky, Sandra Lee (1990). *Feminism and Dominance: Studies in the Phenomenology of Oppression*. New York: Routledge.

Baumgartner, C. (1963). *La Grace du Christ* (*Le Mystère Chrétien: Théologie Dogmatique*, vol. 10.). Paris: Desclée.

De Beauvoir, Simone (1948). *The Ethics of Ambiguity*. Trans. B. Frechtman. Secaucus, N.J.: Citadel.

——— (1980). *The Second Sex*. Trans. H. Parshley. New York: Vintage.

——— (1984). *After the Second Sex: Conversations with Simone de Beauvoir*. Ed. Alice Schwartzer. New York: Pantheon.

Beiser, Frederick C. (1987). *The Fate of Reason: German Philosophy from Kant to Fichte*. Cambridge, Mass.: Harvard University Press.

Bengis, Ingrid (1973). *Combat in the Erogenous Zone: Writings on Love, Hate, and Sex*. New York: Knopf.

Benhabib, Seyla (1986a). *Critique, Norm, and Utopia: A Study of the Foundations of Critical Theory*. New York: Columbia University Press.

——— (1986b). "The Generalized and the Concrete Other: The Kohlberg-Gilligan Controversy and Moral Theory." In Kittay and Meyers, eds., pp. 154-177.

Benhabib, Seyla and Drucilla Cornell, eds. (1987). *Feminism as Criticism*. Minneapolis: University of Minnesota Press.

Benjamin, Jessica (1983). "Master and Slave: The Fantasy of Erotic Domination." In Snitow, Stansell, and Thompson, eds., pp. 280-299.

Benson, Paul (1987). "Moral Worth," *Philosophical Studies* 51: 365-382.

Benson, Peter (1991). "The Priority of Abstract Right: Constructivism in Hegel's Legal Philosophy." In Cornell, Rosenfeld, and Gray, pp. 174-204.

Bergmann, Frithjof (1964). "The Purpose of Hegel's System." *Journal of the History of Philosophy* 2: 189-204.

Bleier, Ruth (1986). "Lab Coat: Robe of Innocence or Klansman's Sheet." In de Lauretis, ed., pp. 55-66.

Blum, Lawrence (1980). *Friendship, Altruism, and Morality*. London: Routledge and Kegan Paul.

——— (1982). "Kant and Hegel's Moral Rationalism: A Feminist Perspective." *Canadian Journal of Philosophy* 12: 287-302.

——— (1994). *Moral Perception and Particularity*. New York: Cambridge University Press.

Bono, Paola and Sandra Kemp, eds. (1991). *Italian Feminist Thought: A Reader*. New York: Basil Blackwell.

Booth, Wayne C. (1982). "Freedom of Interpretation: Bakhtin and the Challenge of Feminist Criticism." *Critical Inquiry* 9: 45-76.

Bowles, Samuel, and Herbert Gintis (1986). *Democracy and Capitalism: Property, Community, and the Contradictions of Modern Social Thought*. New York: Basic Books.

Braverman, Harry (1974). *Labor and Monopoly Capital*. New York: Monthly Review Press.

Brod, Harry (1992). *Hegel's Philosophy of Politics: Idealism, Identity and Modernity*. San Francisco: Westview.

Brownmiller, Susan (1975). *Against Our Will: Men, Women, and Rape*. New York: Simon and Schuster.

Bulkin, Elly, Minnie Bruce Pratt, and Barbara Smith (1984). *Yours in Struggle: Three Feminist Perspectives on Anti-Semitism and Racism*. New York: Long Haul Press.

Butler, Judith (1990). *Gender Trouble: Feminism and the Subversion of Identity*. New York: Routledge.

Butler, Marylou (1985). "Guidelines for Feminist Therapy," in Rosewater and Walker, eds., pp. 32-38.

Calhoun, Cheshire (1988). "Justice, Care, and Gender-Bias." *The Journal of Philosophy* 85: 451-463.

―――― (1989). "Responsibility and Reproach." *Ethics* 99: 389-406.

Card, Claudia (1991). *Feminist Ethics*. Lawrence, Kans.: University of Kansas Press.

Carmichael, Stokely and Charles Hamilton (1967). *Black Power*. New York: Random House.

Caught Looking, Inc. (1986). *Caught Looking*. Seattle: Real Comet Press.

Chernin, Kim (1985). *The Hungry Self: Women, Eating, and Identity*. New York: Harper and Row.

Chesler, Phyllis (1978a). *About Men*. New York: Simon and Schuster.

Chevillard, Nicole and Sebastien Leconte (1986). "Slavery and Women." In Coontz and Henderson, eds., pp. 76-107.

Chodorow, Nancy (1971). "Being and Doing: A Cross-Cultural Examination of the Roles of Males and Females." In Gornick and Moran, eds., pp. 43-66.

―――― (1974). "Family Structure and Feminine Personality." In Rosaldo and Lamphere, eds., pp. 43-66.

Christ, Carol P., ed. (1979). *Womanspirit Rising*. New York: Harper and Row.

Cixous, Helene (1983). "The Laugh of the Medusa." In Abel and Abel, eds., pp. 279-297.

Clark, Lorenne M. G. and Lynda Lange, eds. (1979). *The Sexism of Social and Political Theory: Women and Reproduction from Plato to Nietzsche*. Buffalo: University of Toronto Press.

Clark, Lorenne M.G. and Debra Lewis, eds. (1977). *Rape: The Price of Coercive Sexuality*. Toronto: Women's Press.

Cleaver, Eldridge (1968). *Soul on Ice*. New York: McGraw-Hill.

Code, Lorraine, Sheila Mullett, and Christine Overall, eds. (1988). *Feminist Perspectives: Philosophical Essays on Method and Morals*. Buffalo: University of Toronto Press.

Cohen, Marshall, Thomas Nagel, and Thomas Scanlon, eds. (1974). *The Rights and Wrongs of Abortion*. Princeton: Princeton University Press.

Coontz, Stephanie and Peta Henderson, eds. (1986). *Women's Work, Men's Property*. London: Verso.

Copp, David and Susan Wendell, eds. (1983). *Pornography and Censorship*. Buffalo: Prometheus Books.

Cornell, Drucilla (1988). "Institutionalization of Meaning, Recollective Imagination, and the Potentiality of Transformative Legal Definitions." *University of Pennsylvania Law Review* 136: 1135-1229.

―――― (1991). *Beyond Accommodation: Ethical Feminism, Deconstruction, and the Law*. New York: Routledge.

―――― (1993). *Transformations: Recollective Imagination and Sexual Difference*. New York: Routledge.

Cornell, Drucilla, Michael Rosenfeld, and David Gray (1991). *Hegel and Legal Theory.* New York: Routledge.

Crawford, Donald W. (1974). *Kant's Aesthetic Theory.* Madison: University of Wisconsin Press.

Crowther, Paul (1989). *The Kantian Sublime: From Morality to Art.* New York: Oxford University Press.

Daly, Mary (1978). *Gynecology: The Metaethics of Radical Feminism.* Boston: Beacon.

Darwall, Stephen L. (1986a). "Agent-Centered Restrictions from the Inside Out." *Philosophical Studies* 50: 291-319.

——— (1986b). "Kantian Practical Reason Defended." *Ethics* 96: 89-99.

——— (1988). "Self-Deception, Autonomy, and Moral Constitution." In McLaughlin and Rorty, eds., pp. 407-430.

Davies, Jacqueline MacGregor (1988). "Pornographic Harms." In Code, Mullett, and Overall, eds., pp. 127-145.

Davis, Angela Y. (1981). *Women, Race, and Class.* New York: Vintage.

Davis, Elizabeth Gould (1971). *The First Sex.* Baltimore: Penguin.

Diamond, Irene, ed. (1983). *Families, Politics, and Public Policy.* New York: Longman.

Dietrichson, Paul (1964). "When Is a Maxim Fully Universalizable?" *Kant-Studien* 55: 143-170.

Dobash, R. Emerson and Russell Dobash (1979). *Violence Against Wives: A Case Against the Patriarchy.* New York: Free Press.

Doell, Ruth and Helen E. Longino (1988). "Sex Hormones and Human Behavior: A Critique of the Linear Model." *Journal of Homosexuality* 15: 55-79.

Dove, Kenley R. (1971). "Hegel's Phenomenological Method." In Steinkraus, ed., pp. 34-56.

Duelli Klein, Renate (1983). "The 'Men Problem' in Women's Studies: The Expert, the Ignoramus, and the Poor Dear." *Women's Studies International Forum* 6: 413-421.

Dutton-Douglas, Mary Ann and Lenore E. A, Walker, eds. (1988). *Feminist Psychotherapies: Integration of Therapeutic and Feminist Systems.* Norwood, N.J.: Ablex.

Dworkin, Andrea (1987). *Intercourse.* New York: Free Press.

Dworkin, Andrea and Catharine A. MacKinnon (1988). *Pornography and Civil Rights: A New Day for Women's Equality.* Minneapolis: Organizing Against Pornography.

Dworkin, Ronald (1993). "Women and Pornography: *Only Words* by Catharine A. MacKinnon." *New York Review of Books* 40, n. 17 (October 21): 36-42.

Easton, Susan (1984). "Hegel and Feminism." *Radical Philosophy* 38: 2-8.

Echols, Alice (1989). *Daring to Be Bad: Radical Feminism in America 1967-1975.* Minneapolis: University of Minnesota Press.

Ehrenreich, Barbara and Deirdre English (1978). *For Her Own Good: 150 Years of the Experts' Advice to Women.* New York: Anchor.

Ellison, Ralph (1952). *The Invisible Man.* New York: Random House.

Elshtain, Jean Bethke (1981). *Public Man, Private Woman: Women in Social and Political Thought.* Princeton: Princeton University Press.

——— (1986a). *Meditations on Modern Political Thought.* New York, Praeger.

——— (1986b). "Self/Other, Citizen/State: G.W.F. Hegel and Jane Addams." In Elshtain 1986a, pp. 71-84.

Elster, Jon (1990). "Norms of Revenge." *Ethics* 100: 862-885.

Evans, Judith, Jill Hills, Karen Hunt, Elizabeth Meehan, Tessa ten Tusscher, Ursula Vogel, Georgina Walen, eds. (1986). *Feminism and Political Theory*. Beverly Hills: Sage Publications.

Findlay, J. N. (1958). *Hegel: A Re-examination*. London: George Allen and Unwin.

Fineman, Martha Albertson (1991). *The Illusion of Equality: The Rhetoric and Reality of Divorce Reform*. Chicago: University of Chicago Press.

Finkelhor, David and Bersti Yllo (1985). *License to Rape: Sexual Abuse of Wives*. New York: Free Press.

Firestone, Shulamith (1970). *The Dialectic of Sex: The Case for Feminist Revolution*. New York: Morrow.

Fishkin, Shelley Fisher and Carla L. Peterson (1990), "We Hold These Truths to Be Self-Evident: The Rhetoric of Frederick Douglass's Journalism." In Sundquist, ed., pp. 189-204.

Fiss, Owen (1976). "Groups and the Equal Protection Clause." *Philosophy and Public Affairs* 5: 105-177.

Flax, Jane (1983). "Political Philosophy and the Patriarchal Unconscious: A Psychoanalytic Perspective on Epistemology and Metaphysics." In Harding and Hintikka, eds., pp. 245-282.

Foa, Pamela (1977). "What's Wrong with Rape?" In Vetterling-Braggin et al., eds., pp. 347-359.

Forer, Anne (1978). "Thoughts on Consciousness-Raising." In Sarachild, ed., p. 151.

Foucault, Michel. *The Foucault Reader*. Ed. Paul Rabinow. New York: Panthenon, 1984.

Frankfurt, Harry (1978). "The Problem of Action." In Frankfurt (1988), pp. 58-68.

———— (1988). *The Importance of What We Care About*. New York: Cambridge University Press.

Freire, Paolo (1983). *Pedagogy of the Oppressed*. New York: Continuum.

French, Peter A., ed. (1972). *Individual and Collective Responsibility*. Cambridge, Mass.: Schenkman.

Friedman, Marilyn (1991). "The Social Self and the Partiality Debates." In Card, ed., pp. 161-179.

———— (1993). *What Are Friends For? Feminist Perspectives on Personal Relationships and Moral Theory*. Ithaca: Cornell University Press.

Friedrich, Carl J., ed. (1949). *The Philosophy of Kant: Immanuel Kant's Moral and Political Writings*. New York: Random House.

Frye, Marilyn (1983). *The Politics of Reality: Essays in Feminist Theory*. Trumansburg, N.Y.: The Crossing Press.

———— (1990). "A Response to *Lesbian Ethics*." *Hypatia* 5: 132-137.

Garry, Ann and Marilyn Pearsall, eds. (1989). *Woman, Knowledge, and Reality: Explorations in Feminist Philosophy*. New York: Routledge.

Gauthier, David P. (1986). "The Unity of Reason: A Subversive Reinterpretation of Kant." *Ethics* 96: 74-88.

Gauthier, Xavière (1981). "Why Witches?" Trans. E. M. Eisinger. In Marks and de Courtivron, eds., pp. 199-203.

Gert, Bernard, ed. (1972). *Man and Citizen: Thomas Hobbes's De Homine and De Cive*. Garden City, N.Y.: Doubleday.

Gilligan, Carol (1982). *In a Different Voice*. Cambridge, Mass.: Harvard University Press.

Gornick, Vivian and Barbara K. Moran, eds. (1971). *Woman in Sexist Society*. New York: Mentor.

Grene, David and Richmond Lattimore, eds. (1992). *The Complete Greek Tragedies* (4 vols.). Chicago: University of Chicago Press.

Griffin, Susan (1971). "Rape: The All-American Crime." In Vetterling-Braggin et al., eds., pp. 313-332.

—— (1978). *Woman and Nature: The Roaring Inside Her*. New York: Harper and Row.

—— (1986). *Rape: the Politics of Consciousness*. New York: Harper and Row.

Griffiths, Morwenna and Margaret Whitford, eds. (1988). *Feminist Perspectives in Philosophy*. Bloomington: Indiana University Press.

de Gruyter, Walter, ed. (1902). *Kants gesammelte Schriften: herausgegeben von der Akademie der Wissenschaften*. 29 vols. Berlin.

Guyer, Paul (1993). *Kant and the Experience of Freedom: Essays on Aesthetics and Morality*. New York: Cambridge University Press.

Habermas, Jurgen (1968). *Knowledge and Human Interests*. Trans. J. J. Shapiro. Boston: Beacon.

—— (1973). *Theory and Practice*. Trans J. Viertel. Boston: Beacon.

Hanen, Marsha and Kai Nielsen, eds. (1987). *Science, Morality and Feminist Theory*. Calgary: University of Calgary Press.

Harding, Sandra (1986). *The Science Question in Feminism*. Ithaca: Cornell University Press.

Harding, Sandra and Merrill Hintikka, eds. (1983). *Discovering Reality: Feminist Perspectives on Epistemology, Metaphysics, Methodology and Philosophy of Science*. Dordrecht: Reidel.

Hartsock, Nancy (1984). *Money, Sex, and Power*. Boston: Northeastern University Press.

Heath, Stephen (1987). "Male Feminism." In Jardine and Smith, eds., pp. 1-32.

Hegel, G. W. F. (1955). *Lectures on the History of Philosophy*. Trans. E. S. Haldane and F. H. Simson, 3 vols. Atlantic Highlands, N.J.: Humanities Press.

—— (1956). *The Philosophy of History*. Trans. J. Sibree. New York: Dover.

—— (1953). *Reason in History*. Trans. R. S. Hartmann. Indianapolis: Bobbs-Merrill.

—— (1969). *Science of Logic*. Trans. A. V. Miller. Atlantic Highlands, N. J.: Humanities Press.

—— (1971). *Early Theological Writings*. Ed. H. Nohl. English ed., trans. T. M. Knox. Chicago: University of Chicago Press.

—— (1974). *Natural Law*. Trans. T. M. Knox. Philadelphia: University of Pennsylvania Press.

—— (1975). *Logic (Encyclopedia of the Philosophical Sciences*, Vol. I). Trans. W. Wallace. New York: Oxford University Press.

—— (1977a). *The Difference between Fichte's and Schelling's System of Philosophy*. Trans. H. S. Harris and W. Cerf. Albany, N.Y.: State University of New York Press.

—— (1977b). *The Phenomenology of Spirit*. Trans. A. V. Miller. New York: Oxford University Press.

—— (1979). *System of the Ethical Life*. Trans. H. S. Harris, in Harris and Knox, eds.

——— (1984). *Hegel: The Letters*. Trans. C. Butler and C. Seiler. Bloomington: Indiana University Press.

——— (1985). *Relationship of Skepticism to Philosophy, Exposition of its Different Modifications and Comparison of the Latest Form with the Ancient One*. Trans. H. S. Harris. In di Giovanni and Harris, eds., pp. 311-362.

——— (1991). *Elements of the Philosophy of Right*. Trans. H. B. Nisbet. New York: Cambridge University Press.

Held, Virginia (1972). "Moral Responsibility and Collective Action." In French, ed., pp. 101-118.

——— (1993). *Feminist Morality: Transforming Culture, Society, and Politics*. Chicago: University of Chicago Press.

Henson, Richard G. (1979). "What Kant Might Have Said: Moral Worth and the Overdetermination of Dutiful Action." *Philosophical Review* 88: 39-54.

Herman, Barbara (1981). "On the Value of Acting from the Motive of Duty." *Philosophical Review* 90: 372-373.

——— (1983). "Integrity and Impartiality." *Monist* 66: 236, 240.

——— (1985). "The Practice of Moral Judgment." *Journal of Philosophy* 82: 414-436.

——— (1993). "Could It Be Worth Thinking About Kant on Sex and Marriage?" In Antony and Witt, eds., 1993.

Hinton, William (1966). *Fanshen: A Documentary of Revolution in a Chinese Village*. New York: Vintage.

Hill, Thomas E., Jr. (1980). "Humanity as an End in Itself." *Ethics* 91: 84-99.

Hoagland, Sarah (1991). "Some Thoughts About 'Caring.'" In Card, ed., pp. 246-263.

Hodge, Joanna (1987). "Women and the Hegelian State." In Kennedy and Mendus, eds., pp. 127-158.

Hofmeister, Heimo E. M. (1974). "Moral Autonomy in Kant and Hegel." In O'Malley, Algozin, and Weiss, eds., pp. 141-158.

hooks, bell (1989). *Talking Back: Thinking Feminist, Thinking Black*. Boston: South End Press.

Houlgate, Stephen (1991). "Power, Egoism, and the 'Open' Self in Hegel and Nietzsche." *Journal of the British Society for Phenomenology* 22: 120-138.

Hunter, Susan Kay (1993). "Prostitution is Cruelty and Abuse to Women and Children." *Michigan Journal of Gender and Law* 1: 91-104.

Hyppolite, Jean (1957). "Hegel's Phenomenology and Psychoanalysis." In Steinkraus, ed., pp. 57-70.

Irigaray, Luce (1985). *This Sex Which Is Not One*. Trans. C. Porter. Ithaca: Cornell University Press.

——— (1990). *Je, Tu, Nous: Toward a Culture of Difference*. Trans. Alison Martin, 1993. New York: Routledge.

Jaggar, Alison (1983). *Feminist Politics and Human Nature*. Totowa, N.J.: Rowman and Allanheld.

——— (1989). "Love and Knowledge: Emotion in Feminist Epistemology." In Garry and Pearsall, eds., pp. 129-155.

Jaggar, Alison and Susan R. Bordo, eds. (1989). *Gender/Body/Knowledge: Feminist Reconstructions of Being and Knowing*. New Brunswick, N.J.: Rutgers University Press.

Jardine, Alice and Paul Smith, eds. (1987). *Men in Feminism*. New York: Methuen.

Jenson, Henning (1989). "Kant and Moral Integrity," *Philosophical Studies* 53: 65-77.

Johnston, Jill (1974). *Lesbian Nation: The Feminist Solution*. New York: Simon and Schuster.

Kant, Immanuel (1949a). "Idea for a Universal History with a Cosmopolitan Intent." Trans. C. J. Friedrich. In Friedrich, ed., 116-131.

———— (1949b). *Kant's Critique of Practical Reason and Other Writings on Moral Philosophy*. Trans. L. W. Beck. Chicago: University of Chicago Press.

———— (1949c). *What Is Orientation in Thinking?* Trans. L. W. Beck. In Kant 1949b.

———— (1956). *The Critique of Practical Reason*. Trans. L. W. Beck. Indianapolis: Bobbs-Merrill.

———— (1960). *Religion Within the Limits of Reason Alone*. Trans. T. M. Greene and H. H. Hudson. New York: Harper (1960).

———— (1964). *Groundwork of the Metaphysics of Morals*. Trans. H. J. Paton. New York: Harper.

———— (1965a). *The Critique of Pure Reason*. Trans. N. K. Smith (1965 ed.). New York: St. Martin's.

———— (1965b). *The Metaphysical Elements of Justice*. Trans. J. Ladd. Indianapolis: Bobbs-Merrill.

———— (1965c). *The Metaphysics of Morals*. Part I. Trans. J. Ladd. In Kant (1965b).

———— (1971a). "An Answer to the Question: 'What Is Enlightenment?'" In Hans Reiss, ed., pp. 54-60.

———— (1983a). *Ethical Philosophy*. Trans. J. Ellington. Indianapolis: Hackett.

———— (1983b). *The Metaphysics of Morals*. Part II trans. J. Ellington, in Kant (1983a).

———— (1987). *The Critique of Judgment*. Trans. W. S. Pluhar. Indianapolis: Hackett.

Kaplow, Susi (1971). "Getting Angry." In Koedt, Levine, Rapone, eds., pp. 36-41.

Kappeler, Susanne (1986). *The Pornography of Representation*. Minneapolis: University of Minnesota Press.

Kaufmann, Walter (1956). *Existentialism from Dostoevsky to Sartre*. Cleveland: World Publishing.

———— (1965). *Hegel: Reinterpretation, Texts, and Commentary*. Garden City, N.Y.: Doubleday.

Kelly, Liz (1988). *Surviving Sexual Violence*. Minneapolis: University of Minnesota Press.

Kemp, J. (1958). "Kant's Examples of the Categorical Imperative." *Philosophical Quarterly* 8: 63-71.

Kennedy, Ellen and Susan Mendus, eds. (1987). *Women in Western Political Philosophy: Kant to Nietzsche*. New York: St. Martin's.

Kenny, Anthony (1963). *Action, Emotion, and Will*. London: Routledge and Kegan Paul.

Keohane, N. O., M. Z. Rosaldo, and B. C. Gelpi, eds. (1982). *Feminist Theory: A Critique of Ideology*. Chicago: University of Chicago Press.

Kittay, Eva Feder and Diana T. Meyers, eds. (1987). *Women and Moral Theory*. Savage, Md.: Rowman and Littlefield.

Koedt, Anne (1970). "Some Male Responses." In Tanner, ed., pp. 255-256.

Koedt, Anne, Ellen Levine, and Anita Rapone, eds. (1973). *Radical Feminism*. New York: Quadrangle.

Kojeve, Alexandre (1947). *Introduction to the Reading of Hegel.* Trans. J. H. Nichols. Ithaca: Cornell University Press.

Korsgaard, Christine (1985). "Kant's Formula of Universal Law." *Pacific Philosophical Quarterly* 66: 24-47.

Krell, David Farrell (1989). "Lucinde's Shame: Hegel, Sensuous Woman and the Law." *Cardozo Law Review* 10: 1673-1686.

Kristeva, Julia (1984). *Revolution in Poetic Language.* Trans. M. Waller. New York: Columbia University Press.

Kuflik, Arthur (1984). "The Inalienability of Autonomy." *Philosophy and Public Affairs* 13: 271-298.

Kuykendall, Eleanor H. (1989). "Simone de Beauvoir and Two Kinds of Ambivalence in Action." In Allen and Young, eds., pp. 35-50.

Lasch, Christopher (1977). *Haven in a Heartless World: The Family Besieged.* New York: Longman.

Landes, Joan B. (1982). "Hegel's Conception of the Family." In Elshtain, ed., pp. 125-144.

Laska, Peter (1974). "Kant and Hegel on Practical Reason." In O'Malley, Algozin, and Weiss, eds., pp. 129-140.

de Lauretis, Teresa, ed. (1986). *Feminist Studies/Critical Studies.* Bloomington: Indiana University Press.

Lederer, Laura, ed. (1979). "'*Playboy* Isn't Playing,' An Interview with Judith Bat-Ada." In Lederer, ed., pp. 111-124.

——— (1980). *Take Back the Night: Women on Pornography.* New York: Bantam.

Leidholdt, Dorchen and Janice G. Raymond, eds. (1990). *The Sexual Liberals and the Attack on Feminism.* Elmsford, N.Y.: Pergamon.

Leon, Barbara (1978). "Separate to Integrate." In Sarachild, ed., pp. 152-157.

Levin, Michael (1987). *Feminism and Freedom.* New Brunswick, N.J.: Transaction Books.

Lieberman, Sally Taylor (1991). "Visions and Lessons: 'China' in Feminist Theory-Making, 1966-1977." *Michigan Feminist Studies* 6: 91-107.

Lloyd, Genevieve (1983). "Masters, Slaves and Others." *Radical Philosophy* 34: 2-9.

Longino, Helen (1990). *Science as Social Knowledge: Values and Objectivity in Scientific Inquiry.* Princeton: Princeton University Press.

Lonzi, Carla (1991). "Let's Spit on Hegel." In Bono and Kemp, eds., pp. 40-59.

Lorde, Audre (1979). "The Master's Tools Will Never Dismantle the Master's House." In Moraga and Anzaldua, eds., pp. 98-101.

Lukacs, Georg (1954). *The Young Hegel.* Trans. R. Livingstone. Cambridge, Mass.: M.I.T. Press.

——— (1978). *The Ontology of Social Being: Hegel.* Trans. D. Fernbach. London: Merlin.

McAfee, Kathy and Myrna Wood (1970). "Bread and Roses." In Tanner, ed., pp. 415-433.

MacCormack, Carole P. (1980). "Nature, Culture, and Gender: A Critique." In Mac-Cormack and Strathern, eds., pp. 1-24.

MacCormack, Carole P. and Marilyn Strathern, eds. (1980). *Nature, Culture, and Gender.* New York: Columbia University Press.

MacIntyre, Alasdaire, ed. (1972). *Hegel.* New York: Anchor.

——— (1981). *After Virtue.* Notre Dame: University of Notre Dame Press.

——— (1984). "Is Patriotism a Virtue?" The Linley Lectures, University of Kansas.

———— (1988). *Whose Justice, Which Rationality?*. Notre Dame: University of Notre Dame Press.

MacKinnon, Catharine A. (1979). *Sexual Harassment of Working Women: A Case of Sex Discrimination*. New Haven: Yale University Press.

———— (1982). "Feminism, Marxism, Method, and the State: An Agenda for Theory." In Keohane, Rosaldo, and Gelpi, eds., pp. 1-30.

———— (1987). *Feminism Unmodified: Discourses on Life and Law*. Cambridge, Mass.: Harvard University Press.

———— (1989). *Toward a Feminist Theory of the State*. Cambridge, Mass.: Harvard University Press.

McLaughlin, Brian P. and Amelie O. Rorty, eds. (1988). *Perspectives on Self-Deception*. Berkeley: University of California Press.

Manning, Rita C. (1992). *Speaking from the Heart: A Feminist Perspective on Ethics*. Lanham, Md.: Rowman and Littlefield.

Marcuse, Herbert (1932). *Hegel's Ontology and the Theory of Historicity*. Trans. S. Benhabib. Cambridge, Mass.: M.I.T. Press.

———— (1968). *Reason and Revolution: Hegel and the Rise of Social Theory*. Boston: Beacon.

Marks, Elaine and Isabelle de Courtivron, eds. (1981). *New French Feminisms*. New York: Schocken.

Marx, Karl and Friedrich Engels (1978). *The Marx-Engels Reader*. Ed. R. C. Tucker. New York: Norton.

May, Larry and Robert Strikwerda (1994). "Men in Groups: Collective Responsibility for Rape." *Hypatia* 9: 134-151.

Medea, Andrea and Kathleen Thompson, eds. (1974). *Against Rape*. New York: Farrar, Strauss, and Giroux.

Mehrhof, Barbara and Pamela Kearon (1971). "Rape: An Act of Terror." In Koedt, Levine, and Rapone, eds., pp. 228-233.

Melden, A. I. (1961). *Free Action*. London: Routledge and Kegan Paul.

Merleau-Ponty, Maurice (1945). *Phenomenology of Perception*. Trans. C. Smith. London: Routledge and Kegan Paul.

Meyers, Diana T. (1989). *Self, Society, and Personal Choice*. New York: Columbia University Press.

Migne, J. P., ed. (1841-1842). *Patrilogia Latina*. Paris.

Mills, Patricia Jagentowicz (1979). "Hegel and the Woman Question." In Clark and Lange, eds., pp. 74-97.

———— (1986). "Hegel's *Antigone*." *Owl of Minerva* 17: 131-152.

Moraga, Cherrie and Gloria Anzaldua, eds. (1981). *This Bridge Called My Back: Writings by Radical Women of Color*. Watertown, Mass.: Persephone.

Morgan, Robin (1970). "Goodbye to All That." In Tanner, ed., pp. 269-276.

———— (1977). "Theory and Practice: Pornography and Rape." In Lederer, ed., pp. 125-132.

———— (1989). *The Demon Lover: On the Sexuality of Terrorism*. New York: Norton.

Morgan, Robin, ed. (1970). *Sisterhood Is Powerful: An Anthology of Readings from the Women's Liberation Movement*. New York: Bantam.

Nader, Laura (1984). "A User Theory of Law." *Southwestern Law Review* 38: 951-963.

—— (1985). "A User theory of Legal Change as Applied to Gender." In *Nebraska Symposium on Motivation*. Lincoln: University of Nebraska Press.

Nedelsky, Jennifer (1989). "Law, Boundaries, and the Bounded Self." *Representations* 30: 162-189.

—— (1990). "Reconceiving Autonomy: Sources, Thoughts, and Possibilities." *Yale Journal of Law and Feminism* 1: 7-36.

Nell, Onora. (See O'Neill, Onora.)

Nelson, Mariah Burton (1991). *Are We Winning Yet? How Women Are Changing Sports and Sports Are Changing Women*. New York: Random House.

Nietzsche, Friedrich (1966). *Beyond Good and Evil*. Trans. W. Kaufmann. New York: Vintage.

Noddings, Nell (1984). *Caring: A Feminine Approach to Ethics and Moral Education*. Berkeley: University of California Press.

Nozick, Robert (1974). *Anarchy, State, and Utopia*. New York: Basic Books.

O'Brien, Mary (1981). *The Politics of Reproduction*. London: Routledge and Kegan Paul.

O'Hagan, Timothy (1987). "On Hegel's Critique of Kant's Moral and Political Philosophy." In Priest, ed., pp. 135-159.

Okin, Susan Moller (1989). *Justice, Gender, and the Family*. New York: Basic Books.

Olsen, Frances (1989). "Comments on Davis Krell's 'Lucinde's Shame: Hegel, Sensuous Woman, and the Law.'" *Cardozo Law Review* 10: 1687-1693.

O'Malley, Joseph J., K. W. Algozin, and Frederick G. Weiss, eds. (1974). *Hegel and the History of Philosophy*. The Hague: Nijhoff.

O'Neill, Onora (1975). *Acting on Principle: An Essay on Kantian Ethics*. New York: Columbia University Press.

—— (1989). *Constructions of Reason: Explorations of Kant's Practical Philosophy*. New York: Cambridge University Press.

Ortner, Sherry B. (1974). "Is Female to Male as Nature is to Culture?" In Rosaldo and Lamphere, eds., pp. 67-88.

Packer, Mark (1989). "Kant on Desire and Moral Pleasure," *Journal of the History of Ideas* 50: 429-442.

Pateman, Carole (1980). "Women and Consent." *Political Theory* 8: 149-168.

—— (1985). *The Problem of Political Obligation*. Cambridge: Polity Press.

Pelczynski, Z. A., ed. (1971). *Hegel's Political Philosophy*. New York: Cambridge University Press.

Peterson, Susan Rae (1977). "Coercion and Rape: The State As a Male Protection Racket." In Vetterling-Braggin et al., eds., pp. 360-371.

Petry, M. J. (1983). "Hegel's Criticism of the Ethics of Kant and Fichte." In Stepelevich and Lamb, eds., pp. 125-36.

Pfeiffer, Raymond S. (1985). "The Responsibility of Men for the Oppression of Women." *Journal of Applied Philosophy* 2: 217-229.

Pilardi, Jo-Ann (1983). "On the War Path and Beyond: Hegel, Freud and Feminist Theory." *Women's Studies International Forum* 6: 565-572.

—— (1989). "Female Eroticism in the Works of Simone de Beauvoir." In Allen and Young, eds., pp. 18-34.

Pilardi Fuchs, Jo-Ann. (See Pilardi, Jo-Ann.)

Pippin, Robert B. (1989). *Hegel's Idealism: The Satisfactions of Self-Consciousness*. New York: Cambridge University Press.

——— (1991). "Hegel, Modernity, and Habermas." *Monist* 74: 329-357.

Plant, Raymond (1983). *Hegel: An Introduction*. Oxford: Blackwell.

Pratt, Minnie Bruce (1984). "Identity: Skin, Blood, Heart." In Bulkin, Pratt, and Smith, pp. 11-63.

Priest, Stephen, ed. (1987). *Hegel's Critique of Kant*. New York: Oxford University Press.

Quinton, Anthony (1967). *Political Philosophy*. New York: Oxford University Press.

Rabinow, Paul, ed. (1984). *The Foucault Reader*. New York: Pantheon.

Railton, Peter (1986). "Moral Realism." *The Philosophical Review* 95: 163-207.

Rainone, Nanette (1970). "Men and Violence." In Koedt, Levine, and Rapone, eds., pp. 63-71.

Rawls, John (1971). *A Theory of Justice*. Cambridge, Mass.: Harvard University Press.

——— (1985). "Justice as Fairness: Political not Metaphysical." *Philosophy and Public Affairs* 14: 223-251.

Raymond, Janice (1986). *A Passion for Friends: Toward a Philosophy of Female Affection*. Boston: Beacon.

Redstockings (1970). "Principles." In Morgan, ed., pp. 583-584.

Reiss, Hans, ed. (1970). *Kant's Political Writings*. New York: Cambridge University Press.

Reiter, Rayna, ed. (1975). *Towards an Anthropology of Women*. New York: Monthly Review Press.

Rhode, Deborah (1989). *Justice and Gender*. Cambridge, Mass.: Harvard University Press.

Rich, Adrienne (1976). *Of Woman Born*. New York: Bantam.

——— (1983). "Compulsory Heterosexuality and Lesbian Experience." In Abel and Abel, eds., pp. 139-168.

Ring, Jennifer (1991). *Modern Political Theory and Contemporary Feminism: A Dialectical Analysis*. Albany: State University of New York Press.

Rogers, Arthur Kenyon (1922). *The Theory of Ethics*. New York: MacMillan.

Rogers, Susan C. (1975). "Female Forms of Power and the Myth of Male Dominance: A Model of Male/Female Interaction in Peasant Society." *American Ethnologist* 2: 727-756.

Roiphe, Katie (1993). *The Morning After: Sex, Fear, and Feminism on Campus*. New York: Little Brown.

Rorty, Amelie ed. (1976). *The Identities of Persons*. Berkeley: University of California Press.

Rosaldo, Michelle Z. (1974). "Woman, Culture, and Society: A Theoretical Overview." In Rosaldo and Lamphere, eds., pp. 17-42.

Rosaldo, M. Z. and L. Lamphere, eds. (1974). *Woman, Culture, and Society*. Stanford: Stanford University Press.

Rose, Gillian (1981). *Hegel Contra Sociology*. London: Athlone.

Rose, Hilary (1983). "Mind, Brain, and Heart: A Feminist Epistemology for the Natural Sciences." *Signs* 9: 73-80.

Rosewater, Lynne Bravo (1988). "Feminist Therapies with Women." In Dutton-Douglas and Walker, eds., pp. 137-155.

Rosewater, Lynne Bravo and Lenore E.A. Walker, eds. (1985). *Handbook of Feminist Therapy: Women's Issues in Psychotherapy*. New York: Springer.

Rubin, Gayle (1975). "The Traffic in Women: Notes on the Political Economy of Sex." In Reiter, ed., pp. 157-210.

Ruddick, Sara (1989). *Maternal Thinking: Towards a Politics of Peace*. New York: Ballantine Books.

Russell, Diana E. H. (1977). *The Politics of Rape: The Victim's Perspective*. New York: Stein and Day.

—— (1980). "Pornography and Violence: What Does the Research Say?" In Lederer, ed., pp. 216-236.

—— (1982). *Rape in Marriage*. New York: MacMillan.

—— (1983). "Research on How Women Experience the Impact of Pornography." In Copp and Wendell, eds., pp. 213-218.

Sacks, Karen (1976). "State Bias and Women's Status." *American Anthropologist* 78: 565-570.

Sanday, Peggy Reeves (1981). *Female Power and Male Dominance: On the Origins of Sexual Inequality*. New York: Cambridge University Press.

Sandel, Michael (1982). *Liberalism and the Limits of Justice*. New York: Cambridge University Press.

Sarachild, Kathie (1978a). "Consciousness-Raising: A Radical Weapon." In *Feminist Revolution*: 144-151.

—— (1978b). "The Power of History." In *Feminist Revolution*: 13-43.

Sarachild, Kathie, ed. (1978). *Feminist Revolution* (Redstockings, Inc.). New York: Random House.

Sartre, Jean-Paul (1957). *The Transcendence of the Ego*. Trans. F. Williams and R. Kirkpatrick. New York: Farrar, Strauss and Giroux.

—— (1948). *Anti-Semite and Jew*. Trans. G. J. Becker. New York: Schocken.

—— (1956). *Being and Nothingness*. Trans. H. Barnes. New York: Modern Library.

Schechter, Susan (1982). *Women and Violence: The Visions and Struggles of the Battered Women's Movement*. Boston: South End Press.

Schillebeeckx, Edward (1974). *Jesus: An Experiment in Christology*. Trans. H. Hoskins. New York: Seabury.

Schiller, Friedrich (1967). *On the Aesthetic Education of Man*. Trans. E. M. Wilkinson and L. A. Willoughby. New York: Oxford University Press.

Schlegel, Alice, ed. (1977). *Sexual Stratification*. New York: Columbia University Press.

Schwarzenbach, Sibyl (1987). "Rawls and Ownership: The Forgotten Category of Reproductive Labor." In Hanen and Nielsen, eds., pp. 139-167.

Shafer, Carolyn M. and Marilyn Frye (1977). "Rape and Respect." In Vetterling-Braggin et al., eds., pp. 333-346.

Shklar, Judith M. (1976). *Freedom and Independence: A Study of the Political Ideas of Hegel's Phenomenology of Mind*. New York: Cambridge University Press.

Siep, Ludwig (1983). "The 'Aufhebung' of Morality in the Ethical Life." In Stepelevich and Lamb, eds., pp. 137-155.

Simmons, Keith (1989). "Kant on Moral Worth," *History of Philosophy Quarterly* 6: 85-100.

Simons, Margaret A. (1983). "The Silencing of Simone de Beauvoir: Guess What's Missing from *The Second Sex*." *Women's Studies International Forum* 6: 559-564.

Singer, Marcus G. (1961). *Generalization in Ethics: An Essay in the Logic of Ethics with the Rudiments of a System of Moral Philosophy.* New York: Knopf.

Smith, Adrienne and Ruth Siegel (1985). "Feminist Therapy: Redefining Power for the Powerless." In Rosewater and Walker, eds., 1985, pp. 13-21.

Smith, Dorothy (1981). "The Experienced World as Problematic: A Feminist Method." Sorokin Lecture 12. Saskatoon: University of Saskatchewan Press.

Smith, John E. (1974). "Hegel's Critique of Kant." In O'Malley, Algozin, and Weiss, eds., pp. 109-128.

Smith, Steven B. (1989). *Hegel's Critique of Liberalism: Rights in Context.* Chicago: University of Chicago Press.

Snitow, Ann, Christine Stansell, and Sharon Thompson, eds. (1983). *Powers of Desire: The Politics of Sexuality.* New York: Monthly Review Press.

Solomon, Robert (1983). *In the Spirit of Hegel.* New York: Oxford University Press.

Sommers, Christina Hoff (1994). *Who Stole Feminism?: How Women Have Betrayed Women.* New York: Simon and Schuster.

Spelman, Elizabeth V. (1988). *Inessential Woman: Problems of Exclusion in Feminist Thought.* Boston: Beacon.

——— (1989). "Anger and Insubordination." In Garry and Pearsall, eds., pp. 263-273.

Steinkraus, Warren E., ed. (1971). *New Studies in Hegel's Philosophy.* New York: Holt, Rinehart and Winston.

Stepelevich, Lawrence S. and David Lamb, eds. (1983). *Hegel's Philosophy of Action.* Atlantic Highlands, N.J.: Humanities Press.

Stocker, Michael (1976). "The Schizophrenia of Modern Ethical Theories." *Journal of Philosophy* 63 (1976): 462.

Sundquist, Eric J. (1990). *Frederick Douglass: New Literary and Historical Essays.* New York; Cambridge University Press.

Syfers, Judy (1973). "Why I Want a Wife." In Koedt, Levine, and Rapone, eds., pp. 60-62.

Tanner, Leslie B., ed. (1970). *Voices from Women's Liberation.* New York: Signet.

Tax, Meredith (1973). "Woman and her Mind: The Story of Everyday Life." In Koedt, Levine, and Rapone, eds., pp. 23-35.

Taylor, Charles (1967). "Relations between Cause and Action." *Proceedings of the Seventh Inter-American Congress of Philosophy,* vol. I. Les Presses de L'Université Laval.

——— (1970). "Explaining Action." *Inquiry* 13: 54-89.

——— (1974). "Hegel's *Sittlichkeit* and the Crisis of Representative Institutions." In Yovel 1978, pp. 133-154.

——— (1975). *Hegel.* New York: Cambridge University Press.

——— (1979). *Hegel and Modern Society.* New York: Cambridge University Press.

——— (1983). "Hegel's Philosophy of Mind." In Taylor, 1985a, pp. 77-96.

——— (1985a). *Human Agency and Language: Philosophical Papers 1.* New York: Cambridge University Press.

——— (1985b). *Philosophy and the Human Sciences: Philosophical Papers 2.* New York: Cambridge University Press.

Thomson, Judith Jarvis (1971). "A Defense of Abortion." In Cohen, Nagel, and Scanlon, eds. 1974, pp. 3-22.

Tronto, Joan (1987). "Beyond Gender Difference to a Theory of Care." *Signs* 12: 644-661.

Vadas, Melinda (1987). "A First Look at the Pornography/Civil Rights Ordinance: Could Pornography Be the Subordination of Women?" *Journal of Philosophy* 84: 487-511.

———— (1990). "Dearest Maryann and Other Possible PWC's." *American Philosophical Association Newsletter on Feminism and Philosophy* (90: 1): 139-141.

Vance, Carole S., ed. (1989). *Pleasure and Danger: Exploring Female Sexuality*. London: Pandora.

Vetterling-Braggin, Mary, Frederick Elliston, and Jane English, eds. (1977). *Feminism and Philosophy*. Totowa, N.J.: Rowman and Allenheld.

Walker, Lenore E.A. (1979). *The Battered Woman*. New York: Harper and Row.

———— (1985). "Feminist Therapy with Victim/Survivors of Interpersonal Violence." In Rosewater and Walker, eds. 1985, pp. 203-214.

Walsh, W. H. (1969). *Hegelian Ethics*. New York: St. Martin's.

Westphal, Kenneth R. (1989). *Hegel's Epistemological Realism: A Study of the Aim and Method of Hegel's Phenomenology of Spirit*. Boston: Kluwer.

Willis, Ellen (1983). "Feminism, Moralism, and Pornography." In Snitow, Stansell, and Thompson, eds., pp. 460-467.

———— (1986). "Rebel Girl." *Village Voice*, May 27: 38.

Williams, Bernard (1976). "Persons, Character, and Morality," in Rorty, ed., pp. 197-216.

———— (1978). *Descartes: The Project of Pure Enquiry*. Hammondsworth: Penguin.

Wolf, Naomi (1993). *Fire with Fire: The New Female Power and How It Will Change the 21st Century*. New York: Random House.

Wolf, Susan (1982). "Moral Saints." *The Journal of Philosophy* 79: 419-439.

Wollstonecraft, Mary (1967). *Vindication of the Rights of Women*. Hammondsworth: Penguin.

Wood, Allen W. (1990). *Hegel's Ethical Thought*. New York: Cambridge University Press.

Yovel, Yirmiahu, ed. (1978). *Philosophy of History and Action*. Boston: Beacon.

Zilsel, Edgar (1942). "The Sociological Roots of Science." *American Journal of Sociology* 47.

INDEX

abortion, 187n. 48, 193n. 28, 196n. 24.
  See also birth and reproduction
Absicht. See intention
absolute knowing, 43, 170n. 64, 206-7n. 33
abstraction: and concepts, 38; freedom as, 41;
  impartiality as, 67; and moral principles,
  51, 91, 95, 145; and universality, 24, 58,
  145, 153, 196n. 21. *See also* emptiness; formalism; immediacy; Kant, Immanuel
Achtung. See respect
action theory, 1-5, 157n. 2. *See also* agency
African Americans, 153. *See also* Black Power
  Movement; racism
agency: collective, 2, 7, 26, 158n. 17, 159n.
  27, 179n. 60; ethical, 79; feminine, 57,
  74, 119, 125, 169n. 55, 198n. 6, 199n. 16;
  and moral responsibility, 78, 79, 160n. 29
  (11); sexist, 78, 80-92, 194n. 34; transformation of, 11-13, 29, 31, 41, 84, 131,
  168n. 53, 169n. 56 (29), 178n. 54, 184n.
  21, 201n. 31. *See also* feminine, the; individuality
alienation, 2, 9, 110, 172n. 10
Allen, Pamela, 182n. 7, 204n. 9
Allgemeinheit. See meaning; universality
ambiguity. *See* de Beauvoir, Simone
Anderson, David M., 176n. 40

Anderson, Elizabeth, 163n. 23 (21), 163n.
  23, 179n. 62 (51), 205n. 1
anger, 58-59, 147, 195n. 4 (102)
Anscombe, G.E.M., 155-56n. 2, 156n. 4 (4)
Antigone, xvi, 5-13, 22, 26, 35, 43, 45-48, 93,
  123, 156n. 7, 158n. 18, 165n. 31 (22),
  193n. 29 (91),
  198n. 9, 199n. 13, 16
Arian heresy, 169-70n. 60
Aristotle, 164n. 29, 190-91n. 10
Arnault, Lynne, 167n. 45
Assiter, Alison, 198n. 8
Atkinson, Ti-Grace, 148
Aufhebung (surpassing), 44-45, 158-59n. 22,
  161n. 4, 162n. 12, 176n. 42
Augustine, Saint, 168n. 53
autonomy: Hegel's socializing of, 10-11, 23,
  29-31, 36, 79, 110, 153, 157n. 10, 158n.
  19, 159n. 25, 169n. 58, 59, 190n. 8; Kantian, 1, 10, 21, 23, 35, 58, 77, 100, 153,
  159n. 24 (10), 166n. 41, 166-67n. 43; and
  sexism, 92-93, 95, 205n. 19; and social mediation, 22, 29-31, 51, 95, 165n. 31 (22),
  174n. 25, 178n. 51; and universalizability
  test, 24. *See also* freedom; rationality; reason; self-sufficiency
Avineri, Shlomo, 170n. 61 (30), 175n. 28

223